KNOW YOUR
BERNINA

KNOW YOUR
BERNINA

Second Edition

JACKIE DODSON

CHILTON TRADE BOOK PUBLISHING

RADNOR, PENNSYLVANIA

*Are you interested in a quarterly magazine about creative uses
of the sewing machine: Robbie Fanning and Jackie Dodson are planning
to start one. For more information, write:*

*The Creative Machine
PO Box 2634
Menlo Park, CA 94026*

Published in Radnor, Pennsylvania 19089, by Chilton Trade Book Publishing

Designed by William E. Lickfield
Manufactured in the United States of America

Library of Congress Cataloging in Publication Data

Dodson, Jackie.
    Know your Bernina.
    (Creative machine arts series)
    Bibliography: p. 208
    Includes index
    1. Machine sewing.   2. Sewing machines.   I. Title.
II. Series.
TT713.D63   1988   646.2′044   87–48011
ISBN 0–8019–7876–9 (pbk.)

3 4 5 6 7 8 9 0   7 6 5 4 3 2 1 0

Contents

Foreword

Recently I've been on an anti-clutter rampage, cleaning out closets, boxes, shelves, and files with a vengeance. I call it Playing the Game of Condominium—if I had to move to a condominium and compress all my belongings, what could I give away? The level of clutter surrounding me parallels the messy state of my brain: clean surfaces, clean mind. So I'm ruthlessly cleaning; if I haven't used it, worn it, thought of it for a year or more, out it goes.

But I cannot bring myself to throw away my bulging file of letters from Jackie Dodson, author of this book. Jackie and I met 10 years ago by accident on a tour bus in Chicago. Since then she has showered me with wacky, inspiring letters. This is a woman who is brimming with laughter and ideas, sharing both freely. Most of the letters arrived with swatches of machine-embroidered fabric pinned to them. "Have you tried this?" she'd ask, again and again.

Over the years I have learned about her machine-embroidery classes, her work with the Hinsdale Embroiderers' Guild, her ongoing family escapades. But always her letters have inspired me to run to my machine and play around with new ideas.

When it came time to revise my machine-embroidery book, I knew who to ask for help as a designer and critic: Jackie.

Now you, too, can participate in the output of this creative woman, whether or not you own a Bernina. She has developed a series of lessons that will introduce you to the full range of what you and your machine can accomplish as partners. In this revised edition, Jackie has added three lessons on using decorative stitches, especially Fantasy Stitches on the 1130. She has changed many of the designs, provided new projects, and has made refinements in the directions. By the end of the book, you will truly know your machine. Enjoy the trip!

Robbie Fanning

Series Editor, Creative Machine Arts, and co-author
The Complete Book of Machine Embroidery

Preface

When our children were small, we took long car trips. I remember one that took longer than planned. We all grumbled about being lost, but one of our boys said, "It's just one of Dad's long-cuts."

We loved that new word, so we came up with dictionary meanings.

Long-cut (noun): When it takes longer, but Dad convinces everyone he wanted it that way. A "little something extra." An adventure. An educational side-trip. You are happier when you finally reach your destination. And so on.

What does this have to do with the sewing machine? This book contains long-cuts, those adventurous techniques that help you and your Bernina create something special, something out of the ordinary.

Most of us learned basic techniques of sewing when we bought our Bernina—how to thread it, wind a bobbin, make a buttonhole, sew a straight seam. We were shown each presser foot and how to use it. . . and, I'll bet, except for the zipper and buttonhole feet, you haven't looked at those other feet again.

But there's so much more to learn. Join me on an educational side-trip. By the time you're done with this book, you'll truly know your Bernina.

Let's begin by exploring how we can change a piece of fabric with the Bernina: we can add texture to it, appliqué it, quilt it, stitch across holes in it, draw thread out of it, gather it up and decorate it. We can stitch in space with our Berninas, make cording–but, more importantly, once we understand the Bernina, it makes all our stitching easier.

As we explore all these effects, which are presented in 39 lessons, we'll make small samples for a notebook; make finished 6" squares to fit on a totebag, displaying what we've learned; and make 28 other projects. In the process of stitching the samples and projects in the book, you'll take an educational side-trip as well. You'll learn to adjust and manipulate your sewing machine until you can use it to its full potential.

This workbook of ideas does not take the place of your basic manuals nor of the *Advanced Bernina Book*. Instead, it is to be used as a reinforcement and supplement to what you already know. By working through the lessons, you will come to know your machine better. At the same time, you'll realize what fun it is to stitch with your Bernina.

Yes, there is much more to sewing than straight stitching. And wouldn't you rather go that long-cut route–to make your stitching more interesting and original?

In my classes I often hear this progression: "I can't do that" to "Can I really do that?" to "I can do that!" I hope this book is the next best thing to having me prompting, prodding, patting you on the back in person.

Jackie Dodson
LaGrange Park, Illinois

Acknowledgments

Thank You:

To Judy Baker, Erik Hattenschweiler, and Hans Neuenschwander; Linda Sus and Sandy Marolf who spoke Bernina to me for a week at Bernina University; and to Richard Gannon, JoAnn Pugh, Mary Jo Berglund, Sharon Knudson and Tami Durand from Bernina, who answered my questions and helped me in so many ways.

To Caryl Rae Hancock, Nora Lou Kampe, Gail Kibiger, Pat Pasquini, Ann Price, Diana Schlumpf, Sherrie Coppenbarger, Judy Whitemyer, Ruth Drosen, and Marcia Strickland for sharing ideas; Ladi Tisol who helped me before I had to ask; and Marilyn Tisol, critic, sounding-board, and special friend.

To Chuck, who took photos, and the rest of my family who've learned to accept decorative clothing in place of mended clothing.

To Robbie Fanning, for her optimism, encouragement, and endless support.

And to my students, who kept telling me to write it all down.

CHAPTER 1

Getting Started

This book is organized by the changes you can make to a piece of fabric — add stitches, add texture, subtract threads, and so on. Following this introductory chapter, each chapter consists of several lessons, and some projects. Each lesson asks you to stitch up practice samples for a notebook or for finished projects. The largest project in the book is the tote bag (directions for making it are in Chapter 12). It was designed to show off interchangeable decorative squares, which you'll make as you proceed through the lessons.

For the practice samples, you will want to set up a three-ring notebook — the kind with the largest rings — to keep track of your stitching (Fig.1.1). Buy plastic pockets and blank notebook paper (both available at office supply stores). Write the settings you've used directly on the stitched samples and slip them into the plastic pockets for future reference.

Clip pictures from magazines that trigger ideas. Ask yourself: Could I get that effect if I loosened the bobbin? Which presser foot would I use for that? Which thread

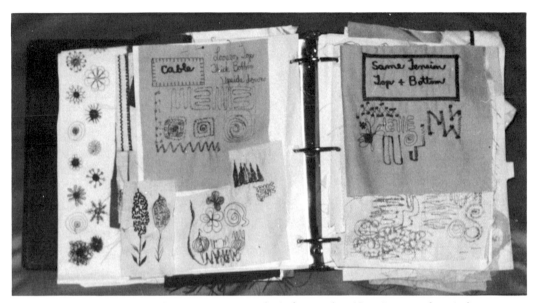

Fig. 1.1 A reference notebook, open to a page of stitch samples. Notations on the stitchery will help you reset the machine.

would produce loops like that? Write notes to yourself with ideas to try and add these to the notebook along with the magazine pictures.

Love your Bernina

When I bought my first Bernina, it never occurred to me that the blind hem stitch could be used for more than putting in a blind hem or that many of the stitches could be sewn freely, with feed dogs lowered, to create a different kind of fill-in stitch from the usual zigzag. Soon after, I discovered books on machine stitchery and began to see the sewing machine in a new way. I knew I had found a type of stitchery that suited the way I worked and had the look I loved. I've concentrated on learning everything I can about machining ever since.

In the books I read and the workshops I took, I noticed that the machine used was almost always the Bernina. The reason is obvious. It is so easy to adjust and manipulate. And it's fun to sew on. The fun comes out of its dependability. We may all choose our machines for different reasons, but we can agree that dependability is the most important.

When I chose my machine, I wanted one that would accept the thickest and most tightly woven fabric made, while at the same time sewing sheers or stitching over open spaces without balking. I can do all of that without changing the tension setting. However, when I want to change tensions for different effects, it's easy to change both top and bobbin and get them back to normal. And while I'm working, I can change the bobbin without taking my fabric off the bed of the machine.

I didn't look for a machine that had built-in animal motifs, but I did want a built-in blind hem, an overlock stitch, and a stretch stitch. The most important automatic stitch, the zigzag, had to produce a perfect satin stitch with even edges and no skipped stitches. (The Bernina is renowned for its satin stitch.)

Everything I wanted is in my Bernina—plus more. I have a machine that accepts any thread, and that threads easily. Another feature I've come to appreciate is changing presser feet in seconds, using only one hand. The presser foot knee lifter, which is unique to the Bernina, has been found on the top-of-the-line models since the early 1960s. By using it, I can lift the presser foot and still keep both hands on my work.

After sewing on other machines, I realize I sometimes take these special features for granted: the slender free arm, the feed dogs that lower by turning a knob, the marks on the needle plate that help me stitch in a straight line, the moderate speed setting for my precision work, and the bobbin that holds more thread than bobbins on other machines.

Those are Bernina generalities. Now let me tell you about specific models. Bernina offers not only mechanical machines (1000 series), but also a computer series (1100). I'll tell you some of the features you'll find on each Bernina model; then I'll tell you why I'm sold on the 1130 computer model.

The top-of-the-line 1130 provides 35 stitches, 11 presser feet, completely automatic buttonhole, needle down, half speed, continuous reverse, pattern start, long stitch, basting stitch, balance buttons, single pattern, mirror image, double (length) pattern, double needle and memory. When you choose one of the stitches, the machine sets up length and width for you and tells you what presser foot to use. Of course, you can override those settings if you wish.

The other computer machine is the 1120, which also automatically sets stitch length and width and tells you the appropriate presser foot when a stitch button is pressed. It offers 14 stitches and 9 presser feet. The long stitch and balancing buttons are included, but you are not able to program stitches on the 1120.

The new 1030 is the top-of-the-line for

the mechanical series. It has 26 standard stitches and the long stitch for basting and top stitching. It has a special buttonhole that sews both beads in a forward direction, which gives them an exact, equal density. Eleven presser feet come with this model. Although the machine does not change stitch width and length settings for you when you press a stitch button, once you have chosen a stitch, the panel at eye level will indicate the appropriate settings to manually set up your machine for sewing.

The 1020 has 22 built-in stitches, 9 presser feet, and the stitch-setting panel to advise you. In the same family of machines is the newest 1010, with 14 stitches and 5 presser feet, but no panel of visuals.

The mechanical 300 and 400 Bernette sewing machines are made in Taiwan, using Bernina specifications. The one I purchased includes straight stitch, zigzag, blind hem, overlock, the triple straight and zigzag stitches, along with a buttonhole. They are a good way to buy Bernina quality inexpensively.

Let me tell you the reasons why I'm sold on the Bernina 1130 computer machine. The list is long. First, I like having the machine set length and width and advise which presser foot to use. It will also set needle position when applicable (e.g., blind hem stitch), and I'm able to use any of the five needle positions for any stitch.

When I change the width and length settings, I can dial the width to 50 increments—length to 100 increments. Not all electronic machines will do that. This Bernina advantage means more and more to me as I try to perfect my French machine sewing, mitered corners, and exact satin stitch width.

I also like the fully automatic buttonhole on the 1130. This foot has a prism in it that can memorize the first buttonhole stitched by measuring length, not by counting stitches as with other computer machines. The prism sends signals to the memory so the second buttonhole is stitched precisely the same as the first, even if one is stitched over two layers of fabric, the second over many bulky layers (e.g., neckband and collar areas). On other machines, the buttonholes sometimes end up different lengths—but not on my Bernina.

The no-stitch-run-on feature is little publicized, but extremely important to anyone demanding sewing perfection. When I lift my foot from the foot pedal, my Bernina stops cold. Another joy is that even at the top speed of 1050 stitches per minute, all the built-in stitches, even the buttonhole, are stitched perfectly. But I also have exact stitch-by-stitch control at slow speed.

When I first learned my 1130, I was not aware of how valuable the altered-memory feature is. (It has nothing to do with the memory button.) Not until I stopped doing samples and actually began to make garments did I discover what a time-saver the altered-memory is. My machine will remember two altered settings. Let's say I want to straight stitch at 4 length (I push straight stitch and dial the length of 4) and then I want to change to a zigzag, stitch width 2, length 3 (I push the zigzag button, then dial my length and width). Now, when I want to return to straight stitch, stitch length 4, I merely push the straight stitch button. The machine remembers I want a 4 stitch length. And when I call up my zigzag, all I have to do is push the zigzag button and the altered settings are already there. For clothing construction, it is wonderful. And when I stitch on Battenberg projects I use it constantly (see Lesson 14). If you put in a third alteration, the machine will drop the first one. In other words, only two stitch alterations are held in the machine at any one time. To erase these altered stitches when I finish using them, I press the clear button or turn off the machine.

I also like the double-stitch pattern button on the computer. When I elongate designs, the entire design is stitched with twice as many stitches as the standard design, so the pattern doesn't lose density.

I can easily change needle positions by pushing a button — and I can use any of the five needle positions with any built-in stitch (which is possible with any Bernina machine).

On both the 1000 and 1100 series, there is a silky thread guide, which prevents slippery threads from sliding to the bottom of the spool and getting twisted around the spool pin.

I also love the feature on the 1100 series of stopping with needle down when I choose to. Satin stitching around appliqués can be done more precisely and I can turn corners on the exact stitch I intended. You'll discover many other applications for this important function as you get to know your Bernina.

On my computer machine, I can begin and end a pattern on the exact stitch without guessing if I use the special function button called "single pattern." Then I can mirror the entire design by pushing another special function button. Or I can combine mirror images with the standard stitches in memory to give me more decorative possibilities. I'm excited about the balancing buttons, not only for fine adjustments on stitches so they are all perfect no matter how thick or thin the fabric I'm stitching, but because I can create dozens of new stitches by combining those buttons with the standard built-in stitches. And I can create new stitch patterns if I use the standard stitches with the long stitch button, which sews every other stitch (see Chapter 11).

The double-needle button narrows stitch designs and instantly sets the correct width when I use a double needle. Another feature of my machine is a rigidly guided needle bar that will move only if it's safe to move. No more needle breakage.

Last, and most important to computer machine owners, is the memory on the 1130. I can place 5 stitches (altering them if I wish) in the memory, so the combinations I can create are in the hundreds — I am not limited to the 35 stitches on the machine.

I love my Bernina! One of the reasons my enthusiasm never wanes is because I have a group of friends who own Berninas. We exchange sewing advice, pass on our creative discoveries, recommend books to each other, and sometimes meet to try new ideas. If you don't have such friends already, you'll find them in classes at your Bernina dealer, where new ideas are taught regularly.

While at the store, check out the books, magazines, and videos there (see Sources of Supply). The *Revised Advanced Bernina Guide Book* was available as of July '88. Bernina issues a "Bernina Sewing Club" magazine twice a year. Also available at your dealer, from Bernina's educational service in Switzerland, are leaflets about each presser foot. Also look for "Footsteps," Bernina of America's pamphlets for individuals or teachers (terrific ideas for classes). Each issue contains projects that teach techniques and offer information about presser feet and accessories. "Footworks" is the name of some videos, which are based on the presser feet (several are explained on each tape). The leaflet of instructions accompanying each video gives you exact settings for the machine. Keep a copy in your notebook, as well as with the video. In addition, I've listed some great stitchery books in the Bibliography.

From the beginning I was sold on my Bernina and I still am. Now that I know my Bernina, I can't think of using any other machine for sewing or machine stitchery. Notice that I did not say "machine embroidery." Embroidery is only one part of machine stitchery, which also includes making lace, needleweaving, appliquéing in creative ways, to name a few we'll touch on in this book.

Presser feet

Each Bernina model comes with standard accessories and presser feet. What is included varies from model to model and many more presser feet are available, as well as such accessories as the ruffler, bias binder attachment, circle maker, Cut'n'Sew, English eyelet maker, and walking foot.

Presser feet on all the 700, 800 and 900 series are interchangeable, but they cannot be used on the 1000 or 1100 series. On the 1000 and 1100 machines, the shape of the cone that slips onto the shaft and holds the presser foot in place is different from that of the other machines and the feed dogs are set wider apart, so the grooves in some of the feet for other machines would

Bernina Feet in
1130 Number Sequence

Note: numbering for foot equivalents (if any) on older machines appears in parentheses.

0	(000)	zigzag
1	(560)	multi-motion
2*	(470)	overlock
3*	(452)	buttonhole
3a*	–	automatic buttonhole
4*	(007)	zipper
5	(016)	blind stitch
6	(030)	embroidery
7	(419)	tailor tack
8	(145)	jeans
9	(285)	darning
10	(492)	edge
11	(499)	cordonette
12	(525)	bulky overlock (knitter's)
13	(038)	straight stitch
16	(508)	gathering zigzag
17	(179)	gathering zigzag
18	(152)	button sew-on
20	(147)	open embroidery
21	(189)	braiding
22*	–	couching
23	(181)	appliqué
24	–	free-hand embroidery
27	(033)	non-automatic buttonhole
28	(272)	wool darning foot
29	–	special darning foot
30	(526)	pintuck, 3 groove
31	(588)	pintuck, 5 groove
32	(525)	pintuck, 7 groove
33	(569)	pintuck, 9 groove
38	–	binding (cordless)
51	(201)	roller foot
52	(142)	Teflon zigzag
53	(468)	Teflon straight stitch
54*	(547)	Teflon zipper
55	(572)	leather roller foot
61	(166)	zigzag narrow hem, 2mm
62	(589)	straight stitch narrow hem, 2mm
63	(252)	hemmer, 3mm
64	(003)	wide hemmer, 4mm
66	(415)	wide hemmer, 6mm
68	(168)	roll and shell hemmer, 2mm
70	(174)	lap hemmer (feller)
71	(178)	lap hemmer (feller), 8mm
75	(177)	long extension (adaptor)
77	(187)	short extension (adaptor)
83*	(018)	circular embroidery device
84	(121)	bias binder, 20–24mm
85	(077)	bias binder
86	(165)	5 stitch ruffler
90*	(578)	Cut'n'Sew
91	(140)	zigzag for jersey
92	(194)	English embroidery
94	(554)	binder foot only
99	–	zigzag with finger guard
–	–	walking foot

*Not suitable for use on models older than 1130.

Chart 1.1
Bernina Presser Feet Included with Machine

Note: Numbering for foot equivalents on older machines (if any) in parentheses

	730	830	930	1020	1030	1120	1130
0 (000) zigzag	x	x	x	x	x	x	x
1 (560) multi-motion			x	x	x	x	x
2 (470) overlock		x	x	x	x	x	x
3 (452) buttonhole	x	x	x	x	x	x	x
3a auto buttonhole							x
3b buttonhole/slide				x	x		
4 (007) zipper	x	x	x	x	x	x	x
5 (016) blind stitch	x	x	x	x	x	x	x
6 (030) embroidery	x	x	x		x	x	x
7 (419) tailor tacking	x	x	x		x		x
8 (145) jeans			x		x	x	x
9 (284) darning	x	x	x	x	x	x	x
68 (168) hemmer	x	x					
70 (174) lap hemmer	x	x					

not be in correct alignment. The new presser feet are constructed to allow for a wider stitch width (5), as opposed to stitch width 4 on the other models. Presser feet for machines up to and including the 900 series aren't being made anymore, but the new presser feet can be used on previous models (700, 800, 900 series).

Chart 1.1 shows presser feet supplied with each model. There's a chart following Chapter 12 that lists additional presser feet and accessories available for each model. If you have a 730 machine, you'll find that the presser feet have no numbers, but they are the same feet as the 830 and 930 models. Only the buttonhole foot for the 730 is slightly different. Machines in the 1000 and 1100 series have a different numbering system from the other machines. I've indicated the *number* of the foot in the charts.

Check prices before you buy extra presser feet. Sometimes the same foot from a different machine will be less expensive and work as well as the Bernina foot if you use an adaptor shank. There are two heights in adaptor shanks, so buy both to be prepared. Even the #178 lap hemmer, which is a Bernina industrial foot, needs one. All presser feet listed, adaptor shanks, and accessories are available at Bernina dealers. Also, I own an "ankle" for my adaptor shanks which enables me to use various clip-on feet from other machines.

New presser feet are introduced often. Use the charts to keep a record of the ones you have. When you've come to know your Bernina well, you will quickly realize that a jeans foot is not just for jeans, a blind hemmer is not for blind hems only, and many feet can do the same job. A chart of presser feet and accessories can be found at the end of the book.

Accessories

Bias binder

Two different accessories are available.
1. The first is a bias binder presser foot to be used with ½" (12.7mm) single-fold bias tape. It can edge quilted or non-quilted fabrics. It works best on straight edges and attaches binding in one operation instead of the usual two steps. The zigzag stitch cannot be used.
2. The second accessory, called the flat bias binder, is used with flat, not pre-folded, bias. The attachment includes a presser foot (ask for the one that fits your particular machine), free arm extension table, and the bias apparatus. The bias apparatus comes in sizes to accommodate different widths of bias.

Circular embroidery device

This attachment clips to the feed dogs and is used to sew circles or half-circles from 1½" (3.8cm) to 14" (35.6cm) in diameter. Use this for making patches, buttons, monograms, and circular decorations. Try decorative built-in stitches with it, as well as straight and satin stitches.

Cut'n'Sew

This accessory is like a serger, but not as fast. It cuts, sews, and neatens edges of fabric in a single operation. Also use it for stay-stitching, overcasting raw edges, for French seams, and to replace ribbed bands on sweaters or T-shirts. Sew on lace edging with it and, if you remove the pin in the foot, roll and whip edges of fabrics. Topstitch using the guide at the side of the presser foot.

English eyelet maker

This attachment can be used to make Battenberg rings as well as English eyelets. The box includes a special foot for eyelet embroidery, a special needle plate with a small (2mm) and a large (3mm) slide with prong. It also includes a screwdriver and a round awl for material, and a square awl for leather and very hard felt.

Ruffler

This attachment ruffles fabric and also pleats it. The ruffler is adjustable and you determine how full you want your ruffle or pleats to be. Always do a sample first, using the fabric you plan to use on your finished project so you can determine how much fabric you will need. The ruffles or pleats are *not* adjustable once they are sewn in.

Walking foot

Although walking feet from other machines may be fit to the Bernina using an adaptor shank, if you have a choice, buy the Bernina walking foot. Another walking foot may not accommodate reverse pattern stitching, as the Bernina walking foot does. I've discovered through my classes that it is not as noisy but, even more importantly, other walking feet do not stand up to the wear that the Bernina foot does. Use it to stitch stripes and plaids together perfectly, to stitch plastics, leathers, foambacks, interlock knits, napped fabrics, slippery fabrics, thick fabrics, and layers of fabrics, such as quilts.

Needle plates

Needle plates other than the zigzag plate that comes with your machine are available. Each is used for a specific function. One that I own and find valuable is the straight-stitch plate. It is very helpful when I want added support around the needle hole so the fabric will not be shoved down under the plate when quilting or sewing fine, filmy fabrics. It's not necessary, but I use the straight-stitch (#038 or #13) presser foot with it for added support when I use the stitch plate.

Supplies

In addition to your Bernina and a good supply of threads, here's a shopping list of what you'll need for the lessons. (Each lesson will give you a detailed materials list). You probably have many of the supplies in your sewing room.

1. Scissors and shears: sharp embroidery scissors, plus shears for cutting fabric and paper-cutting scissors
2. Water-erasable markers for light fabrics; white opaque permanent marker for water-soluble stabilizer; vanishing markers with ink that disappears within 24 to 48 hours — or less, depending on the humidity; slivers of soap or light-colored chalk pencils for dark fabrics
3. T square or 6″ × 24″ (15.2cm × 61.0cm) plastic ruler; 6″ (15.2cm) and 12″ (30.5cm) see-through rulers are also helpful
4. Wood and spring-type hoops in varied sizes, maximum 7″ (17.8cm) for ease
5. Rotary cutting wheel and mat
6. Extra bobbin case (optional)
7. Dressmaker's carbon
8. Stabilizers: freezer paper, water-soluble, tear-away

Have fabric ready for stitching samples. A handy size is a 9″ (22.9cm) square. It will fit in the 7″ (17.8cm) hoop and can be trimmed slightly for your notebook. Cut up a variety of fabrics from extra-light-weight types like organdy, lightweights like calicos, medium-weight poplins, and heavy-weight denim. Extra-heavy-weight canvas scraps will be left over from your tote bag and can be used for experiments.

In the projects, you'll also use felt, transparent fabrics, bridal veil, ⅛″ (3.2mm) and ½″ (12.7mm) satin double-faced ribbon, lace insertion, scalloped lace, lace beading, Battenberg tape, fleece, batting, stabilizers and fusibles. Now let's discuss your choices of threads, needles, and other supplies.

Threads

One of the most useful charts I have in my notebook is a piece of doubled fabric with line after line of satin stitches on it. Each row is stitched using a different type of thread. I recommend that you make one, too. More important than telling you which thread to use, your chart will graphically convince you that what is called machine-embroidery cotton is usually more lustrous and covers an area more quickly and more beautifully than regular sewing thread. It's easy to compare differences among threads.

Generally, sewing threads are not used for machine embroidery. Ordinary sewing threads are usually thicker, stretch more (if polyester), and do not cover as well as machine embroidery threads. However, for durability or when you need a certain color, try using a high quality sewing thread. I never use thread from the sale bin — the ones that are three spools for 88 cents. This thread does not hold up to heavy use; it breaks, shrinks, knots, and, after all the time spent stitching with it, looks sloppy. If I am going to take the time to sew or embroider anything, then it deserves quality thread.

Machine embroidery rayons and cottons are more lustrous and have a softer twist than ordinary sewing thread. Rayon embroidery threads are silky and loosely twisted, but if you use a #90/14 needle and sew evenly and at a moderate speed, they are easy to use. However, don't use rayons or any other machine embroidery threads for clothing construction because they aren't strong enough.

Besides regular sewing threads and those used for machine embroidery, there are others to become acquainted with. The fine nylon used for lingerie and woolly overlock used for serging are just a couple of them. Another is darning thread: It's often used on the bobbin for machine embroidery because it's lightweight and you can get so much more of it wound on. It comes in only a few colors, so it cannot always be used should you want the bobbin thread to be seen on the surface.

Monofilament, another popular thread, comes in two shades. One blends into light-colored fabrics, the other darks. It is not the wild, fish-line type anymore, so don't be afraid of making it work. I use it on the top and bobbin constantly.

If you use silk and silk buttonhole twists as well as fine pearl cottons, crochet and cordonnet, the needle must be large enough to keep the threads from fraying against the fabric and the eye large enough to enable the thread to go through smoothly. Sometimes top-stitching needles are called for. Or you may have to use a needle larger than you normally would embroider with.

Waxed or glacé finished quilting thread should never be used on your machine, as the finish wears off and does your machine no good.

Chart 1.3 is a handy guide, showing which needles and threads to use with which fabrics. More about where to purchase threads can be found in Sources of Supplies at the end of the book.

Needles

It is important to choose the right needle for the job. Match fabric weight, thread and needle size as well as type of material

Chart 1.2
Needle and Thread Chart

Fabric	Thread	Needles
Very heavy (upholstery, canvas, denim)	Heavy-duty cotton; polyester; buttonhole twist; cordonnet	18 (110)
Heavy (sailcloth, heavy coating)	Heavy-duty cotton; polyester	16 (100)
Medium weight (wool, poplin, velvet)	Ordinary sewing cotton and polyester; machine-embroidery cotton and rayon	12, 14 (80, 90)
Lightweight (shirt cotton, dress fabrics, silk)	Extra-fine to ordinary sewing cotton and polyester	10, 12 (70, 80)
Very lightweight (lace, net, organdy, batiste)	Extra-fine sewing cotton and polyester	8, 10 (60, 70)

(Chart 1.2). The lighter the material, the smaller the needle and the finer the thread should be. The heavier the fabric, the larger the needle should be.

Even more important is choosing the right needle for your machine. The 730 and 830 models use the standard sewing machine needle. In America this needle system is called 15 x 1 and in Europe it is called 705B.

Sizes available are:

	Very Fine	Fine	Med. Fine	Med.	Strong	Large	Very Large	Hem-Stitching
U.S.	8	10	11	12	14	16	18	–
Europe	60	70	75	80	90	100	110	120

Bernina 705B needles are available in *pierce point*, used for woven fabrics: and *ballpoint,* used for knits to minimize cutting threads and causing runs in the fabric. You can also use the 130/705H system on the 730 and 830 models. For the 900, 1000, and 1100 models, you must use 130/705H needles or you'll damage your machine.

The 705H is a universal-point needle, an all-purpose needle that can be used for knits as well as woven fabrics. Instead of cutting through the fabric, the slightly rounded point deflects off the threads and slips between them. Because of its versatility, it is the needle in greatest use today. If you need a pierce point, then purchase jeans needles (130/705H–J).

Following is a list of needles and their uses:

Universal Needles (130/705H): All-purpose sewing.
Fine Ballpoint Needles (130/705-SES): Fine fabrics, including knits and wovens.
Medium Ballpoint Needles (130/705 H-SUK): Heavier knitted fabrics.
Medium Ballpoint Needles (130/705 H-S): Special needles for problem stretch fabrics.
Extra-Fine Point Needles (130/705H-J): Used to pierce closely woven fabrics such as canvas or denim; often called jeans needles.
Topstitching Needles (130 N): Equipped with an eye and thread groove larger than a regular needle of the same size. Use buttonhole twist or double thread when topstitching. Use them for embroidery, too.
Magic Needles (130-705 RH): Identified by their black top and the two eyes. They're used for basting with the 730 and 830. The lower eye can be threaded for regular sewing. If you plan to use it for basting, thread the top eye.
Double and Triple Needles (130/705H ZWI and 130/705H DRI): Used for sewing with more than one thread on top. Schmetz double needles come in these sizes: 1.6mm, 2mm, 2.5mm, 3mm, 4mm. All other sizes are being discontinued.
Hemstitching Needles (130/705H ZWIHO and 130/705H WING): Double and single types.
Leather Needles (130/705H-LR): Often

called wedge needles because of their cutting points. Use them on real suede and leather. Or use a regular #110 needle in place of a leather needle.

To keep your machine running trouble-free, change the needle often. Be sure the needle is straight and has no burr on the point. Damaged needles damage fabric and machines.

If your Bernina is noisy and is skipping stitches, change the needle (assuming the machine is oiled and clean). Be sure to use the correct needle system for your machine and be certain you've placed the needle in the machine correctly. Most of the time a damaged needle is the only problem—and an easy one to rectify.

To make it easier for you to prepare appropriate supplies before beginning the lessons, let's discuss items often called for and the terms I'll use.

Batting, fleece, and fiberfill

Batting, both cotton and polyester, is used between fabric layers for quilting. Different weights and sizes are available, as well as different qualities. For our use, most of the projects can be quilted with bonded batting, which holds together firmly, or with fleece, which is a filler that's thinner than bonded batting and about as thick as a heavy wool blanket. Alternative fillers can be flannel, when only a light garment is desired, or a wool blanket. Fiberfill is the shredded batting used to fill toys. Or stuff toys with batting.

Fusibles

Fusibles are used to hold appliqués to background fabrics so edges are held firmly for the final step of stitching them in place. Plastic sandwich bags or cleaner's garment bags can be used. Stitch Witchery, Fine Fuse, Magic Polyweb and Jiffy Fuse are commercial fusible webbings. To use, place them between two pieces of fabric and press with a hot iron until the webbing melts and holds the two fabrics together. Use a Teflon pressing sheet to protect your iron and also to allow you to press the fusible to one fabric at a time. The Applique Pressing Sheet or Teflon sheet has eliminated any problem with the fusible melting on your iron: it looks like opaque wax paper, is reusable, and comes in handy sizes.

A fusible webbing already backed by paper, which saves one step in application, is called Wonder-Under Transfer Fusing Web. Draw your design directly onto the paper and place it over the appliqué fabric. Press for a few seconds, which fuses the webbing to the fabric. Then cut out the pattern and pull the paper away from the webbing. Place the appliqué, fusible side down, on the background fabric. Steam press a few seconds to fuse the appliqué to the background. Then stitch the appliqué onto a background fabric.

Appliqué papers are paper-backed products that look very much like freezer wrap, but act like the transfer web. One side of the paper has a glue finish.

See Chapter 4 for more about fusibles.

Stabilizers

Stabilizers are used behind fabric to keep it from puckering when you embroider. At one time, we used typing paper, but today we have more choices of stabilizers, available at fabric and quilt shops, Bernina shops, and through mail-order (see Sources of Supplies).

The old standby, typing paper, still does the job. Or, use shelf paper when stitching large pictures and adding-machine tape for long strips of embroidery. A problem with paper is that it dulls machine needles faster than tear-away stabilizers do. It's also harder to remove from the back of the embroidery, although dampening the paper will help.

Another stabilizer you probably have in the cupboard is plastic-coated freezer wrap. I find I'm using it more and more. If I'm embroidering a fabric that could be damaged by the hoop, or if I don't want to be encumbered by a hoop, I press freezer wrap to the back of the fabric. The freezer paper adheres to the fabric and stiffens it. When I finish my embroidery, I peel off the freezer paper. I like using it if I have a small piece of fabric to embroider. I iron the small piece to a larger, easier-to-manipulate piece of freezer paper.

Also instead of worrying about hitting the hoop against the side of the machine, or hitting the side of the hoop with the needle, I use freezer paper whenever I can. Large embroideries can be backed; then, as I stitch, they can be rolled up to the right of my needle.

Tear-away stabilizers come in crisp or soft finishes and some are iron-ons. When embroidering, place them between the fabric and machine. When the embroidery is completed, they tear away from the fabric easily.

Don't confuse stabilizers with interfacings. Interfacings are permanent and don't tear away. They can be used, of course, and so can fabrics like organdy, but they are usually used when you plan to leave the stabilizer on the back of the embroidery after it's completed.

One of the newest stabilizers is a thin film of plastic, available by the sheet or the yard, that will dissolve when wet. It's called water-soluble stabilizer. Clamp it into the hoop along with the fabric. It is transparent, and can be used on top of the embroidery, too. It can be marked on, but choose a water-erasable marker or permanent white opaque marker that will not leave ink on your embroidery when the plastic is dissolved. When your embroidery is completed, rinse out the stabilizer. It will become gooey, then disappear. To me, water-soluble stabilizer is the most exciting product that has happened to machine stitchery. Stitch on it as you would fabric. Use it whenever you want to stitch in

space, but need to change the direction of your stitching as you create (see Lesson 16), or when you want the stabilizer to completely disappear after you complete your project.

Dressmaker's carbon

At one time, we worried whether the dressmaker's carbon we used (we had only one choice) would wash out or remain permanently on our garments. Today there are several excellent replacements. One, Saral, advertises itself as the carbonless carbon. It's wax-free, and the tracing lines can be easily sponged out of fabric. The lines produced by another product, Dritz Trace-B-Gone Tracing Paper, will also wash out in water. Dritz Mark-B-Gone Tracing Paper is unique because the lines traced disappear after 24 to 72 hours, depending on fabric, temperature, and humidity. If you can't wait that long, they can also be sponged off with water. (Although both of these products are named "tracing paper," they are both dressmaker's carbons. Don't get them confused with the see-through tracing paper I refer to often in the lessons.)

Helpful hints for sewing

Before beginning to sew, check out the following general helpful hints:

1. Except on the 930, you can wind bobbins while sewing. Place the spool of thread on the closest pin to the bobbin winder (the spool you are sewing with will be on the lefthand pin), slip the thread to be wound into the slot on the bobbin and wind it by hand several turns to hold it in place. As you sew, the bobbin will wind. This is a terrific time-saver for embroiderers.

The bobbins on the 1000 and 1100 series are wound by separate motors. The motor is activated when the lever to the right of the bobbin is pushed to the left. I think it winds too fast to sew while winding, although it is advertised that you are able to do it.

2. Do you know what stitch length really means? Here are the conversions:

Setting	Number of Stitches per 1″ (2.5cm)
0.5	60
1	24
2	13
3	9
4	6
5	5
7	4

3. Please note that the marks on the throatplate (needleplate) to the left and right of the feed dogs are *metric* distances from the needle. So those of us from the U.S. who know that a ⅝″ seam allowance doesn't mean "almost ⅝″" or "slightly more than ⅝″" must mark the throatplate ourselves. I use masking tape or fine-line permanent marker.

Also, now that the new presser feet are wider to accommodate a wider stitch width, you can no longer measure a ¼″ seam by lining up the zigzag foot with the edge of the fabric. That must be marked on the throatplate as well.

4. If you need more room under the presser foot—even if it is in its highest position—take hold of the presser foot shaft and lift up on it to get more clearance. You may need to do this to get a hoop under the darning foot.

5. Every machine has its own idiosyncracies, so the settings I recommend for each lesson are only suggestions; your machine may prefer different ones.

6. Take your Bernina in for a yearly check-up whether you think it needs it or not. Between checkups, keep it cleaned and oiled. It should be oiled after every 10 or 12 hours of use. Or, if your machine starts clacking instead of humming, get out the oil can, but take it easy. There are more problems with over-oiling than with too little. To be sure the oil works its way through the areas that need lubricating (this will vary with the model), oil *before* sewing rather than when your sewing is completed. Check your manuals to learn all the spots on your machine that need oil.

7. No matter what model you have, you must keep the inside free of lint and threads. Take out the bobbin case and remove the hook. Wipe out all the lint. A Q-tip works well. I sometimes vacuum out lint from inside the machine or use canned air to remove it. Remember to clean the feed dogs whenever you finish sewing or during a long period of stitching nappy fabrics such as corduroy, fur, or velvets. Always clean during and after using the Cut'n'Sew accessory.

After the inside has been freed of lint, put a drop of oil in the race and on every other spot that needs lubricating. To replace the hook in the race, turn the hand wheel till the race looks like a smile. Then your bobbin hook will slip in and stay there without falling out before you have clicked it in place.

Now gather your supplies together and begin the adventure—to know your Bernina.

CHAPTER 2

Adding Stitches to Your Fabric

- **Lesson 1. Using built-in stitches**
- **Lesson 2. Using free machining**

In this chapter you'll become acquainted with the range of stitches your Bernina can produce. By the end of it, you'll easily switch back and forth from stitching with the feed dogs up to stitching with feed dogs down. To demonstrate your new facility, you'll make beautiful small buttons and pendants.

Lesson 1. Using built-in stitches

The first thing I did when I bought my Bernina was to try all the built-in stitches. I wanted a reference, so I sewed stitches in rows at different widths and lengths and put them in a notebook, along with notations from the Basic Manual. I was determined to know my Bernina, and this has been so helpful to me that I've made it your first lesson too.

To save you time, practical and decorative stitches have been built into the Bernina: I classify them as "closed" and "open." "Closed" refers to those where the beauty is in stitching it close together (stitch width 4 or 5, stitch length almost 0 to 1/2), like the satin stitch or scallop stitch. "Open" built-in stitches, like the sewn-out zigzag, blind hem, vari-overlock and gathering stitch, are usually sewn at a stitch length longer than 1/2.

To practice the built-in stitches and make a record of them, first set up your machine as indicated in the box at the beginning of the lesson. Then override the settings indicated on your 1000 or 1100 machine and use your imagination to experiment with other settings.

Stitch width: widest
Stitch length: varies
Needle position: center
Needle: #90/14
Feed dogs: up
Presser foot: #147 (#20) open embroidery foot
Tension: *top*, normal; *bobbin*, normal
Fabric suggestion: medium-weight striped cotton
Thread: machine-embroidery to contrast with fabric, different colors in top and bobbin
Accessories: fine-point marker
Stabilizer: tear-away or freezer paper

Stitch lines of the built-in stitches found on your Bernina (Fig. 2.1). The striped fabric will help you keep them straight. Start by using the settings suggested in the manual. Vary the settings as you stitch, making the stitches wider and narrower, longer and shorter. If there is a setting you

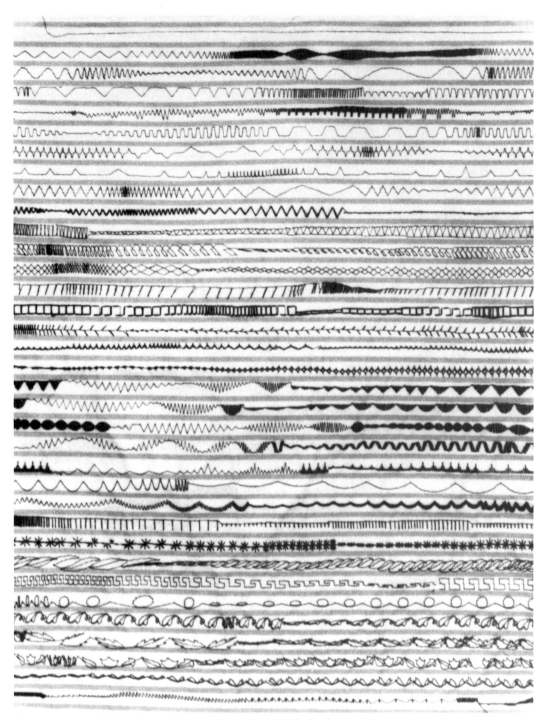

Fig. 2.1 Striped fabric is used to make a record of all the built-in stitches on my 1130.

find particularly useful, mark it right on the fabric with a marker to show where that setting begins.

This is a good time to determine the precise width and length settings for the best-looking closed, decorative stitches.

Using different colors of thread on top and bobbin will help you adjust the machine to find the perfect stitch. Adjust tension by loosening the top tension slightly and leaving the bobbin tension normal, or leaving the top tension normal and threading the bobbin finger. Whichever way you choose, the top thread should be pulled down and show underneath the fabric and should mound slightly on top when making satin stitches.

Start by stitching the zigzag, with the widest stitch width, stitch length 2. Adjust the length as you stitch until the satin stitch is perfect. This will be somewhere between 0 and 1/2 length. Write the setting on the sample.

Also, write on the sample what number stitch you used. Many stitches are the same on all the models we are considering, but there are also differences. Because of this, I will sometimes refer to the stitches I use in this book by name, such as blind-hem stitch, gathering stitch, etc., and sometimes by number, when that seems more helpful.

When you finish your record of the built-in stitches, practice mirror images. If you have the 1120 or 1130, this is as simple as pushing a button. If you have the other models, now is the time to practice and learn to make them. Check your manual.

There are a number of variables with mirror images. Are you feeding the fabric through exactly? Don't pull on one side when the other has been fed through freely. Did you start the second row at exactly the right spot? Just one stitch off will make a difference. Do you have the same thickness of fabric under both sides of the design? If you're stitching on top of a seam

allowance, the needle may go off the two layers.

If you have an 1130 model, you can take this exercise further. Choose one decorative stitch (I chose #34 and used another square of fabric to create the square in Fig. 2.2). Begin by placing a stabilizer such as freezer paper behind your fabric. Begin stitching at the left side and remember to clear all the settings after each exercise:

1. Stitch one line of your chosen stitch, exactly as your machine indicates (*top row*).

2. Next to that, press mirror image and stitch your pattern (*second row*).

3. Elongate the stitch for the next line of stitching (*third row*).

4. Now narrow it by pushing the double-needle button (*fourth row*).

5. Use the memory for the next line of stitching: Push the pattern button, memory, mirror image, memory (*fifth row*).

6. Stitch a single pattern (*sixth row*).

7. Stitch single pattern, needle down, turn fabric and repeat for border as shown (*seventh row*).

8. Stitch #34, Memory, #30, Memory (*eighth row*).

9. Press the pattern button, then the balancing buttons. It is possible to press each at least 30 times, but start with 10 +. Clear, then press pattern button again and 10 − (*bottom rows, left*).

10. To make a decorative square, press these buttons: needle down, pattern, single pattern. After the first design is stitched, raise the presser foot and turn the fabric 90 degrees counter-clockwise; then stitch another pattern. Again, raise the presser foot and turn the fabric. Continue turning and stitching until the square is completed (*bottom row, center*).

11. Repeat step 10, in a clockwise direction (*bottom row, right*).

What we have just done is called *pushing a stitch*. Write on the fabric what buttons you've pushed and in what order.

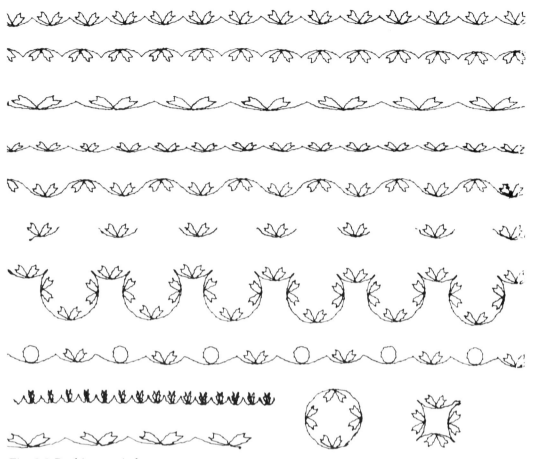

Fig. 2.2 Pushing a stitch.

Place this valuable reference in your notebook.

As you sew line after line of practical and decorative stitches, imagine how they can be used. For example, the blind-hem stitch is used for blind hems and for the tricot scalloped hem. But it can also be an invisible way of stitching on a patch pocket or an appliqué, or use it when couching down heavy cords, or to attach elastic cord to the edge of a garment for button loops.

Lesson 2. Using free-machining: darning, whipping, feather stitching

In free machining, you — not the presser foot — control the movement of the fabric, which in turn determines the length of the stitch. With fabric stretched tightly in a hoop, it is easy to move your work forward, backward, in circles, whatever way you wish.

I suggest working with a wooden hoop when first learning machine stitchery. The one made by Bernina is the best. It has a smooth finish, and because it does not stand as high as other hoops, it slips easily under the darning foot. But whatever wooden hoop you use, be sure it is the screw type, as that will hold the fabric tightly. To be sure that it does, the inside ring of the wooden hoop should be wound with narrow twill tape. This keeps the fabric from slipping. Take a few hand stitches at the end of the tape to hold it firmly.

Fabric is placed in the hoop upside-down from the way you would put it in a hoop for hand embroidery (Fig. 2.3). Pull the cloth as tightly as you can. Tighten the screw; pull again; tighten. Tap on the fabric. If it sounds like a drum, it is tight enough. You may or may not want to use a stabilizer under a hoop, depending upon the effect you want and the weight of the fabric.

You can stitch with a darning foot or the freehand embroidery foot (#24) on, or without a presser foot (but keep your fingers a safe distance from the needle!).

It is possible to stitch freely without a hoop if you use your fingers to hold the fabric taut while stitching. If you don't use

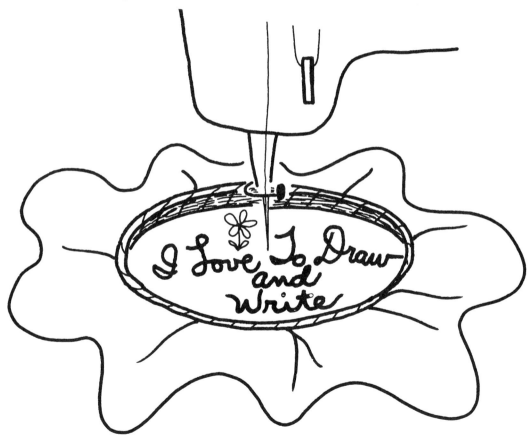

Fig. 2.3 Tighten fabric in a hoop. The fabric rests against the bed of the machine, with the material topside up for machine embroidery.

a hoop—or if you use a spring-type hoop— use the #285 (#9) darning or a freehand embroidery foot (#24) to prevent skipped stitches. It will hold the fabric down each time the machine makes a stitch so the threads interlock correctly underneath. Also, use a stabilizer under the fabric to keep the stitches from puckering.

Stitch width: 0–widest
Stitch length: 0
Needle position: center
Needle: #80/12 and double needle
Feed dogs: lowered
Presser foot: #285 (#9) darning foot or #24 freehand embroidery foot, or none

Tension: *top,* slightly loosened; *bobbin,* normal
Fabric: light-colored, medium-weight fabric, such as poplin—scrap for practice; 18″ x 18″ (45.7cm x 45.7cm) square for your notebook
Thread: one color for top, another for bobbin; both should contrast with fabric
Accessories: wrapped wooden hoop no larger than 7″ (17.8cm), fine-point marker
Stabilizer: tear-away or freezer paper

The two samples in this lesson will give you practice in control and coordination. One sample will be for practice; the other, for your notebook. Keep a record of the

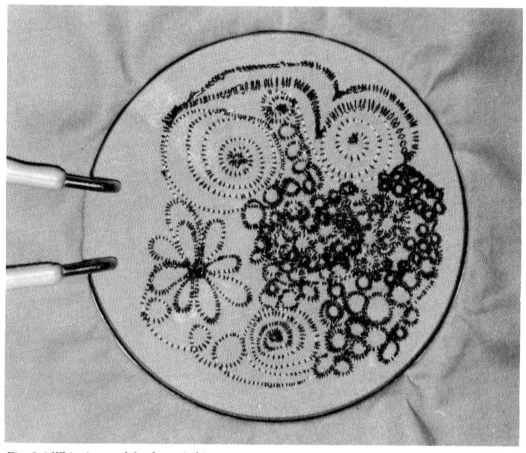

Fig. 2.4 Whipping and feather stitching.

new-found stitches you create with your machine and your imagination.

Free machining—darning, whipping and feather stitching—takes practice, but it is worth every minute. It opens up a new world of stitchery to you.

First, you are going to learn to draw, write, and sketch with your machine. It's called the darning stitch.

Set up your Bernina for darning. If you have a later model 930 machine, tape down the thread cutter so it will not interfere with the movement of the hoop.

Always begin by dipping the needle into

Fig. 2.5 Draw 36 squares on a piece of fabric, then fill them in with the new stitches and techniques you've learned and will learn. Be sure to record machine settings.

20

Tote Bag Squares: (upper left, clockwise) Chapter 4, Lesson 10—Straight Stitch Applique; Chapter 4, Lesson 19—Applique and Quilting; Chapter 4, Lesson 10—Edge-Stitch Applique, Modified Reverse Applique.

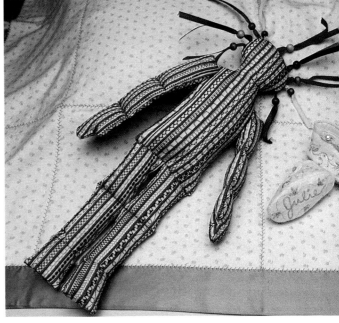

THE MAZE

C. Hickok

Counterclockwise from far left:

Chapter 2, Lesson 2—Pendants are a fast way to practice free machining and satin stitches.

Close-up of Denim Quilt from Chapter 7 by Jackie Dodson.

Projects from Chapter 11—doll with Fantasy Stitches, baby booties, and receiving blanket.

"Flora's Shadow" by dj Bennett, Lake Forest, IL—sheers and needlelace on water-soluble film, mounted ½" above the surface of a 28" circle so shadows are cast on the ground fabric.

"The Maze" by Cindy Hickok, London, England—Rayon machine embroidery on water-soluble fabric, 20 × 20 cm; fabric dissolved and embroidery mounted between layers of Plexiglas.

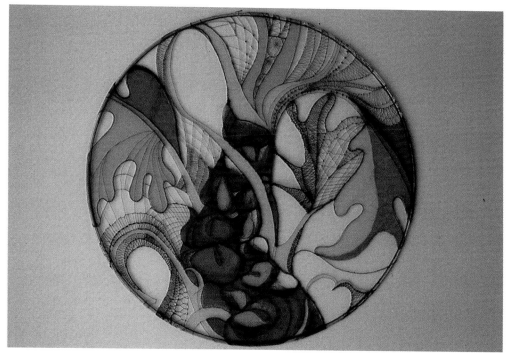

Dress worn to historical society meetings by Deb Wagner, Hutchinson, MN—Battenberg motifs and eyelets were worked in hoopfuls. The entire dress was constructed of water-soluble film from a Vogue pattern; then the motifs were sewn to the stabilizer and put in a bathtub to dissolve it. The dress is connected only at the zipper to a satin sheath underneath; that way, it can be taken apart and washed.

the fabric and bringing the bobbin thread to the top. Hold both threads to the side while stitching in one place several stitches to anchor the thread. Clip off the ends. When you begin your stitchery, start slowly. Practice moving the hoop slowly, as well. You must coordinate the speed at which you move your hoop and your sewing speed. It is not necessary to stitch at top speed—moderate speed is fine. You'll soon learn how fast is right for you and for the particular stitching you are creating.

Move the hoop back and forth, then in circles—remember the old Palmer Method exercises for handwriting? Stitch faster; move your hoop faster. Then write your name, draw a picture of a tree, your dog, an old flame. It doesn't matter how well you draw; you are really practicing control.

Change to zigzag and try it all over again. Yes, it will take awhile to gain absolute control, but don't give up. Stitch tiny fill-in spirals, figure eights and jigsaw patterns.

Now stitch, hesitate, stitch. The bobbin color may come to the top. Good! That's what we want. To make sure it does, tighten the top tension slowly. When you see the bobbin thread, note where the tension dial is set and write this on the sample. This type of stitchery is called whipping. If the hoop is moved slowly and the machine run very fast, a nubby, thickened line of bobbin thread will appear on the surface. It can be used in place of the darning stitch when embroidering—or used with it for variety. Whipping can be seen in the tiny circles of dark bobbin thread in Fig. 2.4.

With the top tension very tight and the bobbin tension loosened, stitch straight lines, circles and spirals. Move the hoop quickly. The top thread is visible as a straight line on top of the fabric. Covering it are looping, feathery bobbin stitches. This is an exaggeration of whipping, which is called feather stitching. This can be seen in the hoop in some of the small circles as I went from tight to tighter top tension, and

in the larger, spiky spirals (Fig. 2.4) that occurred when I loosened the bobbin screw until there was no resistance on the thread.

Practice is the only way to learn control. When you feel you have accomplished coordination between moving the hoop and the speed of the machine, make the following record of what you've learned: On the 18″ x 18″ (45.7cm x 45.7cm) square of fabric, draw a grid of 3″ (7.6cm) squares, six across, six down (Fig. 2.5). Then fill in your squares with examples of free machining—darning, whipping and feather stitching. Use both straight stitches and zigzag stitches in your squares. Try built-in stitches, too. You can stitch your own designs or use mine. But as you practice, write the machine settings on the fabric. Slip this into your notebook. Add new stitches as you discover them and refer to your notebook regularly for stitches you want to use on a project.

For variety, thread your needle with two colors, or try a double needle. But remember to check that your double needle will fall inside the hole of the plate when setting it on zigzag. Or, if you have one of the 1100 machines, push the double-needle button to set the machine on 3mm width.

Project Buttons and Pendants

The following one-of-a-kind projects include free machining and stitching with feed dogs up. Get to know your Bernina by stitching up these small embroideries, shown in the color section.

You have a choice of stitches on the designs and they can be finished as large buttons, earrings, or pendants. Buy button forms at fabric or needlecraft shops. I used a size 75, which is about 2″ (5.1cm) in diameter. And I was inspired by Mary Ann Spawn of Tacoma, Washington, to finish some of them by attaching cords to make pendants (see color section; also Figs. 2.8 through 2.10).

If you use the round design (Fig. 2.10), draw two circles with the same center point on your fabric. One is the area to be embroidered; the other circle, ½″ (12.7mm) outside the first, is the cutting line. It's important to keep the area between the lines free from stitching. Use a piece of fabric large enough to go into a spring hoop and place a piece of tear-away stabilizer underneath.

Embroider, using free machining such as whipping and darning, as well as satin stitches.

Leave a ½″ (12.7mm) margin on the rectangular design in Fig. 2.6, as well. Trace the design on fabric. I used white linen fabric. I chose five colors of cotton machine embroidery thread: light gray, medium gray, red, charcoal black and white. Fill bobbins with those colors, too.

Fig. 2.6 Pattern for rectangular machine-embroidered pendant.

Stitch width: 0–2
Stitch length: 0–2
Needle position: center
Needle: #90/14
Feed dogs: up, lowered
Presser foot: #147 (#20) open embroidery; #285 (#9) darning or #24 freehand embroidery foot
Tension: *top,* loosen slightly, but vary; *bobbin,* vary
Fabric suggestion: medium-weight, tightly woven linen
Thread: cotton embroidery in five colors: white, light gray, medium gray, red, charcoal black
Accessories: wood or spring hoop (or freezer paper stabilizer); button forms or cardboard, batting, craft glue, cord, tracing paper, pencil, dressmaker's carbon, empty ballpoint pen
Stabilizer: tear-away or iron-on freezer paper

Trace the design in Fig. 2.6, then transfer it to the linen with dressmaker's carbon and empty ballpoint pen.

Use red thread on the top and in the bobbin case. Always match thread colors on top and bobbin unless otherwise indicated. Loosen the top tension a bit, feed dogs down, machine set on straight stitch. Stitch in the top red area of the pendant by pulling the design toward you as you stitch, then pushing it away. Go up and back until the area has been filled in with red straight stitches. Change the machine settings to triple zigzag if you have that stitch on your machine. If you don't, you can use a double thread in a topstitching needle and use the single zigzag stitch. Zigzag in red according to the pattern, with stitch width 2, stitch length 1.

Change thread color to medium gray on top, white on the bobbin. Tighten the top tension to bring the white bobbin thread to the top for whip stitching. If it refuses, then loosen the bobbin tension a bit until the white is visible. To do this, turn the bobbin screw counter-clockwise a half turn. Don't be afraid: Mark the location of the notch on the bobbin screw before it's changed by drawing it on a piece of paper, or put a dot of fingernail polish on the bobbin case itself. Then it will be easy to return it to normal tension. Test tension by stitching on scrap fabric. Combine tightening the top tension and loosening the bobbin until the thread on top is a mixture of bobbin and top threads. With feed dogs lowered, stitch tiny circles in the area to build up texture, but leave some of the white background showing.

Turn tensions back to normal and change the settings to stitch width 1, stitch length 1, feed dogs up. Again set the machine on triple zigzag. Following the pattern, fill in the rest of the area with lines of light gray. Then straight stitch with black thread (stitch length 2) between the lines of zigzags as indicated on the pattern.

To complete the pendant, still using black thread, use a straight stitch, feed dogs lowered. The hair is done by stitching small circles along lines of straight stitches. Freely stitch the eye before you change the machine to satin stitch. With stitch width 2, stitch length 1/2, finish embroidering the rest of the hair and face on the pendant.

The other pendants are done much the same way, combining straight stitching with zigzagging. The heart pendant in Fig. 2.7 was done on a silklike polyester with shiny rayon thread. I could have combined decorative stitches with this one, but I didn't. I enjoy drawing freely with my needle, so I scribbled to fill in backgrounds, and sometimes outlined satin stitches with straight stitches of gold thread to give it a bit of glitter. I chose threads that clash: purple, pinks, fuchsia, orange, bright green, gold—but they're terrific together and give the pendant an East Indian look.

The cord was attached at the center of the heart with the free ends pulled through two beads. If you look closely at it, you'll see that it imitates the fisherman's

Fig. 2.7 Use this pattern for a heart-shaped pendant.

knot. In place of the knot, however, I've substituted two beads. No matter how long your cords, you can adjust them to fit you neckline (Fig. 2.9).

The round, white linen pendant in Fig. 2.10 is a combination of freely stitched embroidery and satin stitches. It is different from the others in that it is freer, more creative. Choose to do one or both of the other pendants first—then you'll be better prepared to ad lib embroidering this one.

I chose threads in red, green, yellow and blue. After I traced the pattern on paper, I used markers the same colors as my threads to sketch in where I wanted the colors to occur on the pendant.

After I transferred the design to the fabric, I began stitching in the free-machined areas. First I stitched tiny yellow circles to the right of center. With red thread, I added several small red dots across from the yellow. Then I added lines of green and red, even using the feather stitch freely on the lefthand side. With top tension tightened, a line of spiky stitches were created

23

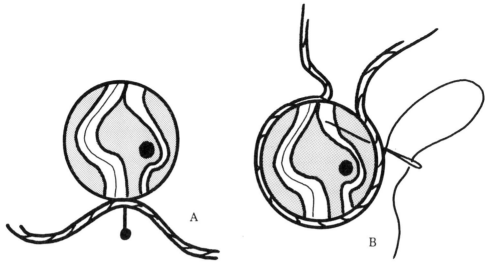

Fig. 2.8 A. *Pin center of cord to center bottom of the pendant. B. Attach cord at edge of the pendant by hand, laying the thread in the twist of the cord as you stitch.*

using that decorative stitch. Instead of straight stitches, I added lines of whip stitches in several of the colors. Then I filled in more yellow—I made sure I used each color more than once on the design.

Once I finished the free-machine embroidery stitches, I changed the settings on the machine to feed dogs up and used blue satin stitches with widths that varied from 1 to 3 to finish my design. At least I *thought*

Fig. 2.9 *Make an adjustable pendant cord by threading both cords through two beads in this manner.*

Fig. 2.10 *Use a button form to make a machine-embroidered pendant.*

I'd finished. But as I looked at it, I began to see areas that needed punching up or toning down, so I added stitches of improvement. Often I wait until the next day to see if I approve of what I stitched. I mention this because you shouldn't hesitate to go back to a piece later and add to it. Or, if you've done too much to it—you have to learn when to stop—then treat this first piece as a sample. No matter how awful it looks, put it in your notebook and start over. When you create, ad libbing as you stitch, your second attempt will be far better than the first (how well I know).

To finish, cut out the shapes. Use large button forms for the round ones, or make a pendant by placing one on a piece of batting over a cardboard circle. Make another circle of plain fabric, batting and cardboard the same way. Use a thick craft glue to glue the fabric backs over the cardboard pieces or use a hand running stitch at the edge of the pendant. Pull up on the thread to keep the batting and fabric in place around the cardboard shape. Then join back-to-back by dabbing glue between and whipping around the edge by hand.

The rectangular designs can be finished by backing them the same way. Measure a length of monk's cord (see Chapter 10), and tie an overhand knot at each end. Stitch the knots to the top or sides of the pendants by hand. Wear your samples; collect compliments.

CHAPTER 3

Adding Texture to Your Fabric

- **Lesson 3. Building up sewing stitches**
- **Lesson 4. Applying thick threads from top and bobbin**
- **Lesson 5. Fringing yarn and fabric**
- **Lesson 6. Adding buttons, beads, shisha**
- **Lesson 7. Smocking and gathering**
- **Lesson 8. Pulling threads together**

Add to or create texture on fabrics by building up sewing stitches, using thick threads, attaching fringe or objects like buttons and beads, gathering fabric for smocking or for utilitarian purposes—to stitch elastic on sleeves or bodices, or to make ruffles for curtains.

You'll make samples for your notebook; stitch up a fabric greeting card; cable stitch a tote bag square; make fabric fringe for rugs and doll hair; and make a framed picture. Both projects and samples will suggest numerous other ways to use these stitches.

Lesson 3. Building up sewing stitches

One of the simplest ways to build up texture is to sew in one place many times. Sounds simple and it is. But you can do this in so many ways that even though it is simple, the results aren't. Texture can look studied and exact or free and wild.

I use the following techniques for landscapes, monograms, and flowers. Practice each one for your notebook, recording your machine settings and any notes on how you might use the stitches later.

Begin with my suggested settings, but change them if they are not correct for your machine or not to your liking.

Stitch width: widest
Stitch length: 0–1/2
Needle position: left
Needle: #90/14

Feed dogs: up, lowered
Presser foot: #285 (9) darning or #24 free-hand embroidery foot; #030 (#6) embroidery or #147 (#20) open embroidery
Tension: *top,* loosened; *bobbin,* normal
Fabric suggestion: experiment with varied weights, types, and colors
Thread: practice with any type, but use machine embroidery thread for good; include several sizes of pearl cotton, cordonnet, yarns and ⅛" (3.2mm) ribbon
Accessories: 7" (17.8cm) spring hoop
Stabilizer: tear-away type

With feed dogs up, using the embroidery foot, anchor the threads first; then use the widest satin stitch. Sew a block of 6 or 8

Fig. 3.1 Use satin stitches for flower centers or fill-in background stitches.

Fig. 3.3 Straight-stitching around blobs.

satin stitches. Anchor them by dialing down to 0 width again and stitch in place. Move the hoop and do another block of satin stitches. Keep them quite close together, but all at different angles (Fig. 3.1). Use these to fill in areas in designs (see Figs. 2.6 and 3.29).

For the next sample, lower the feed dogs and use the darning foot. Anchor the threads by stitching in one place. Use the same wide zigzag, but sew in one place to build up 10 or 12 stitches. Move to another spot close to the first blob of stitches and stitch again. If you wish to achieve the effect in Fig. 3.2, pull the threads into loops as you move from place to place and don't cut them off. You can make flower centers this way. Or finish by clipping between the satin stitches and then, using a different color on top, outlining with straight stitches (Fig. 3.3). Using variegated thread is especially effective.

In the next experiment, dial feed dogs up, place the embroidery foot on, and set your machine on the widest satin stitch. Anchor the threads and sew a block of satin stitches at the left of the practice fabric. Pull the fabric down about three inches and over to the right slightly. Stitch another block of satin stitches. Pull up and over a bit to the right to stitch another block of satin stitches. Pull down and over for the third block. Continue across the fabric. Change threads and come back with another color. Cross the threads from the first pass as you do (Fig. 3.4). This is a good filler for garden pictures—the stitches become hedges of flowers—or use layers of these to crown trees (Fig. 3.5).

Speaking of flowers, try the ones in Fig. 3.6, with feed dogs lowered, using the same machine settings. Anchor the threads.

Fig. 3.2 Blobs and loops.

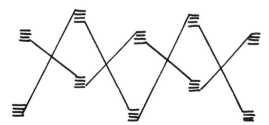

Fig. 3.4 Crossed threads and satin stitches.

27

Fig. 3.5 This tree was stitched on cotton net. The trunk is encroaching zigzags, the crown of the tree is satin stitches and crossed threads.

Stitch one blob of about 10 or 12 satin stitches in one place and, ending on the left side, the needle still in the fabric, turn the hoop. Do another blob and end on the left side. Turn the hoop and do another and another. Lay in about five or six of these to create a satin-stitch flower. The satin stitches will all have that common center—at needle left.

Make the next satin stitch flower (Fig. 3.7) by first tracing around a drinking glass with a water-erasable marker. With feed dogs lowered, anchor the thread and make a satin stitch blob perpendicular to the edge of the circle. Pull the thread across to the other side of the circle and make another blob. Anchor it. Cut off the thread. Go to another place on, just within, or just without the circle and stitch another blob. Pull the thread over to the other side, make another satin stitch blob, anchor it, and cut off the thread. Begin again and continue until you have made a flower head.

Now you'll practice filling in shapes, an-

Fig. 3.7 Create flowers using zigzag stitches and crossed threads.

Fig. 3.6 Zigzag star flowers.

other way to bring texture to your base fabric. Zigzagging is probably the most widely used method to fill in designs. You can use any stitch width, but the wider the setting, the looser the look. I feel I have more control if I use a 2 width—or better yet, I sew with straight stitches to fill in backgrounds. It is more like drawing with a pencil.

The drawback to straight-stitch filling is that the stitches are very tight to the fabric. Sometimes I want a lighter, loopier look, so I may start with zigzagging to fill in a design and then draw on top of that with straight stitches to emphasize a color, to outline, or to add shading to my embroidery. So I've included three ways to add texture to fabric by filling in designs with zigzag stitches.

Method A

In this method you will follow the contour of your design with zigzag stitches, changing a flat circle into a ball shape.

Stitch width: widest
Stitch length: 0
Needle position: center
Needle: #90/14
Feed dogs: lowered
Presser foot: #285 (9) darning foot, #24 free-hand embroidery foot, or use a wooden hoop with no foot
Tension: *top,* slightly loosened; *bobbin,* normal
Fabric suggestion: medium-weight cotton
Thread: sewing thread for practice
Accessories: large hoop at least 7" (17.8cm); water-erasable marker, tear-away stabilizer

Using the marker, draw several circles on the fabric in the hoop (I drew around the base of a large spool of thread). Place stabilizer under the hoop. Zigzag the first circle into a ball shape by stitching in curved lines. To make it easier, first draw stitching guidelines inside the circle (Fig. 3.8, method A, *left*).

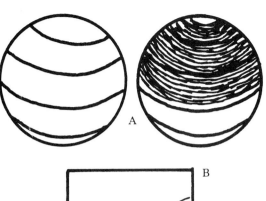

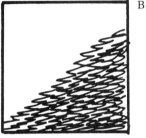

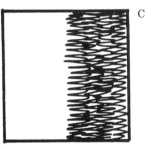

Fig. 3.8 Filling in designs with zigzag stitches. A. Draw guidelines in the circles, then move sideways and back, following the guidelines. B. Stair-step method. C. Encroaching zigzag.

Start at the top of the circle, stitching and moving your hoop sideways and back while following the curves you've drawn (Fig. 3-8, method A, *right*). Move from top to bottom, creating the ball shape as you stitch. Don't build up stitches too fast in one place. Move the hoop evenly, slowly, and practice coordination.

Try other stitch widths on the other cir-

29

cles you've drawn. Put the samples in your notebook.

Method B

This has been described as the stair-step method. Designs can be filled in by zigzag stitching from lower-left corner to upper-right corner and back again (Fig. 3-8, method B). To practice this, set up your machine as you did in method A. Draw several 1½″ (3.8cm) squares on your fabric. Although you will start with the widest stitch, experiment with other widths as you did before. Each line of zigzags blends into the one before it. Add your experiments to your notebook.

Method C

Encroaching zigzag is another way to fill in a design (Fig. 3-8, method C). Set up your machine as follows:

Stitch width: widest
Stitch length: 0
Needle position: center

Needle: #90/14
Feed dogs: lowered
Presser foot: #285 (#9) darning foot, #24 freehand embroidery foot, or no foot
Tension: *top*, slightly loosened; *bobbin*, normal
Fabric: medium-weight cotton
Thread: sewing thread for practice
Accessories: 7″ (17.8cm) hoop, tear-away stabilizer, water-erasable marker

This time, draw only one 2″ (5.1cm) square on the fabric in the hoop, and place stabilizer under it. Keep the hoop in the same position in front of you; don't rotate it. Instead, move it backward and forward as you stitch. Start at the top of the right side of the square you've drawn and stitch down to the bottom, moving the hoop slowly to keep the stitches close together. Move the hoop to the left a bit and stitch back up to the top, overlapping the first stitching slightly. Continue until you have covered the square. Go back and stitch on top of stitches for more texture. Do a sample for your notebook.

Lesson 4. Applying thick threads from the top and bobbin

We created texture with regular sewing threads in Lesson 3, but in this lesson we'll change sewing and machine-embroidery threads for thicker threads, such as pearl cotton, cordonnet, and crocheted cotton. We'll explore four different ways to create texture by attaching these thick threads to fabric, including using them on the top spool, couched down on top of fabric, threaded up through the hole in the throat plate of the machine, and wound on the bobbin.

Adding texture adds interest to sewing and embroidery. Perhaps it's not essential—a dress is still a dress without textured decoration—but it is a long-cut, that something extra that takes your dress from ordinary to special. Adding cords, fringe, objects, and gathers to the background fabric are all easy techniques once you know your machine.

Applying thick thread through the needle

Thread as large as cordonnet can be sewn with a #110/18 needle. Topstitching needles also have eyes to accommodate double threads or thick threads like buttonhole twist, available in #80/12 to #110/18 needles.

Whatever you use, the thread must slip through the needle easily and the needle must make a hole in the fabric large enough to keep the thread from fraying.

Couching thread down on top of fabric

If thread is too thick for the needle, try couching it down on top of the fabric using the #030 (#6) embroidery foot. Pull cord through the hole, front to back, and tie a knot at the back to keep from losing it before you begin. As soon as you start stitching, the thread will be fed through this hole with no help needed. It will stay exactly in place as you satin stitch over it with a zigzag stitch. Cover the cord as closely or sparsely as you wish, using different stitch lengths.

Stitching perfect circles

I feel that owning an #030 (#6) embroidery foot is mandatory. I couldn't sew without it. Covering cord is just one use. I also use it without cord when I want to sew a perfectly straight line of stitches. The center hole is a perfect guide when I line it up with the stitching line on my fabric.

When I sew multiple cords, I use the braiding foot #189 (#21) or bulky overlock foot #528 (#12), lining the cords up next to each other through the slot on top.

You will practice applying thick threads on top of the fabric by making the greeting card shown in the following project. On this card, you will also practice making circles with the circular embroidery device.

If you don't have the circular embroidery device, let me tell you how to stitch a perfect circle. It takes practice and confidence to satin stitch a perfect circle without the circular device, but it isn't necessary to practice stitching one hundred circles. Rather, you gain confidence by using your machine often and by teaching yourself to precision-stitch, even if it is only a simple dress seam. Here's how to stitch a perfect circle if you don't have the circle maker accessory.

Stabilize your appliqué fabric before drawing the circle and cutting it out or, in the case of transparent fabrics, hold them and the background fabric in a hoop and apply using Method A in Chapter 4. If I use regular fabric, I usually use a fusible and Method B in Chapter 4, so there will be no creeping or pleating when the circle is stitched down to the backgrond fabric. Be sure you start by drawing a perfect circle. I've used templates such as spools, cups and plates. If you plan to stitch a lot of circles, buy a plastic template at an art or office supply store (you'll need a fine-line marker or sharp pencil, too). The template is thick, but transparent, with cut-out circles that range from too-tiny-to-be-of-any-use to 3″ (7.6mm). Use the cups and plates for larger circles.

You'll find that large circles are easier to stitch than small ones, and that narrow satin stitches are easier to maneuver than wide ones. Use an embroidery presser foot or appliqué foot. I usually prefer a satin stitch no wider than 3mm for an appliqué, but the embroidery foot #030 (#6) or #147 (#20) for your machine will accommodate the width of your machine's satin stitch. The appliqué foot #181 (#23) is used when stitching a satin stitch no wider than 2mm.

It's important to have a reference point on the foot you use. When I use an open embroidery foot, I cut a piece of transparent tape ⅛″ (3.2mm) wide and wrap it across the toes of the presser foot in front of and very close to the needle. I use a black marking pen to mark a centerpoint on the tape from front to back. When stitching clockwise, to cover the edges of a circle using this foot or the #030 (#6) embroidery foot, I use needle position far left, stitch width 3, stitch length set for satin stitches, and I place the mark I've drawn on the tape, or the right side of the hole in the #030 (#6) embroidery foot, directly above the edge I want to cover. When stitching counter-clockwise, I place the left side of the hole on the edge I wish to cover and stitch with needle far right. Then I watch the mark and fabric edge closely as I guide my fabric around the circle.

The #181 (#23) transparent appliqué foot is a closed foot, which keeps the fabric under it more stable. The center groove, which is visible from the top of the foot, is flared on both sides at the back, behind the needle, to allow you to stitch around curves more easily. The groove in front of the needle is straight. I place the edge of the center groove directly over the edge of the fabric I will be satin stitching—that may be to the left or right side of the groove—depending upon whether I am stitching clockwise or counter-clockwise. This foot should be used with needle position in the center.

To get a more perfect edge when you stitch wovens, use a sharp, sometimes called a jeans, needle; to produce a more beautiful satin stitch, always use machine embroidery thread and back your work with freezer paper or tear-away.

Before I begin stitching my circle, I hand-walk the machine to be sure the needle swing has been set up correctly. I want the needle to go into the background fabric exactly at the edge of the appliqué. The satin stitches are on the appliqué fabric. Never satin stitch out beyond the appliqué, attaching the circle with stitches that barely catch the edge.

Pivot as you stitch around the circle. The smaller the circle, the more pivoting and the harder it is to stitch the perfect circle. Keep this in mind: If the curve is an outside (convex) one, your pivot points will be on the outside of the circle. If your curve is inside (concave) like you find in reverse appliqué, then the pivot points will be on the inside edge. Always pivot whenever you see the satin stitches slanting instead of radiating (imagine your circle has lines radiating from the center and you are stitching only the edges of those lines). You may have to go back to the same pivot point several times as you complete the continuous curve. Do this with needle down in the pivot point, turn the fabric slightly, stitch, needle down in the same pivot point, move the fabric again, and so on, until the curve is smooth and covered evenly with satin stitches. Yes, it is slow going, but never stitch a circle if you are in a hurry—it won't work. Circles are a stitch-by-stitch process, and a slow one if you want a perfect circle.

Practice on several circles, playing with stitch width and the needle position to find what works best for you. Experiment with presser feet as well. Place your samples in your notebook.

Project Greeting Card

Practice perfect circles and applying thick threads by making the greeting card in Fig. 3.9.

Stitch width: 0–4
Stitch length: 1/2–2
Needle position: center
Needle: #90/14
Feed dogs: up, down
Presser foot: #181 (#23) appliqué foot, #528 (#12) bulky overlock, #492 (#10) edging foot, #285 (#9) darning foot
Tension: *top,* normal; *bobbin,* finger threaded
Fabric suggestions: 12″ (30.5cm) square of white polished cotton, 6″ (15.2cm) square of green polished cotton, 12″ (30.5cm) square of yellow organdy
Thread: rayon in rainbow colors—yellow, red, green, purple, blue; #3 pearl cotton in the same colors; monofilament
Accessories: 7″ (17.8cm) spring hoop, Bernina circle maker, water-erasable or vanishing marker, greeting card folder

(available at craft, art, and needlework shops) or picture frame, dressmaker's carbon, empty ballpoint pen
Stabilizer: tear-away

Use the pattern in Fig. 3.10 as a guide, changing measurements to fit the card folder or frame. Trace the pattern from the book, then place the drawing on top of the white background fabric, with dressmaker's carbon between. Transfer it, using the empty ballpoint pen.

Cut a piece from the green fabric large enough for the area at the bottom of the design, plus 1″ (2.5cm). Fold under the top edge of the green about ½″ (12.7mm) and press it. Hold it in place with pins and apply it using the edging foot, with monofilament thread on the top and bobbin, and the machine set on a blind hem stitch — stitch width 1, stitch length 2 (or #26 on 1130).

Next, stretch three layers of yellow organdy over the white and green fabric and put them all in a spring hoop. Back this with tear-away. Set up the circle maker on your machine. Poke the tack through at the center of the three layers of organdy. Place the appliqué presser foot on the line of the inner circle. Stitch on that line around the circle with a straight stitch. Take the fabric out of the hoop and cut back only the top layer of organdy to the stitching.

Place the greeting card back in the hoop, with the tack back in its original hole. Satin stitch with the machine set on a width of 2, length 1/2, or the setting on your machine for smooth, close satin stitches.

Then move the tack so the line of the next circle will be centered under your presser foot. Straight stitch around the circle, cut back and satin stitch again as you did with the first. Do the same for the last layer of organdy.

Take the fabric out of the hoop while you stitch over the cords, but place tear-away stabilizer underneath. Each cord is a different color; use the bulky overlock foot to guide the pearl cotton. Stitch over the cords, using close satin stitches. I prefer to stitch in two passes, attaching the cord first, then stitching in close satin stitches to cover it evenly and smoothly on the second pass.

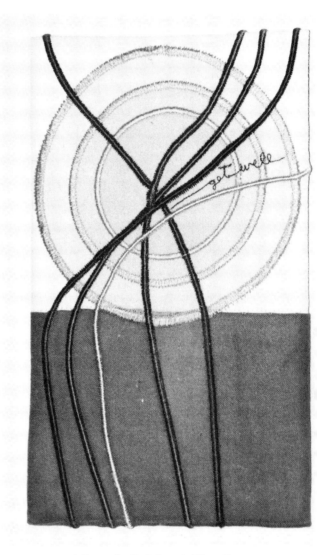

Fig. 3.9 "Even the Rainbow is Upset" greeting card.

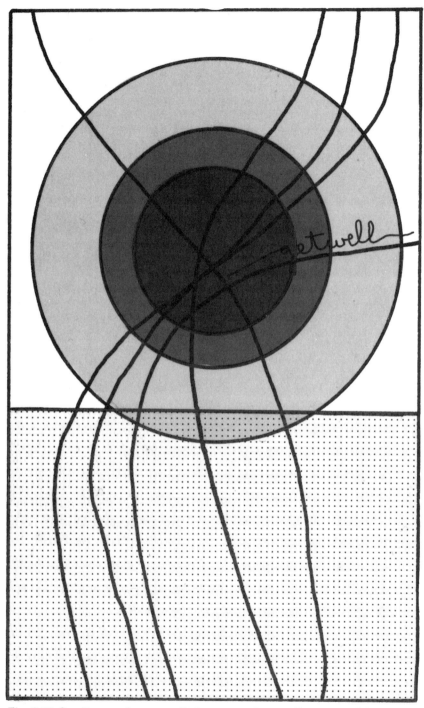

Fig. 3.10 Greeting card pattern. Enlarge or reduce to fit your card folder.

When the last cord has been covered, change to the darning foot, feed dogs down, straight stitch. Use the color you have on your machine—unless it's yellow—to write a message along the top of one of the cords. I wrote "get well," and on the inside I'll write the message: "Even the rainbow is upset."

Finish the edge with a straight stitch. Trim close to stitches and slip into the card folder or finish it for a framed picture.

Also try the #528 (#12) foot for sewing down bulky yarn or cords invisibly. Choose either the vari-overlock stitch or the blind hemming stitch (Fig. 3.11). Set up your machine as follows:

Stitch width: 1–1/2
Stitch length: 1–1/2
Needle position: half right (blind hem stitch);
    half left (vari-overlock stitch)
Needle: varies
Feed dogs: up
Presser foot: #528 (#12) bulky overlock
Tension: *top,* normal; *bobbin,* normal
Thread: monofilament on top, polyester on
    bobbin
Stabilizer: tear-away

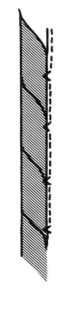

Fig. 3.11 Use the blind-hem stitch to attach cord invisibly.

Stitch alongside the cord. At the wide bite of the needle, the cord is sewn down with a tiny, almost unnoticeable stitch. When the line of stitching is completed, go back and gently nudge the cord over toward the stitching line. Now your monofilament will be completely hidden.

Or, still using the #528 (#12) foot, line up several threads of pearl cotton next to each other. Pull them through the center slot to the back. Use a zigzag or built-in stitch to attach them with monofilament or with a colored thread.

Soutache is like a thick cord, and can be attached perfectly using the #189 (#21) braiding foot. It is not easily done without this special foot, as there is no way to hold the braid in place so the needle will enter exactly in the center each time. It's possible to feed other narrow braids or rickrack through the hole in this foot. To attach soutache, trace the design on the topside of your fabric, using a water-erasable pen. Place stabilizer under the fabric.

Corners are not impossible if you walk the machine around them. Stop at the corner, needle down, presser foot raised. Turn the fabric 45 degrees, lower the foot, take one stitch; then, needle down again, raise the presser foot, turn the fabric to complete the corner. You'll get a good angle. If you can, though, choose a design with undulating curves, which are easier to accomplish. Look at the braiding foot. You'll see a groove cut along the right side, which helps turn corners. It is easiest to turn corners against the left side, which is not cut out.

Use soutache and other braids down jacket and vest fronts, around sleeves, to decorate belts and handbags.

If the braid crosses and recrosses itself, threading in and out like a Celtic interlacing cord, it is still possible to use the braiding foot. The braid will not be threaded through the foot, but will be hand basted in place on the fabric, then fit within the groove as you carefully ride over it and stitch it down.

Fig. 3.12 Stitch alongside, then across, in the twist, to attach cord.

For your next sample, use the #272 (#28) wool darning foot when freely couching down yarn. This darning foot has a slot in the front to guide the yarn along as you freely attach it. The trick is to keep the yarn in the slot as you turn your work. Therefore, to get the feel of the foot, use straight lines or gentle curves on your first samples. Try a smooth, sport-weight yarn for your first experiment. Add the result to your growing notebook.

Here's another invisible way to attach thick, twisted cord or yarn to fabric (Fig. 3.12). Leave the machine set up for free machining, but remove the presser foot. Use monofilament thread on top. Iron a piece of freezer paper onto the fabric. Begin by drawing the bobbin thread to the top and anchoring the threads. Stitch the end of the cord down. Then move along one side of the cord with a straight stitch. When you reach a twist in the cord, follow it to the other side by stitching in the twist. Once on the other side, follow along that side for a few stitches until you reach the top of the next twist. Cross over again, fol-

lowing the twist. Continue in this manner until the cord is attached.

Attaching cord pulled through the needleplate

You can also attach thick cords to the surface of fabric by threading them through the hole in the needleplate on the bed of the machine. Of course, this method attaches the cord underneath the fabric so you must stitch with the top-side of the fabric against the needleplate.

Depending on the machine, take the top of the free arm or the needleplate off the machine. This makes it easier to thread the cord through the hole. Open the bobbin door to thread the cord through the bobbin area, up through the needleplate. Leave the bobbin area open—don't close the door on the cord. Once you have it threaded through, tie a knot at the end so it does not slip out again. Re-attach the free-arm or the plate to the machine.

I've used this method of attaching cords through the needleplate for collages, when I want to add long lines of thick cords easily and fast. I draw on the stabilizer, which is on top of the wrong side of the fabric, to indicate where I should stitch. The cord is fed evenly through the plate and attached to the fabric with straight or zigzag stitches.

Stitch a record of your experiments with straight stitch and zigzag. Also try cord through the needleplate with some of the built-in stitches intended for decorative edgings, like the scallop stitch.

You can also apply round elastic with this method.

Use pearl cotton through the needleplate for pintucking with double needles (see Chapter 5). Make samples using each pintuck foot you own. Stitch many rows, spacing them according to the spacing on the pintuck feet. Mark them for your notebook.

Using thick thread from the bobbin

Cable stitching is an embroidery technique using thick thread on the bobbin. The topside of the fabric will be against the bed of the machine. It can be done with feed dogs up, using an embroidery foot for straight or built-in stitches, or it can be done freely with feed dogs down, using a darning or freehand embroidery foot or using no presser foot at all.

Cabling can look like a tightly couched thread or like fluffy fur, depending on the thread you choose. A hard twist thread like crochet cotton will lay flatter, with less beading or looping than a soft, loosely twisted yarn like mohair. The effects you get will depend not only on top and bobbin tension, but on stitch width, stitch length, color and size of cord, color of top thread, feed dogs up or down, color, weight, and type of fabric, how fast you stitch and how fast you move the hoop.

When I say you can use thick threads, I'm not kidding. Did you know that you can use up to a four-ply yarn in the bobbin? Of course, the thicker the yarn, the less you can wind on the bobbin. Usually the bobbin can be put on the machine and wound slowly while you hold the yarn or cord to control it. If you find the yarn must be wound by hand, do so evenly without stretching it.

To use the thicker threads this embroidery requires, you must override that panicky feeling that accompanies loosening and tightening the tension spring on the bobbin. Perhaps you've already discovered, as you've changed bobbins, that you can recognize the feel of normal tension. If not, put a bobbin full of sewing thread into the bobbin case and click the thread into the spring. Hold on to the end of the thread and let the bobbin case hang from it like a yo-yo. It should drop slowly when jerked. Memorize how this feels with normal tension before you begin to loosen the bobbin

spring for cabling. Loosen the spring over an empty box, as the screw has a tendency to pop out and disappear forever. I've purchased several extra screws just in case.

When adjusting tension for heavy threads, remember that the cord must feed through the bobbin case smoothly. Loosen the bobbin tension by turning the screw counter-clockwise until the tension feels normal to you.

Practice cabling on a piece of scrap fabric. Set up your machine with feed dogs up, using an embroidery thread on top or regular sewing thread. Place your fabric in a hoop and use the #147 (#20) embroidery foot. Stitch and then look under the fabric to be sure the tension is set correctly—do you want tight, stiff stitches or loosely looping ones? Manipulate the bobbin tension for different effects.

Don't forget the top tension. It must be loose enough so the bobbin thread stays underneath the fabric; but if it is too loose, it may keep the stitches from staying neatly in place.

Write on your sample fabric which is the topside, which the back. Also record bobbin and top spool tensions by using + and − signs.

Most embroiderers I know buy an extra bobbin case to use for embroidery only. There is a case made in Japan that costs about $10. (The Bernina case is approximately $30.) Buying an extra case is a good idea. It's possible to tighten and loosen the spring screw—or even remove the spring altogether—without the time-consuming adjustments needed to return to normal sewing tension.

Whatever you choose to do, don't be afraid of your Bernina. Change tensions, lengths, speeds, and use it to its full potential. Get to know your machine.

Now prepare a cabling sample for your notebook. Choose a medium-weight cotton or blend. Use several open and closed built-in stitches with #3, #5, and then #8 pearl cotton. Try ribbon and yarn as well. Keep the stitch long enough to prevent the cord from bunching up under the fabric. Open built-in stitches work best and simple zigzag is most effective. I like the zigzag opened up to a 2 or 3 length and a 4 or 5 stitch width. It gives a rickrack effect.

Stretch a piece of fabric in a hoop, but don't use a stabilizer underneath. Instead, use a stabilizer on top to keep your stitches from pulling. Draw lines or designs on the stabilizer. This is actually the back of your work.

Dip the needle into the fabric, drawing the bobbin thread or cord to the top. Hold the threads to the side as you begin. If you can't bring the cord up through the fabric, then pierce the cloth with an awl or large needle and bring it up. Don't anchor the threads with a lockstitch at the beginning or end. Instead, pull the threads to the back each time you start; when you stop, leave a long enough tail to be able to thread it up in a hand-sewing needle and poke it through to the back. Later you can work these threads into the stitching by hand.

It is also possible to quilt with this technique. Using a white pearl cotton in the bobbin and a top thread to match the fabric, you can get an effect which looks much like Japanese Sashiko (Fig. 3.13).

Apply ⅛" (3.2mm) double-faced satin ribbon as shown in Fig. 3.14. Wind the ribbon onto the bobbin. The end of the ribbon does not go through the tension spring. Rather, thread the ribbon from the bobbin into the square hole in the bobbin case from inside to outside — then place the bobbin in the case. Place the ribbon between the two teeth at the end of the case spring. Use the regular presser foot, needle right, stitch length about 4. On the 900, 1000 and 1100 models, use the top stitch setting.

When you start and stop in this type of couching, the ribbon is brought to the underside and finished off by hand. This technique is used on the infant's bonnet in Chapter 5.

Next try cabling with free embroidery. Place a medium-weight fabric in a hoop

Fig. 3.13 Stitching in the style of Japanese Sashiko.

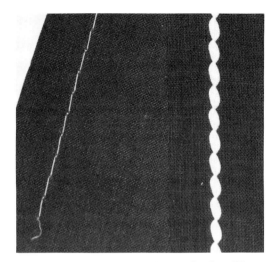

Fig. 3.14 The top and underneath of a ribbon attached by machine stitching.

with a stabilizer on top. Lower the feed dogs and, using a darning foot or bare needle, freely straight stitch, then zigzag.

Plan the lines of stitching before you begin. As you work, sew and peek under your hoop so you can regulate the bobbin and top tensions to your liking. Practice turning, pushing and pulling the hoop, sewing circles and straight lines. When your stitching changes direction, the tension is also changed, so practice how fast you should move your hoop for the effects you want. Often a design can be seen from the back of printed fabric. Take advantage of that to stitch a sample piece for your notebook. Stretch the fabric in a hoop. Water-soluble stabilizer can be used underneath if the fabric is washable. Otherwise, don't use a stabilizer. Instead, be sure your fabric is very taut, and use the darning or freehand embroidery foot. Embellish these prints by outlining the designs with pearl cotton or thick rayon thread on the bobbin.

Use bridal veiling as your fabric and create original lace. Or, decorate velveteen using velour yarn on the bobbin and monofilament thread on the top.

Project
Tote Bag
Square (Cabling)

This flower garden design in Fig. 3.15 is one I use in machine-embroidery classes. It serves two purposes: Students practice control but, more importantly, they are required to come up with their own free-machined stitch ideas or incorporate the ones I've taught them when filling in the barest of outlines. Built-in stitches are allowed, as are built-in stitches used freely.

The same design can be used for cabling. In fact, it is more interesting in cabling because of the texture that's achieved by using thick threads on the bobbin. Here is a chance to see what effects can be created by pearl cotton in sizes #3, #5, and #8. But don't limit yourself to those. Try any thick threads you have, such as buttonhole twist, stiff carpet thread, lightweight yarns, cordonnet and buttonhole gimp.

Stitch width: 0–widest
Stitch length: 0–2
Needle position: center, left
Feed dogs: up, lowered
Presser foot: #147 (#20) open embroidery, #285 (#9) darning or #24 freehand embroidery
Tension: *top,* normal, loosened; *bobbin,* normal, loosened
Fabric suggestion: 9″ (22.9cm) square white linen
Thread: *thick threads,* purple buttonhole twist, pink cordonnet, rosy-red, pale green, medium green, dark greens, variegated blue, yellow, green pearl cotton; *sewing threads,* yellow, greens, light blue, pink, red, purple
Accessories: dressmaker's carbon, empty ballpoint pen, tracing paper and pencil
Stabilizer: 10″ square freezer paper

Trace the outline in Fig. 3.15. Transfer it, using dressmaker's carbon and empty

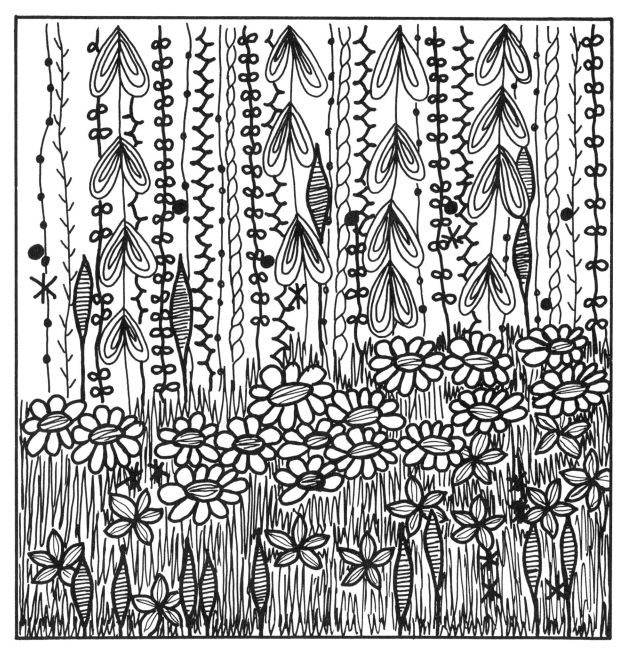

Fig. 3.15 Flower garden pattern for tote bag square.

40

ballpoint pen, to the piece of freezer paper. Press the freezer paper to the back of the fabric you've chosen for the square. Prepare another piece of linen and freezer paper to do sample stitches before you include them on your square. Be sure you write on this sample what kind of cord, what size, what settings you've used, and place this in your notebook later. It is a good idea to staple a few inches of the cords you've used next to your samples.

Many variables influence the look of your cabling: weight and twist of thread, tensions on top and bobbin, sewing speed, speed at which you move the hoop. Sometimes there are noticeable changes in the cabling if you pull rather than push the hoop, or if the top tension is looser than normal, especially if you use jerking movements or move the hoop quickly, then hesitate to let the thick thread build up.

Now fill this square with my ideas or your own. When you finish the square you will certainly have a clear understanding of how texture is achieved by cabling, what threads are effective, what settings are best for the effects you want to achieve.

Stitch in the background first, working from the top down. Remember to choose a pale thread for backgrounds (you want the color to recede), and darker colors for the foreground.

I began with pale blue pearl cotton on the bobbin and sewing thread of the same color on top, then straight stitched lines from top to bottom, adding tiny circles approximately every ¼″ (6.4mm). Stitch several of these across the square.

With medium-green pearl cotton, stitch figure 8s from the top of the square down to the large flowers. Again, stitch several across the square.

Next, use either the feather stitch (#16) or a zigzag stitch. Try narrowing, elongating, sewing it freely. Move the fabric side-to-side to get an uneven, spiky stem effect. Next, if you have the feather stitch, go back and stitch rows of feather stitches with feed dogs up, embroidery foot in place. Then I chose #28, and pushed the double-needle button to make it narrower. If you have neither #16 nor #28, then choose an alternative, such as a honeycomb stitch, or try #12 with every other stitch a mirror image. Don't strive for complete realism as you fill in the background to look like a field of weeds and wildflowers.

The final stems and leaves are freely stitched with medium-green pearl cotton. Stitch down the length of the stem, then up to the first large leaf. Outline it and then fill it in. Go to the next leaf outline and fill it in. Stitch to the next leaves and fill those in. Stitch in the remaining stem and leaves the same way. Add more of these leafed stalks across the square.

The area beneath is stitched with a pale green to look like a grassy background for the large flowers. With the widest zigzag, I turned the square on its side and stitched freely from the top to the bottom of the area.

The large oval flowers were filled in next. I used purple silk buttonhole twist in the bobbin for half of them, merely stitching loops around a centerpoint. Rosy-red pearl #5 was used for the rest of the flowers. While I had that color pearl in the bobbin, I went back to the top long-stem area and stitched in tiny circles of rosy-red to add color to the greens and blue.

The centers of the large flowers are the widest zigzag stitched with yellow variegated thread. To do this I stitched in one place five or six times to build up the center, then I moved from one side to another to fill in the centers.

The bottom area is filled in much like the pale grassy area, but I set the machine on straight stitch and loosened the tensions. I used pale green on the bobbin, dark green on the top. When I move the hoop quickly up and back, the grasses became long green lines, with spikes of dark green top thread holding the lines in place.

Satin stitch flowers are next. I used variegated blue pearl cotton, needle position left, feed dogs lowered, and stitched five satin stitches in one place, turned the hoop to stitch five more and so on until six petals had been stitched.

With a dark pink gimp, I stitched in single-pattern star flowers (#27). These are not clearly defined when using thick thread, but when a contrasting top thread is used on the bobbin, they have points that sparkle and I added these tiny stars for color. If your machine doesn't have star flowers, then stitch small circles as you did before.

Changing to #8 yellow pearl cotton, I used stitch #21, elongated and narrowed. Most machines have this cattail-like stitch. Remember altered memory on the 1130? It comes in handy here. For example, set the machine on stitch #21, double needle, elongated and single pattern. The machine will narrow, elongate, and stitch one motif, then stop. Change to straight stitch and sew to the bottom to make a stem. Push #21 again. The alteration is already in. Do another motif, close to the first, change to straight stitch and stitch the stem. Stitch the next and the next. There's a definite rhythm to it as you move across the square. I used these cattails at the top and at the bottom of the square.

If you don't have this stitch on your machine, then create it as follows: Start with stitch width 0, stitch length 1/2 (satin stitch). Stitch slowly, gradually increasing the stitch width to 3, then back to 0, and straight stitch to the bottom.

When completed, I clipped the threads I hadn't clipped as I progressed and I dotted each one with Fray-Check. If I were cabling on clothing or something that would get wear and tear, I would thread up a darning needle and work each thread to the back of the square and hand-stitch it under the stitching at the back before I clipped it off.

Finish this square as shown in Chapter 12.

Lesson 5. Fringing yarn and fabric

In this lesson you will learn to make fringe with a fringing fork, as well as with strips of fabric sewn together and clipped into fringe. Start by using a fringing fork to make yarn fringe. It can be used for wigs, costumes, rugs, and decorating edges of garments. Fringing forks are available in many different sizes. Or, you can make your own using wire, ranging from the thickness of a coat hanger to fine as a hairpin.

Wrap the fork as shown in Fig. 3.16, sew down the center, pull the loops toward you, and wrap some more. If making yards and yards of fringe, use Robbie Fanning's method of measuring. Robbie measures the length she wants from a roll of adding-machine tape and stitches her fringe right to the tape. This also keeps the fringe from twisting. When you're finished, tear off the paper and apply the fringe.

Sometimes you may not want the fringe sewn in the middle (Fig. 3.16A). Stitch it at the edge of the fork to make fringe twice as wide as that made by sewing down the center (Fig. 3.16B). As you work with the fork, you will understand when to use each method. And don't limit yourself to yarn or string alone. Try fabric. I used it for doll hair for my denim doll.

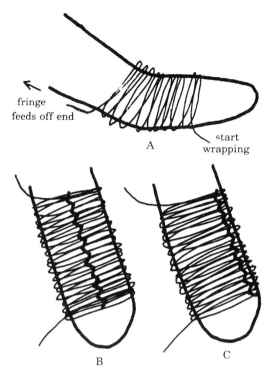

fringe feeds off end

A

start wrapping

B

C

Fig. 3.16 The fringe fork. A. Wrap with yarn or fabric strips. B. Sew down in the middle. C. Or sew at the side of the fork for wider fringe.

chine tape. Use the triple zigzag stitch (for more strength) if your machine has this capability. When I had enough for hair, I tore the paper off the fringe and pinned the hair to her head in various ways to decide what hairdo I liked best. I sewed it on by hand; I could have left it as it was, but I decided to clip the loops (Fig. 3.17).

But you can achieve almost the same effect with fabric without using the fringing fork. Work with strips of fabrics, but don't clip them into fringe until after they are sewn to the item you are making.

Project
Fringed Denim Rug

This fabric-fringe project, a little rug, ate up yards of old jeans and denim remnants I picked up at sales; I kept cutting 2½″ (6.4cm) strips on the bias until I had finished the rug.

Stitch width: 0
Stitch length: 2
Needle position: right
Needle: #110/18 jeans needle
Presser foot: #007 (#4) zipper
Tension: *top*, normal; *bobbin*, normal
Fabric suggestion: denim, cut into 2½″
    (6.4cm) bias strips of blues and red; use
    remnants and old jeans to cut quantity
    needed for rug size you want; heavy up-
    holstery fabric for rug backing
Thread: matching polyester thread
Stabilizer: 1″-wide (2.5cm-wide) fusible web-
    bing (measure circumference of rug)

You'll need a piece of heavy fabric the size of the finished rug, plus an inch all around. Measure the perimeter and cut a piece of 1″-wide (2.5cm-wide) fusible webbing. Using a Teflon pressing sheet, press

Stitch width: 4 or 5
Stitch length: 1
Needle position: center
Feed dogs: up
Presser foot: #147 (#20) open embroidery
    foot
Tension: *top*, normal; *bobbin*, normal
Fabric suggestion: 1″-wide (2.5cm-wide) bias
    strips, several yards
Thread: polyester to match bias
Accessories: large fringe fork
Stabilizer: adding machine tape

I wrapped the fork with red denim and sewed down the center over adding-ma-

Fig. 3.17 The doll's hair is fabric fringe, her eyelashes are thread fringe done with the tailor-tacking foot.

the fusible webbing to the topside of all the edges and fold them back on the topside of the fabric, pressing again (Fig. 3.18). This is the top of the rug, so the edges will be finished when the last strip is stitched down.

Fold the first bias strip lengthwise to find the center, but open it again and place it ⅛″ (3.2mm) from the edge of the upholstery fabric. Stitch down the center crease of each strip from top to bottom (Fig. 3.19). Fold the left side of the strip to the right. Push the next strip as close as you can get it to the first. Sew down the center again; Fig. 3.19 shows the first three fabric strips stitched down. If you run out of fabric for a strip, add another by overlapping the last strip at least 1″ (2.5cm).

When you're all done stitching, clip each strip every ½″ (12.7mm), staggering the clips for each row. My rug (Fig. 3.20) went into the washer and dryer to soften.

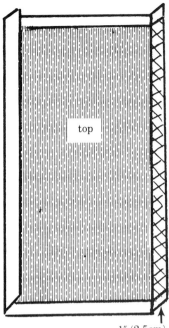

*Fig. 3.18
Place a 1"
(2.5cm) strip
of fusible web-
bing along
each edge.
Fold toward
the topside of
the fabric and
press in place.*

top

1" (2.5cm) strip
fusible webbing

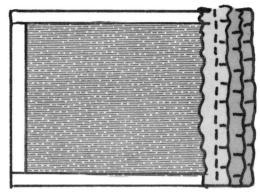

Fig. 3.19 Stitching bias strips onto the rug.

*Fig. 3.20 The bias
strips are clipped
into fringe.*

45

Lesson 6. Adding buttons, beads, shisha

Attaching buttons

Once you've attached a button by machine, you won't want to do it any other way, it is so speedy. If you are applying buttons to a garment you've made, be sure the button area is interfaced. Dab glue stick on the underside of the button and position it.

Stitch width: space between holes in the button
Stitch length: 0
Needle position: far left
Needle: #80/12
Feed dogs: lowered
Presser foot: #152 (#18 or #19) button foot, #419 (#7) tailor tack foot, #470 (#2) vari-overlock
Tension: *top,* normal; *bobbin,* normal
Thread: polyester
Accessories: button elevator or toothpick are optional, transparent tape, glue stick, scrap fabrics, buttons, beads and shisha mirrors (see Sources of Supply)

To use the #152 (#18) presser foot, place the button foot on top of the button and stitch in the hole to the left 3 or 4 times to anchor the threads (stitch width 0). Raise the needle and move the stitch width so the needle clears the button and falls into the hole at the right. On that setting, stitch back and forth several times. When you have finished, move the stitch width to 0 and anchor again. That's all there is to it.

Or use the new button sew-on foot (#19) if you have it. Screwed on to the front of the foot is an adjustable, metal L-shaped pin. When the presser foot is lowered to hold the button for stitching, the base of the L is between the holes of the button. The pin is raised or lowered, depending on the height of the button shank you want to sew.

If the garment fabric is thick, such as coating, you will need to make a button shank; otherwise, the buttonhole will pucker whenever the coat is buttoned. If you don't have the #19 button sew-on foot, raise the stitches to create a shank by taping a darning needle or round toothpick between the holes on top of the button before you stitch (Fig. 3.21A). When finished, pull off the tape and remove the darning needle. Leave a long thread to wrap around the shank and anchor with a hand needle, strengthening the shank.

Button elevators, available at notions counters, can be used to raise the button off the fabric and create several shank heights. The #419 (#7) tailor-tacking foot can also be used, but it will give you a very high shank, so experiment first.

Another foot to use for a higher shank is the #470 (#2) vari-overlock foot. Place the bar in the middle of the button, then adjust the needle position and stitch width as needed.

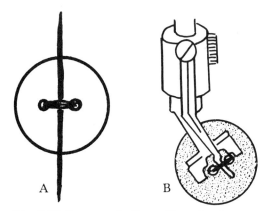

Fig. 3.21 Sew on a button with a shank. A. Use a toothpick on top of the button. B. Or use a #19 button sew-on foot and adjust the height of the button shank by moving the center pin of the presser foot up or down.

Attaching beads and baubles

Beads can be attached by machine if the hole in the bead is large enough and your needle fine enough. The thickness of the bead also matters. If in doubt, hand-walk the machine first to see if the needle will clear the bead, and if the sizes of the bead and needle are compatible. Attach the rim of the bead to the fabric by first holding it in place with a dot of glue from a glue stick. Anchor the thread in the center of the bead by stitching in place three or four times. Raise the needle. Move the fabric over to anchor the thread on the side of the bead. Go back to the center and anchor again. Repeat until the bead is securely sewn in place and will stand up (Fig. 3.22). Nudge the bead to stand on its outside rim when you finish stitching. Wipe off the glue.

If you go back and stitch down the other side as well, your bead will lay flat, hole up (Fig. 3.23).

Attaching seed beads, or other fine or oddly shaped beads can be done in the following way. First string the beads onto a thread. Using monofilament, stitch one end of the beaded thread down on the fabric. Stitch along the thread the width of one bead. Push the first bead near that end and then stitch over the thread to keep the bead in place. Stitch again the distance of the next bead. Push the bead up to the first, stitch over the thread and repeat, as shown in Fig. 3.24.

Or sew beads down by stringing them

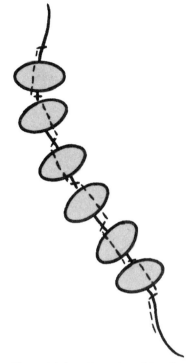

Fig. 3.24 A string of seed beads, attached by machine, along dotted line (solid line is thread).

singly on thick threads and stitching both ends of the threads down (Fig. 3.25).

You can attach beads invisibly, using monofilament thread to couch them down or to string the beads on. Or choose your thread wisely and use the stitching as a part of the decoration.

Fig. 3.22 If beads are stitched down on only one side, they can be nudged to stand up.

Fig. 3.23 Stitching down both sides to make beads lie flat.

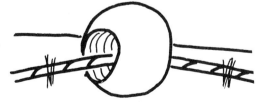

Fig. 3.25 Attach a large bead by threading a cord through it and stitching on either side of the cord.

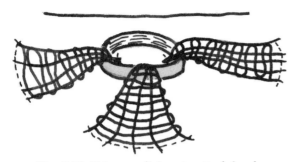

Fig. 3.26 Using needlelace to attach beads.

Another way to hold down beads is to first stitch strips of needlelace on water-soluble stabilizer. When the lace has been stitched, merely pull off the excess stabilizer and hold your work under a faucet to wash out most of what remains; leave a bit of the sticky residue. When it is almost dry, shape the needlelace strips and they will dry in that shape. Use two or three of these strips to hold down beads or washers (Fig. 3.26). Thread a strip through the object and stitch down one end. Move the bauble

Fig. 3.27 "The Flop Box," made by Pat Pasquini, has a machine-embellished top by the author. It includes beads held down with needlelace, other beads strung with cord and porcupine quills and couched in place, textures created by stitching cords down, using a double needle to pintuck suede, and stitching blobs and satin stitches in the background. Photo by Robbie Fanning.

down over your stitching. Arrange the strip, twisting it if you wish. Then stitch down the other end freely and invisibly. Use this method, as I have, on decorative box tops and collages (Fig. 3.27).

Another method of using stones and jewels for wall hangings or pictures is to cover them with net or transparent fabrics, and then stitch down the fabric. Then cut holes in the fabric large enough to let the objects show through and small enough so they don't fall out.

Or make needlelace in the center of wire bent into a circle, rectangle, or other shape. Stretch the lace over an object placed on a background fabric. Attach the lace to the fabric by stitching freely, close to the wire, around the inside of this frame, and cutting off the wire. Embroider the edges if you wish.

Attaching shisha mirrors

Shishas are small pieces of mirrored glass. They are about 1″ (2.5cm) in diameter, but are never exactly circular. It is possible to attach them to fabric if you follow the methods Caryl Rae Hancock of India-

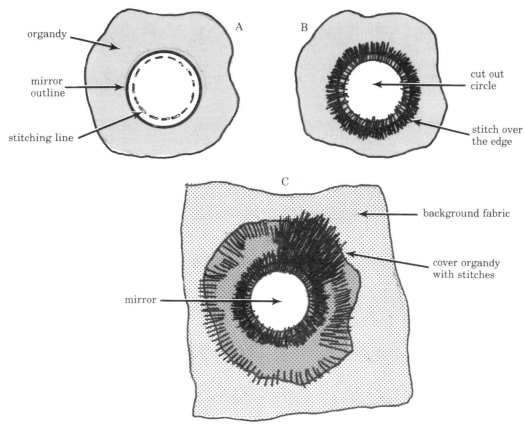

Fig. 3.28 Glue the shisha to the background fabric. A. On organdy, stitch around a circle slightly smaller than the shisha. B. Cut out the center and embroider over the edge. C. Place the organdy over the shisha and stitch it in place on background fabric by straight stitching. Embroider the background to conceal the edge.

49

napolis, Indiana, and Gail Kibiger of Warsaw, Indiana, invented.

This is Caryl Rae Hancock's method, illustrated in Fig. 3.28. First, stretch organdy in a hoop. The shisha is placed on top of the organdy and its outline traced. The back of the shisha is dabbed with glue stick and placed on a background fabric, not the organdy.

Sew around — and about ⅛″ (3.2mm) inside — the drawn circle. Stitch around two more times. Without taking the fabric out of the hoop, cut out the circle of fabric within the stitching. After anchoring threads, the machine should be set on a medium width zigzag and the circle stitched freely around the cut edge. Turn the hoop as you sew around it, letting the stitches radiate from the edge of the hole to about ½″ (12.7mm) beyond. The organdy must be covered with stitches at this time. Anchor threads and take the organdy out of the hoop. Cut very closely around the outside stitching.

With the machine changed back to straight stitch, place the piece of embroidery over the shisha and background fabric and pin organdy in place. Stitch around outside edge of the shisha. Be careful: if you stitch into the glass, the needle and probably the shisha will break.

Leave the machine as set or change to zigzag again and stitch over those straight stitches, following the radiating direction of the original zigzagging. Blend the outside edge of the organdy with the background fabric by radiating stitches onto the background fabric.

Gail Kibiger has a slightly different method. She applies shisha by first placing the mirror on the background fabric, not on organdy, and tracing around it. Removing the shisha, she stitches ⅛″ (3.2mm) within this circle three times and cuts out the circle. Gail embroiders on the background fabric as Caryl Rae did the organdy.

The shisha is then glued to a piece of organdy and placed under the finished hole. After pinning it in place, she straight stitches around the mirror to hold it in place.

One of Gail's variations is to work a spiderweb across the hole before the edges are zigzagged.

Silver bangles, the large sequins found in craft and knitting shops, are an excellent substitute for shisha. Not only are they exactly round, unlike the uneven shape of shishas, but they are durable. If you sew into them, your needle doesn't break. Make a record for your notebook of how you have applied buttons, beads and shisha.

Project
Bird Collage

I work with transparent fabrics almost exclusively, so I collect them. Besides fabric stores, garage sales and thrift shops are wonderful sources. I check out the chiffon scarves, colored nylons, lingerie, curtains, as well as glitzy dresses — though it takes courage to buy some of these because of the double-takes at the checkout counter.

This is a beadwork project, which includes appliqué as well. Bird shapes are my favorites. I like them plump like baby chicks, sleek like soaring eagles, even whimsical like African Dahomey appliqués. I've used them on quilts, wall hangings, and in fabric collages.

In this small picture, shown in Fig. 3.29, I added small clay beads by machine to the appliquéd picture.

Stitch width: 0
Stitch length: 0
Needle position: center
Needle: #90/14
Feed dogs: lowered
Presser foot: #285 (#9) darning foot or #24
    freehand embroidery foot

Fig. 3.29 Bird collage.

Tension: *top,* slightly loosened; *bobbin,* normal

Fabric suggestions: green and gold suede or felt for bird's body and wings; transparent fabrics, such as organdy, chiffon, yellow mesh grapefruit bag, for the wings; moss green bridal veiling to cover the picture; 12" (30.5cm) square of coarse beige upholstery linen for background; loosely woven taupe-colored fabric for the nest; gold lamé for the eggs; nude-colored nylon stocking

Thread: several strands of brown and beige coarse thread or string, cut into 1" (2.5cm) pieces; brown, green and beige shiny rayon; monofilament

Stabilizer: iron-on freezer paper

If this sounds overwhelming, you can substitute any colors you wish, and use only one, instead of a variety, of transparent fabrics. Although I used transparent thread for most of this collage, I added browns, greens and beiges in rayon stitches when my piece was almost complete.

Begin by pulling off a half-dozen threads from the square of background fabric. Cut these threads into small lengths of 1 and 2 inches (2.5–5.1cm) and add them to the other threads you've cut—you will need several dozen. Put them aside.

Iron freezer paper to the back of the linen fabric for stability, as you will not use a hoop for this project. Although not necessary, I always cut the background fabric at

51

least 6"–8" (15.2–20.3cm) bigger than the finished size so I can practice stitching or layering on the edges. Also, I plan my pieces so they look as if they go on beyond the frame. I don't want them to look as if they end inside it.

Fig. 3.30 shows the arrangement, and Fig. 3.31 is the pattern; cut out the fabric pieces as follows: Cut out the oval nest from the taupe fabric and place that slightly below the center on the background. When I cut fabric for collages, I use a cut/tear method. By pulling slightly on the fabric as I cut, I fray the material a bit to keep the edges soft. The bird should be cut from green suede or felt so it will not roll when you cut it out. Be sure to use fabric that has some body, so it will be easy to control. Place the bird on the nest (Fig. 3.30). Cut a gold wing from suede and position that on the bird. Cut out the transparent wings. Place one on top of the gold wing, but shift it a bit so it is not exactly in the same place as the first. Do the same with the other sheers. Your wings will cross, meet, blend, as if in a watercolor.

Over the last wing you will use one cut from a yellow mesh grapefruit bag or a coarse yellow net. Rearrange until the wings look pleasing to you.

Cut the foot and top off a nude-colored nylon stocking and slit the stocking from top to bottom. Stretch it over the picture and pin it down just beyond the image area. As you stretch the stocking, it will lighten in color. It should be almost invisible, but not stretched so tightly it buckles the picture. This holds all the pieces in place, and softens, but does not change, the colors of your picture.

Lower the feed dogs on your machine. Use a darning foot or freehand embroidery foot, as you will have many layers to stitch together. Begin by freely sewing around the bird with transparent thread. Stitch just off the edge of the body and wing pieces. It is not important to be completely accurate; it's fine if you stitch into the body or wings. You might want to stitch in a few feathers on the gold wing as well, giving the bird an attractive, padded look. Stitch to the outside of the nest and sew

Fig. 3.30 Follow this design for assembling the bird picture.

52

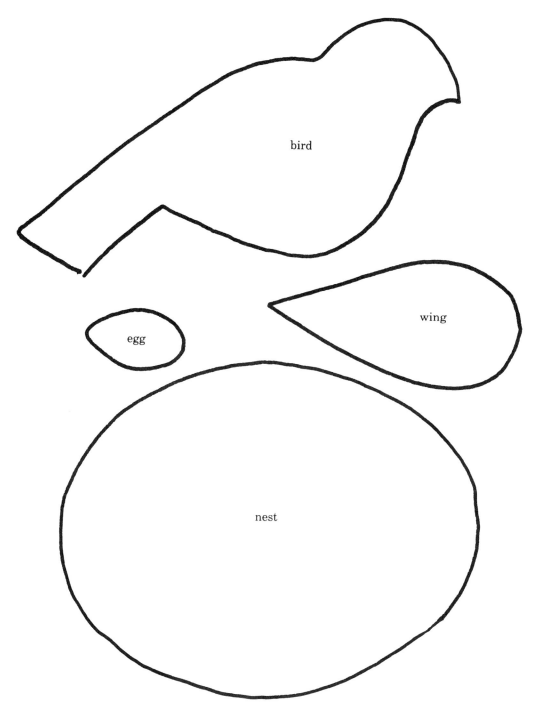

bird

wing

egg

nest

Fig. 3.31 Patterns for the Bird Collage.

that down freely. Then sew all around the outside edge of your picture. Cut off the stocking from the outside edges.

Add three gold lamé eggs under the bird. Over the edge of the nest, scatter half the thread pieces you've cut. Hold all this down by laying a piece of moss green bridal veiling over the picture and pinning it in place.

Again, with transparent thread and a free machine, sew around the eggs, around the outside of the bird and around the nest, managing to catch threads to anchor them. Yes, you will be sewing in a haphazard manner around the nest—and you do not have to sew every thread in place. With a very fine embroidery scissors, cut out the veiling from in front of the bird and the eggs.

String the small clay beads onto some of the remaining "nest" threads. Arrange the threads around the nest on top of those you have already sewn in place. Be very careful as you sew these threads in place; you don't want to hit beads with the

darning foot. With transparent thread, sew above and below the beads to hold them in place (see Fig. 3.25).

An alternative method is to remove the presser foot. Press the fabric firmly against the needle plate as you sew down the threads. Be careful of your fingers. Thread up with a shiny brown rayon thread. With your machine still set up for straight stitching, add texture and color to the nest by stitching a blob, lifting the presser foot lever and pulling the picture to stitch again in another spot. Cross and recross threads. I change colors several times (browns, beiges and greens). This also helps anchor the coarse threads.

The bird's eye can be added by sewing on a gold bead by hand, or with your machine, by building up a blob of thread. Your picture is complete. Pull off the freezer paper, or leave it in place. Cut off that extra margin from around your piece. Stretch the picture over a piece of batting and plywood and frame it. These pictures are so much fun to put together, and no two are alike.

Lesson 7. Smocking and gathering

Smocking

In hand smocking, fabric is gathered tightly into channels and embroidery is worked on top of the channels. Stitches chosen are open and stretchy.

Smocking by machine, on the other hand, will not be stretchy like hand smocking. After gathering with thread or cord, machine embroidery stitches usually hold the gathers in place. But if you use elastic, the gathering will stretch—but then, of course, you won't embroider over it.

There are at least a dozen ways to smock on your Bernina, varying the method of gathering or embroidering, or varying the threads used. Here are several methods you can try. In each one, start with at least 2½ times the width needed for the finished

pattern. For any garment, do the smocking first and then cut out the pattern.

Stitch width: 0–widest
Stitch length: varies
Needle position: center
Needle: #90/14
Feed dogs: up
Presser foot: #147 (#20) open embroidery
Built-in stitch: zigzag or open type
Tension: *top,* normal; *bottom,* varies
Fabric: 2 or more 18″ × 45″ (45.7 × 114.3cm) pieces of medium-weight cotton; 1 yard (.9m) strip for gathering ruffles; several 12″ (30.5cm) or larger pieces of scrap fabrics
Threads: machine embroidery; monofilament

Accessories: water-erasable or vanishing
marker

Stabilizer: water-soluble, tear-away type

Simple gathered smocking

First draw at least four lines across the
45″-wide (114.3cm-wide) fabric with a water-erasable or vanishing marker. The
lines should be about ½″ (12.7mm) apart.
Leave the seam allowances free of stitching. Anchor the threads, and then straight
stitch along your drawn lines, leaving long
ends of thread at the ends of the rows (Fig.
3.32A). Pull on the bobbin threads to gather the fabric to 18″ (45.7cm) and knot every two threads together. Pin this to tear-
away stabilizer.

Choose a decorative stitch and embroider across the fabric between the gathering lines of stitching (Fig. 3.32A). Then
take out the gathering stitches.

Smocking with cordonnet

Use another piece of 18″ × 45″ (45.7 ×
114.3cm) fabric. Thread the cordonnet
through the throatplate of the machine.

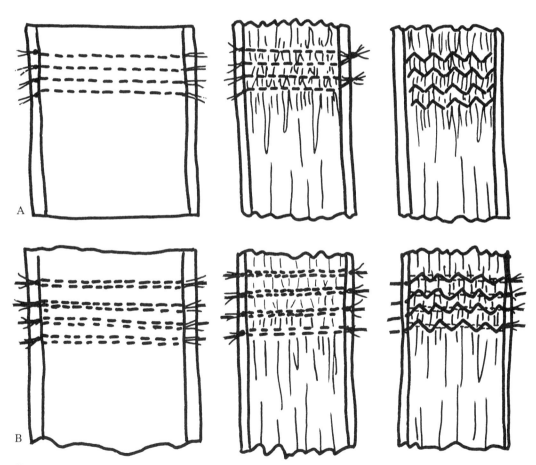

Fig. 3.32 Two ways to machine smock. A. Gather up rows of stitching and embroider
between them. B. Gather the fabric using a cord and double needle and embroider over
the gathers.

To gather, sew across the fabric, using a double needle (1.6mm) and the nine groove pintuck foot (Fig. 3.32B). Again, leave the seam allowances free of stitching. Use the presser foot as a width guide to sew at least three more rows. Stitch an even number of rows, at least four. Leave tails of cord at the beginning and end of each line.

Tie off pairs of the cords at the start. Pull the cords to gather the material to 18" (45.7cm). Then tie a knot at the end of each. Remove the cordonnet from the throatplate.

Place a stabilizer under your work. Embroider over the cords.

Embroidering with thick thread in the bobbin

This may be used with either of the preceding methods for gathering. First complete the gathering. Turn the fabric over, topside down on the bed of the machine. Place water-soluble stabilizer under the gathers.

Stitch width: widest
Stitch length: varies
Built-in stitch: zigzag or open type
Needle position: center
Needle: #90/14
Feed dogs: up
Presser foot: #147 (#20) open embroidery foot
Tension: *top,* normal; *bobbin,* varies with cord
Fabric: medium-weight cotton
Thread: monofilament or sewing thread for top; #5 or #8 pearl cotton for bobbin
Stabilizer: water-soluble

When you stitch up the samples, sew, look underneath to see if the pearl cotton is attached evenly and smoothly. Adjust tensions as necessary.

Open built-in stitches look best — the simple zigzag is effective.

Smocking with elastic

Wind the bobbin with fine, round elastic. Do this by hand so it doesn't stretch. Again, stitch down rows ½" (12.7mm) apart, gathering as you sew. The thread on top will show, so choose the color carefully. You can use this for bodices of sun dresses, nightgowns or swimsuits. This works best on delicate to lightweight fabrics.

Another way to make fabric stretch, giving a shirred effect, is to use a round elastic through the hole of the throat plate. Use regular thread on top and bobbin, and a zigzag setting that clears the elastic.

Alternately, stitch with a double needle and a straight stitch. Stitch several rows across the fabric using the presser foot as a guide, or draw the rows on the fabric with

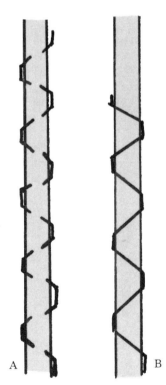

A   B

Fig. 3.33 Two ways to attach flat elastic. A. Lycra stitch. B. Universal stitch.

a water-erasable or vanishing marker before stitching. Don't pull the elastic for gathering until all the stitching is completed. I use this method at the top of children's knit skirts, as well as on waistlines of T-shirt dresses.

With ⅛" (3.2mm) flat elastic, use either the universal stitch or lycra stitch, width 4, length 2. If your machine does not have the lycra stitch (Fig.3.33A), use the sewn-out (three-step) zigzag (Fig. 3.33B). Thread the elastic through the opening in the #189 (#21) braiding foot or use the groove in the #147 (#20)open embroidery foot to guide it.

With the lycra or sewn-out (three-step) zigzag settings, the gathers can't be changed after they are sewn in, because the needle stitches into the elastic. Stretch the elastic while sewing. The more you stretch it, the more gathers it will create.

The universal stitch will sew on either side of the flat elastic and will not pierce it as the lycra stitch does. After stitching, adjust the gathers.

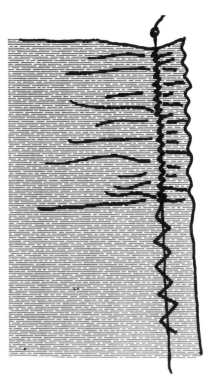

Fig. 3.34 Use the #030 (#6) embroidery foot when zigzagging over cord to gather fabric.

Gathering

Using cord

To gather light to heavyweight materials, use this, my all-time favorite method.

Stitch width: 2
Stitch length: 2
Needle position: center
Feed dogs: up

Zigzag over a cord, such as gimp or cordonnet, that has been threaded through the #030 (#6) embroidery foot (Fig. 3.34). Pull up the cord to gather the fabric. Leave the cord in the fabric.

I use this for everything from skirts to dust ruffles to slipcovers. You won't break the gathering stitch as you often do when pulling on a basting thread. It saves hours.

Using elastic

Using the same settings as you did for cord, thread the elastic through the hole in the #030 (#6) foot. Knot the elastic in back. Pull on it from the front while sewing a zigzag over it. I use this for quick sleeve finishes for little girls' dresses. If sewn about 1" (2.5cm) from the finished edge, it creates a ruffle.

Using the #508 (#16) gathering foot

Gathering yards of ruffles is easy with this gathering foot. It simultaneously gathers and applies the gathers to another flat piece of fabric. The only drawback is that without seeing your fabric, I can't give you an iron-clad formula for how much fabric is needed to gather into, say, a 15″ (38.1cm) ruffle.

The key to your estimates is to stitch a sample. Work with the same material you're going to use for the ruffle. Finer materials need to be gathered more fully than heavy fabrics do. Gathering depends upon fabric weight, tension and stitch length. The tighter the tension, the more gathering. The longer the stitch, the more fullness that can be locked into each stitch and the tighter the gathers—and the more fabric you'll need. I admit I'm a coward and always add inches to be sure.

Even though this foot will gather a ruffle and apply it to fabric at the same time, I prefer gathering and attaching the gathers in two steps because of the difficulty in estimating the yardage I'll need for the ruffles. But, to do both steps at once, place the fabric to be attached to the ruffle in the slot of the gathering foot and the ruffle fabric under the foot. Keep the edges of the fabrics even with the right side of the foot.

This does not exhaust the methods of gathering and smocking on the machine. Check your manuals for others.

Lesson 8. Pulling threads together

Satin stitching on top of loosely woven fabric builds up texture quickly by drawing the threads of the fabric together into ridges. Then you can connect the ridges for even more texture. As you can see in the sample (Fig. 3.35), this technique looks like lace.

Stitch width: 0–widest
Stitch length: 0
Needle position: center
Needle: #90/14
Feed dogs: lowered
Presser foot: #285 (#9) darning foot or #24 freehand embroidery foot
Tension: *top,* slightly loosened; *bobbin,* normal
Fabric: loosely woven cheesecloth type
Thread: machine embroidery, desired color top and bobbin
Accessories: spring hoop

To learn this technique, stitch an imaginary tree of satin stitches and lacy straight stitches. It's not necessary to trace my design as this is done freely.

Put the fabric in a hoop. It must be stretched tightly. Bring the bobbin thread to the top and anchor the threads. Using the widest stitch setting, sew up and down

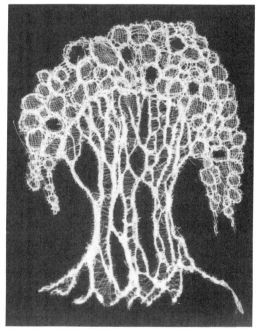

Fig. 3.35 Straight stitch and zigzag over loosely woven fabric produced both lacy and textured embroidery.

in straight lines. At the down points, move the fabric over a bit and go up and down again. Continue until you have three or four rows of satin stitches. Then go back over them, zigzagging in between. This draws the previous lines together. Cut fabric threads if there is too much pulling and puckering.

Create branches on top and, when you come down to the bottom again, flare the line of stitching to resemble roots. Use the widest zigzags to stitch up and down again. Go back and zigzag over the whole tree again and again until the stitches are built up to your liking.

Change to a straight stitch and begin to stitch small circles at the top to crown the branches. Go from one to another. Cut or poke out the centers of some or all of the circles to give a lacy look to the tree top.

In the sample, I trimmed the tree from the background to show you the type of appliqué I add to my collages. It has a lacy look you can see through, which adds depth to the embroidery it's placed over. But sometimes I place the untrimmed appliqué over a background fabric and stitch it in place. After trimming it back to the stitches, I freely embroider over it with more satin stitches, with more ridges, building up more and more texture.

If you do a large enough square of threads pulled together with satin stitches, it can be used as a design for your tote bag. Or leave it untrimmed and still in the hoop for a window hanging.

CHAPTER 4

Adding Fabric to Fabric: Appliqué

- **Lesson 9. Methods of applying appliqués**
- **Lesson 10. Appliquéing with feed dogs up**
- **Lesson 11. Appliquéing with feed dogs lowered**

I can produce perfect satin stitches on my Bernina, but believe me, there is so much more to appliqué. And once you know your machine as I know mine, you won't be satisfied stitching down all your appliqués with satin stitches. This chapter will show you several ways to place an appliqué onto a background successfully and teach a variety of methods for stitching it in place.

You'll make tote bag squares, Carrickmacross lace, and shadow work in these lessons. You will also work samples for your notebook to practice other appliqué methods.

Lesson 9. Methods of applying appliqués

Applying fabric to fabric takes two steps. Both are equally important. The first is to place the appliqué on the background in a way that keeps it in place, without puckering the fabric and with edges held down firmly, to enable you to do a perfect final stitching. The second step is the stitching. In Lessons 10 and 11, we'll try blind hems, straight stitching, blurring, scribbling and corded edges.

In appliqué, the best results are achieved when the applied and background fabrics have similar properties. For example, if using a cotton background fabric, it is best to use a similar weight appliqué fabric, and one that can be washed like the cotton. If washable, prepare the fabrics by washing and ironing them. They may be easier to work with if they are starched.

Match the grain lines of the appliqué to those of the background fabric. It's usually necessary to use a stabilizer under the fabric to prevent puckers when stitching. There are several methods for the first step. The first one wastes fabric, but the results are worth it.

Method A

Stretch both fabrics tightly in a hoop. I use a wooden hoop for this step because the fabric can be stretched and held more tightly than in a spring hoop. The fabric for the appliqué should be underneath–on the bed of the machine–with the topsides of both fabrics down. Draw the design on the wrong side of the base fabric, or place a paper pattern in the hoop, either pinning it there or catching it in the hoop with the fabric.

With the machine set up for free machining, single stitch around the design. Take the fabric out of the hoop, turn it over and cut the applied fabric back to the stitching line. Place the fabric back in the

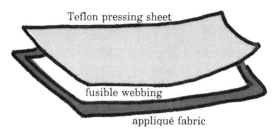

Teflon pressing sheet

fusible webbing

appliqué fabric

Fig. 4.1 To prepare an appliqué with fusible webbing, first place a piece of the fusible on the back of the appliqué fabric, cover it with the special Teflon sheet, and press in place.

hoop with the appliqué on top this time. Use one of the methods for final stitching discussed in Lessons 10 and 11.

Method B

For the next method, fusible webbing and a Teflon pressing sheet are needed. This will produce a slightly stiffer appliqué than the first method, but if done correctly, it will never produce a pucker.

Cut a piece of fabric and a piece of fusible webbing slightly larger than the appliqué (Fig. 4.1). With the fusible webbing on top of the appliqué fabric, place the Teflon sheet over it and iron until the fusible web-

bing melts (Fig. 4.2). When it cools, the Teflon can be peeled away. Cut out the appliqué from this piece of fabric and then iron it to the background fabric, using a Teflon sheet on top to protect your iron.

Method C

An alternative to fusible webbing is the appliqué paper backed with "glue." To use this paper, cut a piece of it and fabric approximately the size of the appliqué. Draw the design on the non-adhesive side of the paper, then iron the paper to the back of the fabric. After it adheres and cools, cut around the design and fabric, then peel the paper off the appliqué. The glue will have been transferred from the paper to the fabric. Iron the appliqué to the background.

Or use what can best be described as a combination of fusible webbing and appliqué paper: Wonder-Under Fusible Webbing (see Chapter 1).

Method D

Plastic sandwich bags can also be used as a fusible—or try cleaners' garment bags. Cut out a piece of plastic the size of the ap-

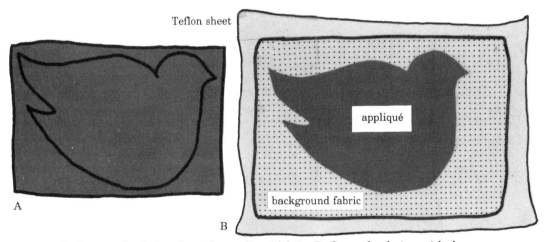

Teflon sheet

appliqué

background fabric

A

B

Fig. 4.2 A. Cut out the design from the appliqué fabric. B. Cover the design with the Teflon sheet again to press in place on the background fabric.

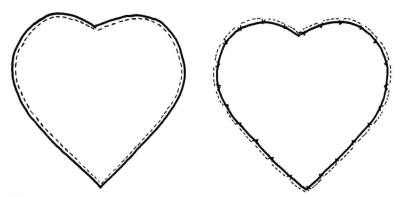

Fig. 4.3 To prepare and apply an appliqué for blind hemming, stitch all around it ¼" (6.3mm) from the edge (top). Fold under on the stitching, apply to the background and blind-hem-stitch in place (bottom).

pliqué and place it between the backing fabric and appliqué.

Put brown wrapping paper over and under this "sandwich" so any plastic that is peeking out will be ironed onto the brown paper and not your iron or ironing board. Press it with an iron hot enough to melt the plastic and fuse the fabrics together.

Method E

If you wish to blind hem around the edge of an appliqué for step two, the appliqué must be prepared in another way (Fig. 4.3).

First, straight stitch around the appliqué on what will be the fold line. Cut the appliqué from the fabric, leaving a ¼" (6.3mm) seam allowance. Clip the edges and turn under on the stitched line. Trim off more seam allowance wherever fabric overlaps and creates bulk. Baste with stitches or a glue-stick. Press the edges

flat. Baste in place on the background fabric—I find it more accurate when done by hand. Now you can blind-hem the appliqué to the foundation, or use stitch #26 on the 1130 (narrow the stitch to barely penetrate the appliqué fabric on the wide bite, straight stitch on backing fabric only).

If the appliqué is to be embroidered, it is sometimes best to do it first to prevent puckers in the background fabric. Embroidered patches can be appliquéd in many ways, the most common being satin stitching around the edge. But another way is to leave the edge almost devoid of stitching, cut out the appliqué and apply it with the same free stitches as the embroidery, to blend it into the background.

Even if fabric is to be heavily embroidered, embroider first on another piece of fabric, cut it out, and make it an appliqué. Use a glue stick or pin it in place. These appliqués are usually too thick to attach with fusible webbing.

Lesson 10. Appliquéing with feed dogs up

Satin stitches three ways

When I compare the satin stitches done on my machine with those done on any

other, I know why I could never part with my Bernina. Mine are always smooth and even, with never a skipped stitch.

Standard method

Keep a few things in mind when attaching an appliqué with satin stitches: First, the stitch width should not overpower the appliqué. I almost always use a setting no wider than 2, along with the #181 (#23) transparent appliqué foot, because the satin stitches fit perfectly inside the groove on the underside of the foot. The groove guides my stitching so that satin stitches are perfect. If I use a wider stitch setting, then I use a foot with a wider groove — such as the #147 (#20) open embroidery foot or #030 (#6) embroidery foot.

Stitch width: 2–4
Stitch length: 1/2 (satin stitch) or adjust for
    your machine
Needle position: center
Presser foot: #181 (#23) appliqué foot or
    #147 (#20) open embroidery foot or
    #030 (#6) embroidery foot
Feed dogs: up
Tension: *top*, normal; *bobbin*, finger thread-
    ed — or *top*, slightly loosened; *bobbin*,
    normal

On the 1100 machines, the basic settings are automatically provided when you indicate the stitch you want. (They can be changed.) The widest stitch setting on the 1000 and 1100 series is 5; on other models it is 4.

A perfect satin stitch also comes from the matching of fabric, needle, and thread. Always sew a sample, using the same fabric, needle and thread that will be used on the finished piece. Don't watch the needle, but keep your eyes on the line you'll be stitching. Check to see if the fabric is being fed through evenly. Open or close the length of the zigzags. Each machine has its own personality, so you must work this out for yours.

I prefer to cover the edge of an appliqué in two passes rather than one. Instead of a 1/2 length, start with 3/4. At the same time, dial the first pass slightly narrower than the final one. Instead of 4 width, dial down to 3 3/4 for the first pass.

Use a needle appropriate for the thread. The needle must be large enough to let the thread pass through freely and it must punch a large enough hole in the fabric to prevent the thread from fraying. For example, with rayon embroidery thread I use a #90/14 needle; on cotton embroidery thread, I use a #80/12 needle. On woven materials, I use a pierce-point needle instead of a universal point because I feel it gives me a more perfect edge. (The universal point is slightly rounded, so it deflects off the fibers and slips between them. When satin stitching on closely woven materials, this needle may create an uneven edge.

Stained-glass method

Stained-glass is a type of satin-stitch appliqué in which your satin stitches are gray to black and usually extend out from the appliqué to the borders of the design. It is important to remember this, since not every design is appropriate for stained-glass.

Project
Bird Patch

When stitching the design in Fig. 4.4, do all the short lines first; then go back and do the long lines. Usually a wider-than-normal satin stitch is used for stained-glass work because the emphasis is on the "leaded" effect. My bird design is small, however, so I used a narrow stitch in order not to obscure parts of the design.

The sample can be used on the tote bag if the background fabric isn't cut off (it must be square to fit in the frame).

Stitch width: 2
Stitch length: 0–1/2 (satin stitch)
Needle position: center
Needle: #90/14

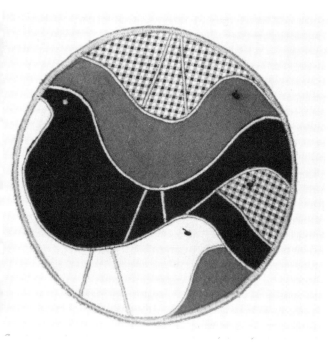

Fig. 4.4 This bird patch is applied by either the fusible webbing method or reverse appliqué method.

Feed dogs: up
Presser foot: #181 (#23) appliqué
Tension: *top*, normal; *bobbin*, finger thread-
　　ed—or *top*, slightly loosened; *bobbin*,
　　normal
Fabric suggestions: lightweight cotton, 10″
　　(25.4cm) squares of red, white, black,
　　and black-and-white checkered fabric
Thread: gray and black machine embroidery
Accessories: 8″ (20.3cm) wrapped wooden
　　hoop; Bernina circle maker; water-eras-
　　able marker; fusible webbing; dress-
　　makers' carbon; empty ballpoint pen
Stabilizer: tear-away type

Trace the design from Fig. 4.5 onto tracing paper. Use dressmaker's carbon between the design and the white background fabric. With the ballpoint pen,
transfer the design to the white fabric.

Then cut apart the bird design on the
tracing paper. Using the pieces of the design, cut out fabrics for the shapes, each
slightly larger than the finished size. Using a Teflon sheet on top, iron fusible webbing to the backs of all the pieces of appliqué fabric except white. Then cut out the
actual pattern pieces from the fabric in
this manner: Start with the top checkered
fabric. Cut out the top shape following the
pattern, but cut the bottom edge to allow a
⅛″ (3.2mm) seam allowance. Press this
and the following shapes onto the white
background as they are cut out. Next, cut
out the red bird by cutting the top exactly
as the pattern indicates, but leaving a ⅛″
(3.2mm) seam allowance on the bottom
curve. The checkered area to the right
should be cut next, with a seam allowance
on both the top and bottom curve. The
small red area is cut, leaving a seam allowance on the top curve at top. Finally, cut
out the black bird and place it on the design. Then cut out the white bird on the
seam line. By cutting out the design in this
manner, you will always be stitching on
only one raw edge. It eliminates the jigsaw
fitting problem when you try to butt fabrics together.

Once all appliqués are in place, draw in
the short lines with the marker. Also, indicate the bird's eyes.

Place the background fabric and appliqué into the hoop. Use tear-away stabilizer
under it.

Set up for a satin stitch and do all the
short lines, then stitch in the longer lines
with gray thread. Thread up with black
thread and satin stitch in place about ten
times for each eye.

Take the fabric out of the hoop and find
the center of the appliqué. To do this, fold
the circle in half. Hold it up to a window to
see that the left side meets the right side.
Crease lightly. Then fold up from the bottom to meet the top edge. Crease again.
Open the fabric to find the place where the
folds cross. Use a water-erasable pen to

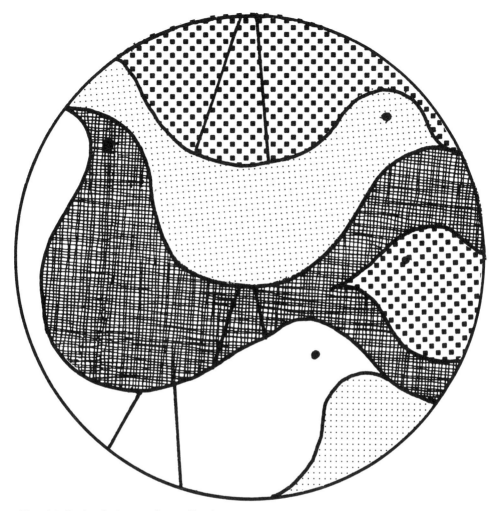

Fig. 4.5 Stained-glass style appliqué.

mark this point. Place the fabric back in the hoop.

Clip the circle-maker accessory to the needleplate and place the tack up through the center mark on the fabric. Adjust the tack so the machine needle is at the edge of the circle. Don't stitch yet. Raise the needle so it is slightly above the fabric. Turn the hoop and watch the needle's position at the edge of the appliqué to make sure that the needle will stitch into the appliqué all the way around.

Then straight-stitch around the edge. Cut the background back to the stitches. Slip a piece of stabilizer under and extending past the bird patch. Put it back on the tack in the same place. Satin stitch two passes over the line of straight stitching, letting the stitches go off the edge on the right swing to cover the cut edge with stitches. The stabilizer will drop away after stitching, or it can be pulled off.

For an alternative finishing method, use the corded edge found at the end of Lesson 10.

Reverse appliqué

Reverse appliqué is the technique of layering from one to many fabrics on top of a background material. A design is straight stitched through the layers, then the fabric is cut out of portions of the design to reveal the fabric beneath. It is finished by satin stitching over the straight stitches. It can be combined with appliqué from the top as well. For fun and a challenge, try the Bird Patch project using reverse appliqué.

It is sometimes easier to use reverse appliqué for one layer of fabric. To do a perfect reverse appliqué, put both fabrics in a hoop, topsides up, your appliqué fabric underneath. Draw the design on the top fabric or place the paper pattern in the hoop and straight stitch around the design. Remove the paper.

Take the fabrics out of the hoop and cut out the top fabric inside the design area. Put the fabric back in the hoop, slip stabilizer between hoop and machine, and then satin stitch the edges. When finished, you may want to cut away the extra appliqué fabric on the back to eliminate bulk.

This method often affords better control of the appliqué when applying small pieces to a design.

Project
Tote Bag Square (Reverse Appliqué)

See color section for the finished reverse appliqué square.

Stitch width: 0–3
Stitch length: 1/2 (satin stitch) to 2
Needle position: center, left, right

Needle: 80/11
Feed dogs: up
Presser foot: #030 (#6) embroidery
Tension: *top*, normal; *bobbin*, finger threaded and normal
Fabric suggestion: 9″ (22.9cm) square each of royal blue, green, orange, red, yellow
Thread: red machine-embroidery cotton to match red fabric
Accessories: tracing paper and pencil, dressmaker's carbon and empty ballpoint pen, fine-pointed scissors
Stabilizer: Wonder-Under, iron-on freezer paper, Teflon pressing sheet

Begin by backing all the fabrics except blue with Wonder-Under.

Trace the pattern in Fig. 4.6, using the tracing paper and pencil. Then place dressmaker's carbon between the tracing paper and fabrics to transfer the pattern to each color, using the empty ballpoint pen. Then read through the following directions first before you begin to construct the square.

Place a Teflon pressing sheet on your ironing board. Cut out the areas indicated on the green fabric (we'll fuse this top fabric piece to the yellow under it, and continue working from the top down to the backing fabric). Line up the cutting lines with those on the yellow fabric underneath and place both of these, fusible-side-down, on the Teflon pressing sheet to steam press in place. Next, cut out the yellow areas as shown on the pattern, then place the green and yellow fused fabric on top of the red—paying close attention to the design marked on the red fabric. Fuse these fabrics together, as you did the first. Cut out the areas from the red as shown on the pattern. Place the fabrics on top of the orange 9″ square next, fuse, then cut out the center as shown. Then place this piece on the blue background. Fuse again so all the layers may be handled as one when you satin stitch. By layering and cutting this way, not only do the layers fuse better, but

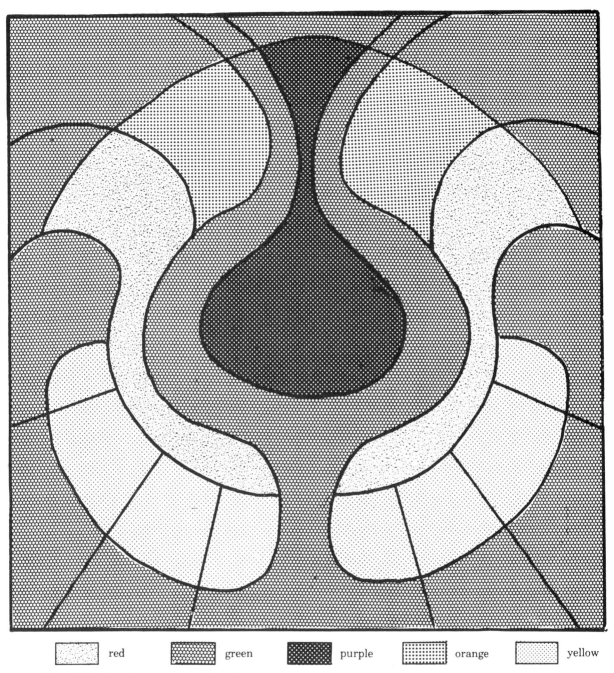

| | red | | green | | purple | | orange | | yellow |

Fig. 4.6 Pattern for reverse appliqué tote bag square.

it's easier to cut through layers without mistake.

Continue by satin stitching all the edges with red machine-embroidery cotton, top tension normal, bobbin finger threaded. Although this is not necessary, I always go over my satin stitches one more time. The first time, I use a slightly narrower stitch width and longer stitch length than the finished satin stitch should be (stitch width 2 1/2, stitch length 3/4). On the next pass, I use stitch width 3, and a stitch length which will give me a close, smooth satin stitch).

To stitch a perfect edge, place the hole of the cording foot on the raw edge of the appliqué. I line up my fabric directly under the right side of the hole when stitching in a clockwise direction or if the raw edge of the fabric is at the right (change needle position to left). If stitching counter-clockwise, the edge of the fabric is to the left and should be under the left edge of the cording hole (change needle position to the right). Always stitch with the needle just off the edge of the fabric on one swing, but covering the edge on the next. Stitch slowly. When the stitches begin to slant, stop and turn the fabric slightly, stitch again, turn, and continue in this manner until the curve is covered smoothly.

If you have the 1130, you will appreciate the machine's remembering the last altered stitch. I take advantage of this by first pushing the straight stitch button (1) to set the stitch length at 0. Then I push the zigzag button (2) and set the stitch length and width. Now I can begin stitching by anchoring (straight stitch button #1) my threads in one place before I begin to satin stitch (#2).

At the end of a line of satin stitches, I press #1 again and anchor, sewing several stitches in one place. When appliquéing, I like this method better than sewing in reverse and doubling back on my stitching. When I change my satin-stitch settings, the machine accepts this change, but retains the straight-stitch setting. The settings will remain as changed unless you change them again or turn off the machine.

After you finish stitching all the raw edges, go back and stitch the straight lines through the yellow and green areas.

Back your square with another piece of fabric and finish it as described in Chapter 12.

Blind hemming

A second way to attach appliqués to a background is with the blind hemstitch. Use the #492 edging foot or #016 blind-stitch foot. Prepare the appliqué in Method E (see Fig. 4.3) and use monofilament thread on the top. Use your machine's blind-hem built-in stitch; length and width are determined by you, but start with a stitch width 1 and a stitch length 2. Stitch around the appliqué, letting the straight stitches fall just outside the appliqué, with the bite of the widest stitch catching the edge. You can set up the machine to give the look you want. Do you want a wide bite? Then set the width to a higher number. The length of the stitch determines the closeness of those two stitches that go up and back, holding the appliqué in place. Find the right length by doing a sample. Use this method to attach patch pockets and to couch down heavy threads and cords. Usually monofilament is used on the top because it is almost invisible.

If you change the monofilament to a thread that will contrast with the fabric, this stitch gives the look of buttonholing by hand. On the 1130, use decorative stitch #26 also. I mirror the stitch because I'm more comfortable stitching down the rightside of the appliqué, but leave the settings the computer tells me to use.

A line of blind hemstitching is used in the greeting card project in Lesson 4 (Fig. 3.9).

Straight stitching

To apply fabric with a straight stitch, you will place the appliqué on the background as you did for blind hemming (if you are working with non-wovens like suedes or felt, don't press the edges under). Use the #492 (#10) edging foot or #016 (#5) blind-stitch foot. Set the straight stitch at a 2 length and stitch width at 0.

With the black bar riding along the fold of the appliqué, set the needle position to slightly within the appliqué. Stitch around the motif.

Project
Tote Bag Square (Edge-Stitch Appliqué)

See color section for the finished edge-stitch appliqué tote square.

Stitch width: 0
Stitch length: 0–2
Needle position: center, right
Needle: #80/11, #110/18
Feed dogs: up, lowered
Presser foot: #007 (#4) zipper; #285 (#9) darning or #24 freehand machine embroidery foot
Tension: *top,* normal; *bobbin,* normal
Fabric suggestion: 9″ (22.9cm) white felt square; felt scraps of red, green, gray, royal blue, and yellow; small dots of blue, pink and orange felt (see Fig. 4.7 for sizes)
Thread: monofilament for the bobbin; red, green, and gray sewing thread; royal blue cordonnet
Accessories: fine-pointed scissors; glue stick; pins; two pieces of tracing paper and pencil; Wonder-Under; vanishing marker; dressmaker's carbon; empty ballpoint pen
Stabilizer: freezer paper

Trace each design element in Fig. 4.7 onto tracing paper *twice* and cut out the patterns on one sheet.

Press Wonder-Under to back of each piece of felt, except white. Cut out the designs from the colored felt, using Fig. 4.7 as a guide. The tiny dots of pink and orange on top of the pins and the blue dot on the scissors can be held in place with glue stick.

Press freezer paper to the back of the square of white felt. With dressmaker's carbon behind the second tracing, transfer the design to the white felt, using the ballpoint pen.

Place each piece of the design on the white felt background, using the carbon marks as a guide. Lay the tracing over it to double-check placement. Remove all the design pieces except the pincushion. Fuse this piece by steam pressing. I chose the zipper foot instead of the edge foot for stitching because the appliqué is small and has intricate curves. The edge of the zipper foot is placed on the edge of the appliqué. I am more comfortable with needle right and I stitch that way throughout. However, should you prefer needle left, then stitch with needle left instead. But remember, whichever direction you stitch, the zipper foot is on top of the appliqué at all times.

Stitch the edge of the pincushion to attach it, using green thread on top and monofilament on the bobbin. Then continue by stitching the curved lines from top to bottom, as shown. After the pincushion is attached, arrange the rest of the design, placing the tracing over it to be sure the pieces are in the correct places. Fuse and stitch as you did before. Use green thread to attach the spool. Then change to gray for the large needle and the pins. Use red thread for the embroidery scissors. The

Fig. 4.7 Pattern for edge-stitch appliqué square.

yellow	green	orange	red
gray	blue	pink	

tiny circles on the pins and the scissors are held in place by stitching around them freely (lower feed dogs, clip darning or free machine-embroidery foot in place, use stitch width 0).

Change the needle to #110/18 and use blue cordonnet in the spool. With the machine still set up for free machining, begin stitching the cordonnet to one side of the spool appliqué—but don't anchor it. Stitch a line of straight stitches across the top of the spool, down the side 1/8" (3.2mm), over to the other side, down and over again, until you have covered the thread area. Cut the cordonnet, leaving a few inches of thread to be worked into the back later.

Go to the top middle of the square. Again, leave a long end of cord as you stitch over the line drawn on the square. When you reach the eye of the darning needle, pull out thread from the machine needle so you can clip this and bring the ends to the back later. Hold on to the loop and put the needle back in the fabric. Continue sewing to the scissors. When you reach the blades, cross over them as you did the needle. Keep straight stitching on top of your line, stitch in the Bernina name, then continue up to the spool. Cut the cordonnet, leaving a few inches to be poked to the back later. When the appliqué is complete, go back to clip the center of the loops, leaving two long threads. Then thread up a large-eyed darning needle and poke all the thread ends to the back of your appliqué. Clip back to about an inch long (2.5cm) and leave them; they won't show, as you will leave the freezer paper in place.

Finish the square as described in Chapter 12.

Project
Tote Bag Square
(Straight Stitch)

The next sample also uses straight stitches to hold appliqués in place, but is otherwise quite different (see color section). Instead of stitching at the edges of the appliqués, they are held in place with lines of straight stitches which run from top to bottom across the square.

Stitch width: 0
Stitch length: 2
Needle position: center
Needle: #80/12
Feed dogs: up
Presser foot: #000 (#0) zigzag foot
Tension: *top*, normal; *bobbin*, normal
Fabric suggestion: lightweight, closely woven cottons: 9" (22.9cm) square green; scraps of red, yellow and royal blue (see Fig. 4.8 for sizes)
Thread: green machine embroidery on top, green sewing thread on bobbin
Accessories: Wonder-Under, vanishing marker, two pieces of tracing paper, pencil
Stabilizer: freezer paper

Apply Wonder-Under to the back of the red, blue and yellow scraps. Trace the design in Fig. 4.8 and put aside. With the other piece of tracing paper, trace the three design elements. Use these patterns to cut out the appliqués. Arrange them on the green background fabric. Place the first tracing over your arrangement to be sure the appliqués are in their proper places. Steam press in place.

With the vanishing marker, draw lines from top to bottom every 1/2" (12.7mm) across the square. Starting at the top right corner, straight stitch to the bottom on the first line. Turn the square and stitch back to the top on the next line. Continue across the square.

Go back and stitch between those lines. If you wish, make one last pass and stitch between the lines again.

Instead of row after row of straight stitches to hold appliqués in place, try satin stitches or use a double needle. Also try couching down metallics and thick cords.

Finish the square following the directions in Chapter 12.

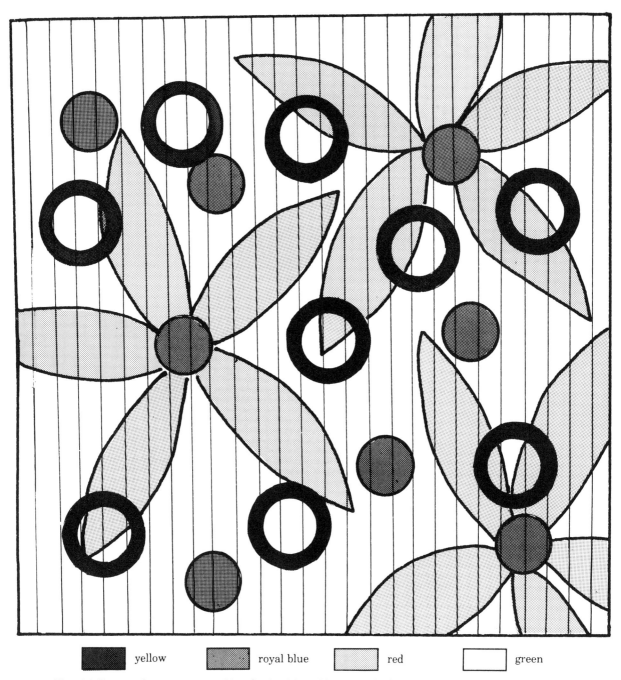

| yellow | royal blue | red | green |

Fig. 4.8 Pattern for tote square. Use the fusible webbing method to attach design to the background fabric, then stitch evenly spaced lines of straight stitching to hold them there.

72

Cording edges

Corded edges give appliqués and decorative patches a neat, exact finish. Use the #030 (#6) foot if cord is fine enough to be threaded through it.

When finishing patches, sew the corded edges in two passes. Place the patch over typing paper or tear-away stabilizer. It must be large enough to extend past the edge of the patch.

On the first pass, apply the cord, sewing at a narrower stitch width, and with stitch length slightly longer than the final pass. When you near the end, clip the cord on an angle and keep satin stitching to hide the cord in the stitches.

The final stitching is done with a close satin stitch, the needle stitching down in the fabric on one side of the cord, but stitching off the cord and fabric on the other side. If the stabilizer has pulled apart from the edge, slip another piece underneath or stitch the second pass without the stabilizer beyond the satin stitches. The edge will be wrapped with your satin stitches, which will cover the tiny bits of stabilizer caught in the threads from the first pass. You'll love the smooth, professional appearance. Leave enough cord at the beginning and end to poke to the back and work into the stitches if you didn't clip it off already. Use a needle with a large eye to do this by hand.

It is not necessary to cover the entire cord if the cord itself is decorative or is a color that adds to the effect you wish to achieve. When I had to appliqué dozens of velveteen crosses to a woolen ecclesiastical garment, I used a velour cord and an open zigzag, and sewed with a thread the color of the velour. When finished, the velour edges looked like an extension of the velveteen.

Lesson 11. Appliquéing with feed dogs lowered

In this lesson, the appliqués are sewn in place freely; sometimes edges are not completely covered.

Set up your machine by lowering the feed dogs, using either a hoop or ironed-on freezer paper, and loosening the top tension slightly.

Blurring

What is blurring? Apply a fabric to another by starting to stitch within the appliqué. Then, following the shape of the appliqué, stitch around and around it, extending the stitching out into the background fabric. It's difficult to tell where one begins and the other leaves off. That is called blurring.

Although the sample here uses transparent fabrics, blurring can be done with any type of fabric. I chose to combine blurring with sheers and overlays to show you how to create pictures that look like watercolors. Thread color is usually the same as the appliqué, but never limit yourself. Use other colors as well.

When working with transparent fabrics, use pins to hold the appliqués in place. If possible, hold both in a hoop while sewing. Attach one layer at a time, sewing a straight stitch around the appliqué and then cutting back to the stitching. Then stretch the next transparent fabric in the hoop, stitch and cut away excess.

To blur it, find any point inside the appliqué. Stitch round and round, in ever-widening circles, until the edge of the appliqué is reached. But don't stop. Keep stitching past the edge and into the background. Three transparent circles applied in this way, one overlapping the next, the

Fig. 4.9 Blurring the edges of appliqués.

third overlapping the others, makes a good sample (Fig. 4.9). Possibilities will grow from this one idea: try many colors, overlapping them to make other colors; give depth to a picture by overlapping so that the color becomes more intense as the layers are built up, and recedes where only one layer is used.

Project Flower of Sheers and Overlays

Use this floral piece as a pillow top or slip it into your notebook. To do the flower sample (Fig. 4.10), set up the machine.

Stitch width: 0–widest
Stitch length: 0
Needle position: center
Needle: #80/12
Feed dogs: lowered
Presser foot: #285 (#9) darning foot or #24 freehand embroidery foot
Tension: *top,* slightly loosened; *bobbin,* normal
Fabric suggestion: 10″ (25.4cm) square medium-weight white fabric for the background; ¼ yard (22.9cm) green transparent fabric; ⅛ yard (11.4cm) pink transparent fabric; 12″ (30.5cm) square off-white bridal veiling
Threads: machine embroidery in yellow, green, and pink; green sewing thread
Accessories: 7″ (17.8cm) spring hoop (optional)
Stabilizer: iron-on freezer paper

Use the circle and leaf shape to make the patterns. Cut out several dozen 1″ (2.5cm) circles in pink transparent fabric. Also cut the same number of 2″ (5.1cm) long leaf shapes from green transparent fabric. Patterns are provided in Fig. 4.11. You may not use all of these petals and leaves: It will depend upon how much they are overlapped and how large an area you're covering with the design.

Press freezer paper to the back of the white fabric if you don't use a hoop. If you use a hoop, first arrange and overlap the leaves in a circle on the background fabric, points toward the center. Plan your design well, so the circles and leaves will fit within the hoop if you use one, keeping the leaves at least an inch (2.5cm) inside. If the presser foot gets too close to the edge, it will be difficult to sew around the appliqués without hitting the darning foot on the hoop. If you work with freezer paper, you will not be encumbered with the hoop, and the placement of your appliqués is not as critical.

Lay down the circles of color for the flower head, starting in the middle of the leaves. New colors pop out for the leaves and petals as you overlap, arrange and re-arrange. Leave the center of the flower open. Don't pin down any of these small pieces.

After completing the arrangement of the sheers and overlays, cover with the piece of bridal veil to help hold them all in place. Pin the veiling down in several places near the center of the flower and at the edges of the fabric. Lift this carefully from the table and place it in a hoop if you use one. Slip stabilizer under it.

Start by sewing around the petals of the flower. Use pink thread on the top, green sewing thread on the bobbin. Stitch the petals very freely. Bring the stitching out past them, or inside, or make stitched circles between them. Stitch circles within circles.

Then change the top thread to green. Stitch around the leaves in the same free-flowing way. Go up the centers and down, stitching in veins on some and leaving others without.

Remove pins as you go, whenever they are no longer necessary to hold the pieces together.

Now only the center is left to stitch. Change the top thread to yellow and set stitch width to the widest zigzag, stitch length 0, needle position to the left. Anchor your threads in the center of the flower. Stitch in the same spot at least a dozen times to build up a nubby "seed" (see Fig. 3.2). Anchor the threads again. Lift the presser foot–use the knee lift–and move to another place. Do another seed. There's no need to clip threads until all the seeds are completed. Keep building up the nubs and moving your needle from one place to the next until the flower center is to your liking. Then clip the threads between the zigzag areas.

Change the top thread back to green. Set stitch width back to 0, needle position center. Sew around the seeds. Go from one to another until all are outlined. When the

Fig. 4.10 Use bridal veiling to hold small pieces of appliqué fabric in place.

picture is complete, take it out of the hoop if you've used one. Remove all the pins, if you haven't done this already. Most of the stabilizer will drop away; the rest can be pulled off (or left on, since it won't show).

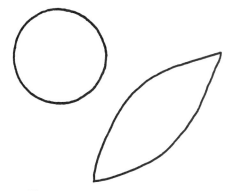

Fig. 4.11 Patterns for the flower design.

75

The bridal veil can be left as is. However, I often clip out areas to create color changes.

Scribbling

Scribbling is like darning over appliqués, but you will use both straight and zigzag stitches. It's a good way to lay in big areas of color without having to cover the areas with heavy embroidery.

The appliqué picture in Fig. 4.12 was placed on the outside of a tote bag. Use the patterns in Fig. 4.13 as a guide, enlarging or reducing to fit your purpose.

Stitch width: varies
Stitch length: 0
Needle position: center
Needle: #90/14
Feed dogs: lowered
Presser foot: #285 (#9) darning foot or #24 freehand embroidery foot
Tension: *top,* slightly loosened; *bobbin,* normal
Fabric suggestion: medium-weight cotton
Thread: machine embroidery on top; sewing or darning thread on bobbin
Accessories: glue stick
Stabilizer: iron-on freezer paper

Apply the appliqués with a dab of glue stick and begin to stitch the edges down freely with either a straight or a zigzag stitch. Sew freely over the entire appliqué first to anchor it before embroidering the designs. Stitch inside and over the edges of the appliqués. If you can live with raw edges, then don't be too particular about covering them exactly. Here is a good place to blur edges. Add to the design by laying in different colors with the same free machining. Add as much stitching as you wish, but don't cover the entire appliqué, as that would defeat the purpose. Let most of the color show through. It's like sketching with colored pencils.

Stitching Carrickmacross

Carrickmacross is an Irish lace made with appliqués of batiste. Tiny pops, or eyelets, are embroidered in the fine hexagonal net which is used as the ground, and it has a picot edge. If hand done, this type of lace is very fragile, but our machine version is both beautiful and sturdy (Fig. 4.14).

Fig. 4.12 This is part of a design that has been appliquéd to a tote bag, using free-machining to hold the appliqués in place.

Fig. 4.13 Use these patterns to create one element of the design shown in Fig. 4.12.

Fig. 4.14 Appliquéd lace (Carrickmacross), is made quickly using organdy and fine hexagonal net.

Project
Carrickmacross Doily

Instead of batiste, we'll use organdy. I've used a polyester for the veiling, so my fabric will be the same. It will be white on white, typical of Carrickmacross lace.

Stitch width: 0
Stitch length: 0
Needle position: center
Needle: #70/9
Feed dogs: lowered
Presser foot: #285 (#9) darning or #24 free-hand embroidery
Tension: *top*, slightly loosened; *bobbin*, normal

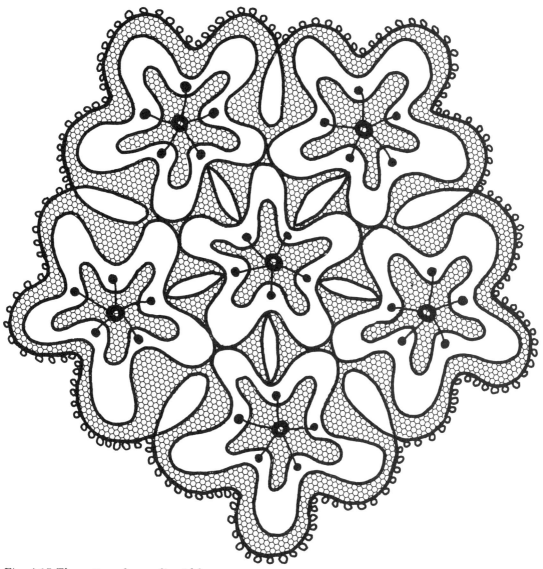

Fig. 4.15 The pattern for appliquéd lace.

Fabric suggestion: white polyester organdy; fine white polyester hexagonal veiling

Thread: white cotton machine-embroidery thread

Accessories: 9″ (22.9cm) hoop, large darning needle, water-erasable pen, white opaque marker

Stabilizer: water-soluble

Place water-soluble stabilizer in the hoop. Trace the design in Fig. 4.15, using the white opaque marker. Slip the veiling underneath the organdy and put them both into the hoop over the water-soluble stabilizer.

Set up your machine for free embroidery. Don't anchor stitches — it isn't necessary, as you will be stitching around each motif several times. Begin by stitching around each flower and around each leaf three times. Stitch twice around the centers of the flowers.

It is easy to plot the course of your needle so that you can go from one flower to the next when you stitch. When you stitch the centers, lift up the presser foot and move from one place to another. Stitch around the edge three times, and around the inside edge twice.

To add pops to the centers of the flowers, stitch three times around each tiny center circle. With the darning needle, poke through the center of each circle. Set your machine to stitch width 1 1/2. Zigzag around each circle by letting the needle stitch into the center on one swing and over your three lines of stitching on the other. Rotate the hoop slowly as you stitch the eyelet. You will be almost hand-walking the machine in order to satin stitch closely around the tiny circle.

When finished, take the design out of the hoop and cut out all the areas that are to be free of organdy, but don't cut around the edge of the doily yet. Use sharp, fine-pointed scissors when cutting out the fabric. It helps to lift areas away from the net with the point of a seam ripper and then clip. Also clip unnecessary threads and thread ends.

Should you cut the net, don't panic. Put it back under the needle, sew a few lines of straight stitching over the cut, blending it into the other stitches already there. If the cut is too large, carefully remove the whole section and place another piece of veiling underneath (be sure to arrange the veiling so it matches the direction of the veil in the hoop). Stitch around the damaged area to attach the patch. Cut the veil back to the stitching lines.

Put the work back in the hoop and finish the flower centers by stitching from the inside line up to the center pop, then back down again. Stitch a small blob of thread there by stitching in a circle to build up a tiny pindot. Travel along the inside line to the next spot. Stitch to the center and back to the inside line again. Make another dot, then continue on to the next. Continue like this until all the flower centers have been completed.

Now remove the embroidery from the hoop. Cut back on the net only, leaving the organdy and stabilizer. Put the lace back in the hoop. With a water-erasable pen, mark small dots every 1/8″ (3.2mm) along the edge to use as a guide for the picots. Following the edge, stitch around each dot three times, making small loops on top of each other at each mark.

Again, take the embroidery out of the hoop and cut away the stabilizer and the organdy up to the picots — including the few threads of fabric that remain between each picot. Wash the remaining stabilizer and blue pen marks out of the fabric.

What we've made is a small doily but, if you're like me, you are not big on small doilies. This is a fast technique, so think big. Try it for the edge of a bridal veil or for the bodice and puffed sleeves of the wedding dress itself. Now that's what I call a long-cut, but definitely worth it.

Layering transparent fabrics

Shadow work is my favorite. I love the painterly effects of combining colors and toning down with whites. It's done using sheers and overlays. In the picture made in the following project, the color does not come from a colored cotton fabric layered between organdies; instead, these flowers are created only from transparent fabrics.

Project
Shadow Work
Picture

In this project, I switch from feed dogs up to feed dogs lowered, but most of the stitching is done freely, so I've put it in this lesson. This design (Fig. 4.16) will give you an idea of what can be done with only white, mauve and green organza.

Stitch width: 0–4
Stitch length: 0–1/2
Needle position: center
Needle: #70/9
Feed dogs: up, lowered
Presser foot: #181 (#23) appliqué, #147 (#20) open embroidery, #285 (#9) darning foot or #24 free-machine embroidery foot
Tension: *top,* normal; *bobbin,* finger threaded — or *top,* slightly loosened; *bobbin,* normal
Fabric: white, mauve, and green organza
Thread: machine embroidery, green
Accessories: spring hoop; water-erasable marker
Stabilizer: water-soluble

Fig. 4.16 Layers of transparent fabrics give a painterly effect to shadow work.

Place the white organza over the design (Fig. 4.17) and trace it off with a water-erasable marker. Layer two mauves behind each flower on the white organza and pin them in place. Put this in a hoop.

With the machine set for free machining, without anchoring the threads, straight stitch around the flowers twice. Lift the needle and go to the flower centers. Stitch twice around each center, also: The lines should be next to each other, not on top of each other. Cut back to the stitching around the outside edge, but not too close.

Place the green organza behind the leaf areas and stitch in place with two lines of

stitching. Cut back to the stitching at the edges.

Set up your machine for normal sewing. Put feed dogs up and use the appliqué foot. Use stitch width 2, stitch length 1/2 or a setting that will produce a smooth satin stitch. Sew around the flowers and leaves. Be careful: sew too closely and the stitches will cut the fabric.

From the front of your picture, cut the white organza from one flower, the white and one mauve layer from another. Turn the hoop over. Cut out one layer of mauve from the back on another. Or from the back, cut out both layers of color, leaving only the white organdy and the flower cen-

Fig. 4.17 Shadow work design.

ter intact. Can you imagine the combinations and shades of mauve you can create?

The large leaf is divided into four sections. In the first section, cut out the top white layer and place a layer of green behind the remaining green layer to darken it. In the second area, cut out the white and leave just green. In the third, place white behind the section to make it three layers. The fourth is left as is, the white in front of the green.

Once you have finished the flowers and leaves, go back to the flower centers and blur them out by stitching spirals from the centers out to the edges. Or start at the edges and travel to the outside of the flowers. Leave some flowers with only the first stitching around the center.

Satin stitches should be sewn through at least two layers of fabric. Ordinarily, we'd add stabilizer, but tear-away could leave specks in the fabric that might show through. To prevent this, use green organza as a backing for the stems. The lines are satin stitched, then the stabilizing organza is cut back to the stitching.

Finish up with straight stitching. Set up again for free machining. Using water-soluble stabilizer behind the fabric, set the machine on stitch width 0, stitch length 0, to sew in the accent lines.

If one of the fabrics has pulled away from the satin stitches, don't give up. Layer a piece of transparent fabric underneath and stitch it on. Then cut away the original one. Or put a piece of organza underneath, use straight stitching or zigzags to sew in some lines, and pretend you wanted it that way. On the flowers, too: If by mistake you cut through two layers instead of one, leave it or layer something behind it. Sometimes blurring out more lines of stitching will attach and hide any mistakes.

Keep the stitching light and airy, with no wide satin stitches. There should be more fabric showing than stitching. When finished, wash out the stabilizer and pen marks.

This type of shadow work is quite fragile and I suggest using it for pictures or window hangings, rather than for clothing.

Project
Stitching Three-Dimensional Appliqués

One of the prettiest dresses I've ever seen was at a fraternity dance back when we though we had to wear yards of tulle and gobs of ruffles. This dress was a beautiful white organdy exception. Over the entire skirt were scattered lavender and peach pansy appliqués of organdy. They were attached only at the centers. It was a plain dress except for this scattering of flowers.

Detached appliqués do not need a heavy satin stitch edge, and I think you'll agree that straight stitching on fine fabric is easier and more beautiful. After all, that was a long time ago and I've never forgotten that dress.

Stitch width: 0
Stitch length: 0
Needle position: center
Needle: #70/9
Feed dogs: lowered
Presser foot: darning foot or no presser foot; tailor-tacking (optional)
Tension: *top,* loosened; *bobbin,* normal
Fabric suggestion: mauve and green organdy
Thread: machine embroidery thread to match
Accessories: spring hoop
Stabilizer: water-soluble

Place a layer of water-soluble stabilizer between two layers of mauve organdy. Clip this into the spring hoop. Draw the design in Fig. 4.18 on it with a water-erasable marker. You will copy the petal design twice. The small sample is done in pieces and combined later (Fig. 4-19).

Set the machine on moderate speed for accuracy. Stitch three times around the edges with a straight stitch. Lines should be close together, but not on top of each other. Use a colored thread that matches or is a shade darker than the fabric. Cut out the petals close to the stitching, but not too close.

The leaves should be worked in the same way on green organdy. Stitch only straight stitches as you follow the pattern. Go into the centers and stitch the veins as well. Cut out the leaves.

Place the flower petals on top of each other, staggering them so the petals un-derneath are not hidden by the top layer. Place this over the leaves and stitch them together with mauve thread, following the stitching in the center of the petals. You may go a step further and fringe the center. Using the tailor-tacking foot, green thread, stitch width 2 and stitch length almost 0, stitch in several places in the center of the flower. Finish by holding the flower under the faucet and rinsing out some, but *not* all, of the stabilizer. Shape the flower and leaves carefully and let them dry. They will be stiff, as if heavily starched, and will retain their shapes. How can you use these three-dimensional appliqués? Add a band of them to a bodice of Carrickmacross lace. Make a fake corsage or a flowered hat. Add the flower to a cord for a necklace.

Fig. 4.18 Three-dimensional appliqué design.

Fig. 4.19 Pattern pieces for floral 3-D appliqué.

Helpful hints for appliqué

If an appliqué bubbles, fix it by taking it out of the hoop and nicking the base fabric beneath the appliqué, which will then allow the base to lay flat.

Or slit the back a bit and fill the appliqué area with cotton. This is called trapunto. Hand whip the slit closed. Machine stitch on top of the appliqué to add to the design and hold the batting in place.

Another way to keep appliqué puckers from showing is to hide them by hand or machine embroidering over the appliqué.

When layering net, there is sometimes a moiré look to it that spoils the effect of your picture. To eliminate it, change the direction of one of the layers.

Don't limit yourself to fabric appliqués; thread appliqués are also effective. Work spider webs in another fabric, cut them out, and apply.

Work lace in space inside a small ring. Apply it to a background by free machining all around the inside edge of the ring. Then cut the ring from the lace.

Check out Lesson 6 on beads, baubles, and shishas.

Do pulled and drawn threads with the machine on one fabric and attach them to another background.

With an 1100 model, you can make appliqué stitching much easier by using "needle down." Stitching will be smoother, as there will be no moving the fabric by mistake when you stop. And don't you love that the machine does not run on once you've stopped stitching?

The most helpful hint of all is to remind you to use the presser foot lifter. It raises and lowers the presser foot with the right knee so both your hands can guide your work. When satin stitching around curves or turning corners, it is indispensable.

CHAPTER 5

Stitching Across Open Spaces

- **Lesson 12. Cutwork and eyelets**
- **Lesson 13. Free-machined needlelace**
- **Lesson 14. Battenberg lace**
- **Lesson 15. Hemstitching**
- **Lesson 16. Stitching in rings**
- **Lesson 17 Making Alençon lace**

Don't let the title of this chapter scare you. When stitching across open spaces, your Bernina will behave beautifully.

People have been stitching in space for a hundred years; you can, too. However, if you are nervous about doing it, stitching on water-soluble stabilizer usually produces the same effects with even better results. Water-soluble stabilizer is so thin and pliable that placing multiple layers of it in a hoop, along with fabric, is no problem. Another reason I am sold on it is that, once the design is drawn on the stabilizer, it can be stitched exactly, as if stitching on fabric. That isn't possible when actually stitching in space. I use it for cutwork because it holds the cut edges in place while I stitch them and sometimes I use it on both sides of the fabric to give it even more stability.

I use stabilizer when stitching in rings,

too. It keeps threads in place until they are anchored. There is no problem with slipping, as often happens when stitching in space. Practice on water-soluble stabilizer, but once you feel you know your machine, graduate to open space and try that. There are occasions for both techniques.

This chapter includes cutwork, stitching in rings, creating needlelace, and stitching both Battenberg and Alençon laces. Hemstitching is included, as well. Be sure to keep all your samples in your notebook. You may not use an idea today or tomorrow, but maybe next year you'll refer back to your notebook and find just what you're looking for to make a special gift, or welcome a new baby. My notebook is especially valuable when I want to find machine settings for a technique I haven't used in weeks. No matter how well you know your machine, you can't remember everything.

Lesson 12. Cutwork and eyelets

Cutwork

Cutwork is the forerunner of all needlemade laces. It was common as early as the sixteenth century. In handmade cutwork, part of the background fabric is cut away and threads are stretched from

one side of the open area to the other. Bars of buttonhole stitches are worked over the stretched threads and the cut edges. Cutwork can be done by machine, using satin stitches in place of buttonhole stitches.

Fig. 5.1 Cutwork blouse, designed by Sherrie Coppenbarger. Shown with jacket, and in closeup detail.

Project Cutwork Blouse

I first saw Sherrie Coppenbarger's cutwork blouse in a style show. To me, it was the highlight of the show. Sherrie's meticulous stitching on this original creation, shown in Fig. 5.1, is incredible, and I especially liked her blouse cutwork echoing the design woven into the jacket and shorts. It's an inventive idea to copy, whether your fabric is flowered or geometric, as is Sherrie's. Her method of creating the cutwork blouse follows.

As you stitch any cutwork, remember the altered-memory potential (it has nothing to do with the memory button) on the 1100 series. What it means is that you can change two built-in stitches at a time by using different stitch widths and lengths from the basic settings in the machine. As you stitch and call up the narrowed zigzag or the longer straight stitch, for example, the machine will remember them: you simply push the straight-stitch button or the zigzag button. When I zigzag, I often leave the straight-stitch setting on stitch width 0, stitch length 0, to anchor stitches at the beginning and end of my zigzagging by merely pushing the straight-stitch button. When I want to continue my zigzag, the machine remembers the altered length and width. I only need press the zigzag stitch. It may be necessary to change the alterations a couple of times during the course of one pattern, but altered-memory, if used to its full potential, is always a timesaver.

Stitch width: 0–2
Stitch length: 0–satin stitch
Needle: #70/10
Feed dogs: up, lowered
Presser foot: #285 (#9) darning foot, or bare needle; #147 (#20) open embroidery foot

Tension: *top,* slightly loosened; *bobbin,* normal
Fabric suggestion: linen
Thread: cotton or rayon machine embroidery
Accessories: 7" (17.8cm) spring hoop; dressmaker's greaseless carbon paper or Mark-B-Gone Tracing Paper; sharp embroidery scissors; chalk pencil; permanent white marker; pearl cotton cord #5
Stabilizer: water-soluble

Cut out the bodice first, from the pattern you selected (a simple shell is best). Sherrie stabilized all the edges, except the neckline, by serging them, but you can also use the sewn-out (three-step) zigzag. Transfer the cutwork pattern in Fig. 5.2 to your fabric, using dressmaker's greaseless carbon paper or Mark-B-Gone Tracing paper. Pin the cutwork pattern to the bodice front, lining up center front and shoulder seam lines. Carefully slide the carbon paper between fabric and pattern, and mark one side of the pattern with a ballpoint pen. Slide the carbon paper to the remaining portion and complete the transfer. Remove the pattern. If any portion is too faint to see, it can be remarked with a chalk pencil.

Before beginning to sew, practice a few cutouts of similar shape on a scrap of the same fabric, using the same thread, stitch settings, and stabilizer you'll use for the garment; check thread color and satin stitch density, as well as get a feel for stitching the fabric.

Place the stabilizer under an area of the bodice, and the larger ring of the spring hoop under both. Carefully slip the inner ring down into the outer ring so you don't distort the fabric's grainline. Set up your machine by lowering the feed dogs, removing the presser foot, and lowering the presser bar to engage upper thread tension. Start straight stitching at a corner of the design at one side of the hoop. Tap on the presser foot with your heel to bring up the bobbin thread, and hold both threads

89

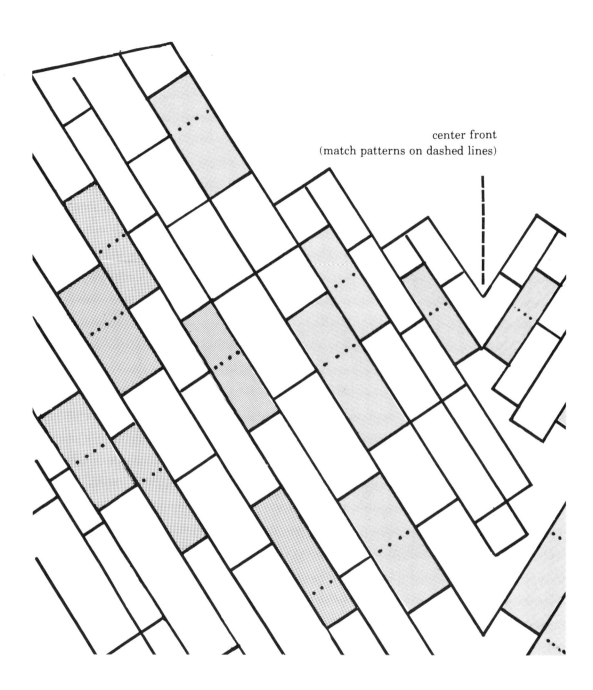

center front
(match patterns on dashed lines)

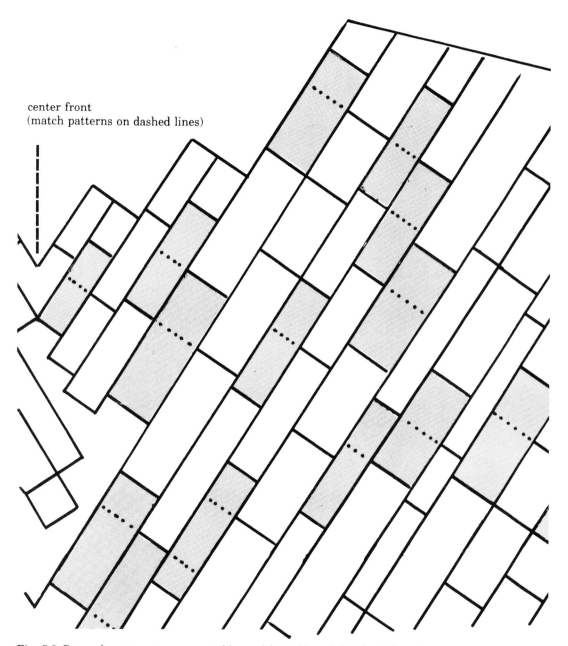

center front
(match patterns on dashed lines)

Fig. 5.2 Cutwork pattern to trace onto blouse fabric. Place left side of the pattern over the right side and match at center front. Then finish drawing the right side of pattern as a mirror image of the left. Shaded areas indicate cutouts; broken lines indicate Richelieu bars.

to one side. To stabilize the fabric and build a cushion for the satin stitches, gently slide the hoop along, straight stitching twice around each rectangle that is to be cut out. (Don't stitch in the bars yet.)

Now you are ready to cut out the design. Snip an opening in the fabric to ease the scissors blade between the fabric and stabilizer. Trim away each rectangle close to the stitching, but leave the stabilizer. If you snip any of the stabilizer, then pin another piece to the back at that area. Do not cut neckline opening at this time.

Brides or *Richelieus* are names for the bars of stitches that keep large areas in place. To mark the Richelieus, line up the hoop over the pattern portion you are working on; trace the Richelieus onto the stabilizer with a permanent white marker. To begin, pull bobbin thread up as before and anchor it in the straight stitches at one of the Richelieus. With the same machine setup, straight stitch across the opening into the other stabilizing stitches. Stitch back across on the same line, anchoring threads, until three or four strings have formed the bar. Change to zigzag stitch, width 1 1/2, and cover the strings with satin stitches. Move slowly so the stitches are packed closely. When you reach the stabilizing stitches, push straight-stitch button to anchor the threads. Follow the rectangle edge to the next Richelieu and repeat the procedure until you've completed all the bars.

At this point you will change the machine setup. Use the open embroidery foot with feed dogs raised and stitch width 2. Stitch the short ends of the rectangles first. Position the fabric under the presser foot so the needle zigs into the fabric and zags into the cutout. Begin stitching deep into the corner to allow for overlap of the longer lines of satin stitching. Finish the ends of the design cutouts and all other short connecting lines.

Then complete the long lines of satin stitching in this segment of the design, moving from the top of the hoop to the bottom. Anchor the thread with a few stitches. Each long line can be continued if needed when the hoop is moved.

Finish the blouse by next trimming the neckline opening close to satin stitching and sew shoulder seams of the blouse. For the final touch, a second row of satin stitches is applied with pearl cotton added for firmness. Start at the back keyhole opening and straight stitch several stitches to anchor thread. Lift presser foot and bring work forward so the open embroidery foot is once again at the starting position. Satin stitch, stitch width 3, and guide the cord along the very edge of the fabric. Position the presser foot so the needle zigs into the fabric, and zags across the previous stitch and cord. Pivot the fabric at inside corners while holding the cord. On outside corners, sew within half the zigzag width from the edge. Turn work so the edge is in the center of the presser foot. Turn to stitch width 0. Sew slowly and at the same time increase stitch width to 3. Continue around to the back opening, leaving a tail of cord to form a buttonhole loop.

Eyelets

Bernina makes an accessory called the English eyelet maker, but it is expensive, so most stitchers don't buy it unless they do a large quantity of eyelets. I've used this accessory in my embroideries, clumping eyelets together for a center of interest, and one of my teachers uses them to decorate lovely bed linens. But try one before you invest.

There are less expensive substitutes for the English eyelet maker. One is a Japanese-made "flower stitcher." It makes eyelets and can be programmed to do decorative floral stitching around them.

I also have a buttonholer with different-sized templates that clamps onto my machine. Of course my machine makes gorgeous buttonholes, but the Bernina does not have a keyhole buttonhole and I need one. Among the templates is an eyelet to be used for lacing. The difference between this eyelet and the one made with the Ber-nina accessory is that there is only one size and it is flat on the top and bottom, where-as both eyelets made by the Bernina acces-sory are typical, round eyelets.

Lesson 13. Free-machined needlelace

The terms *cutwork, lacy spiderwebs,* and *openwork* all describe a machine stitchery technique far removed from darning holes in socks or shredded elbows. But, like darning, they do entail stitching across open spaces.

Stitch width: 0
Stitch length: 0
Needle position: center
Needle: #80/12
Feed dogs: lowered
Presser foot: #285 (#9) darning foot, #24 freehand embroidery foot, or no presser foot
Tension: *top,* normal; *bobbin,* normal
Fabric suggestions: any weight
Thread: one color, machine embroidery or polyester
Accessories: 6″ (15.2cm) wrapped wooden hoop

Openwork is done in a hoop with the fab-ric stretched tightly. Place the hoop, fabric side down, on the machine bed. Draw a cir-cle on the fabric: Circles are easier to con-trol than the squares, crescents and pais-ley shapes you may want to try later.

Start stitching at the edge of the circle by bringing the bobbin thread to the top. Anchor the threads by sewing a few stitch-es in one spot. Guide the hoop slowly as you stitch around the circle three times (Fig. 5.3A). Take the hoop off the machine and, without removing the fabric from it, cut out the circle close to the stitches. Re-place the hoop and secure the threads once again at the edge of the hole.

Now you will begin to lay in a network of spokelike threads across the space. To do this, begin by stitching across from one side of the hole to the other side. Move the hoop slowly, but run the machine moder-ately fast to strengthen and put a tighter twist on the spoke. When your needle en-ters the fabric again, move along the circle to another spot, secure threads, and sew directly across the hole again. Continue in this manner until you have as many spokes as you wish. On the last pass, go up to the center and backstitch right at the center of the wheel to strengthen the web. Starting at that backstitch, fill in the spokes by sewing in ever-widening circles around the center until the "button" is the size you wish it to be (Fig. 5.3B). Sew a few stitches into the button to lock the thread in place and again move to the outside to anchor the threads and complete that spoke.

Would you like a lacier filling? Sew one backstitch over each spoke after crossing it as you stitch around the center. This keeps the threads from slipping to the center. Travel around and around in wider circles till you reach the edge of the hole (Fig. 5.3C).

Although there are as many ways to fin-ish off the edges of the spaces as there are ways to fill them with stitches, one of the softest looks is accomplished by straight stitching from the edge of the hole, out past it and back again, moving the hoop back and forth as if stitching sun rays. You can also use the widest zigzag and accom-plish the same rays. Or, satin stitch around the edge and combine that with other embroidery. These are only a few ideas; try some of your own.

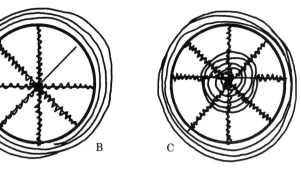

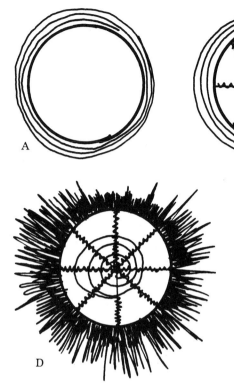

Fig. 5.3 Making needlelace. A. First sew around a circle three times. B. Cut out the center, embroider across the hole, creating spokes. C. Add circles of stitches around the center. D. Stitch radiating lines over the edge, into the fabric.

Create your own samples by placing a piece of medium-weight cotton in a hoop and drawing several circles on it. Stitch around one circle three times. Cut out the center. Stitch a spider web in the hole and finish it off on the edges. Go to the next circle and stitch both the center and the edges in a different way from your first sample. Then do another and another until you have many needlelace samples for your notebook. Or back them with another fabric as squares for your tote bag.

Lesson 14. Battenberg lace

Battenberg lace was popular in the late 1800s. Straight, machine-made tape was shaped into a design and basted to stiff paper. Then the open spaces were filled with bars and embroidery stitches, which held the tape in shape. After the stitchery was completed, the paper was removed and the Battenberg lace could be used to decorate dresses, curtains or linens.

Project
Small Lace
Motif

This lesson will teach you how to make one small piece of Battenberg (Fig. 5.4). From there, you can go on to bigger projects, but let's see if you like Battenberg lacemaking by machine.

Battenberg tape is available in a variety of white, off-white, silver, gold, black, and other colors, by mail (see Sources of Supplies) or from some needlework shops.

Should you create your own design, choose a tape that doesn't overpower the pattern. The one I used is ⅜″ (9.5mm) wide, but my design is quite large. On each side of the tape is a thread that is thicker than the others. Pull gently to curve the tape into the shape that you want.

Place two pieces of water-soluble stabilizer in a 7″ (17.8cm) hoop and over the design in Fig. 5.5. Trace the outline of the tape with a white permanent marking pen. Pull up the thread on the tape, pinning in the shape on the stabilizer as you go. Use a glue stick to hold the tape in place as you shape it. Hide the tape ends by slipping

Fig. 5.4 Battenberg is embroidered after narrow tape has been shaped into a design.

Fig. 5.5 Battenberg pattern.

them behind and across the tape on top. Extend the ends a bit beyond the top tape — until the lace piece is completed and they can be cut back. Glue between the tapes to hold them in place.

Baste both sides of the tape to the stabilizer to prevent curling. Use wash-away basting thread if you have it, or use a fine thread in the same color as your tape. I find it more satisfactory to baste by hand than by machine. When the tape is in place, put the hoop over the pattern again. Draw in the stitching lines: Extend them by drawing dots onto the tape with a water-erasable pen. At times, the stabilizer will be cut out and these dots can be used for reference.

Set up your machine for free embroidery.

Stitch width: 0–1 1/2
Stitch length: 0
Needle position: center
Needle: #90/14
Feed dogs: lowered
Presser foot: #285 (#9) darning or #24 free-
hand machine embroidery foot
Tension: *top,* normal; *bobbin,* normal
Thread: #50 white machine embroidery, wa-
ter-soluble basting thread (optional)
Accessories: 7″ (17.8cm) spring hoop; water-
erasable pen; white permanent marker;
3/8″ (9.5mm) Battenberg tape
Stabilizer: doubled water-soluble stabilizer,
large enough for hoop

If you are stitching on the 1100 models, make use of altered-stitch settings. Leave the straight stitches set at 0, but change the zigzag to 1 1/2 stitch width. Then it will be easy to merely push buttons as you change from straight to zigzag stitches. If you don't have an 1100, it may be easier for you to do all the straight stitching for each section first, then go back and do all the zigzags. That way, you will not have to reset the stitch width and length as often.

Start by straight stitching around the tape at the inside. After the design is attached, cut out the stabilizer in the bottom loop. (Continue to cut out one section at a time as you embroider to give your lace more stability while stitching.) Anchor your thread by stitching in one place several times where the two tapes cross. Stitch one long pass from that point down to the center of the loop, then zigzag back up to the starting point. Move the hoop quite fast. Don't build up thick bars as in cutwork.

Follow the side of the tape with straight stitches. Stitch to the first branch and then to the center. Take a stitch backward to anchor, then stitch to the other side. Change to zigzag and cover those branches as you did with the stem. Straight stitch to the next branch. Stitch to the center, anchor and go to the other side. Again, zigzag

over the branches and anchor your thread in the tape by straight stitching in place three or four stitches.

Cut out the stabilizer in the spider web loop at the top, then lay in your threads and zigzag over all of them except the last one. Zigzag to the center of that thread, then stitch in circles of straight stitches out toward the edge (Fig. 5.6A). End at the thread that has not been zigzagged, change settings to zigzag, and finish covering the threads. Anchor the thread in the tape.

Cut out the stabilizer from the lefthand loop at the bottom. Anchor, then straight stitch from one side of the tape to the other across the area; zigzag back with stitch width 1 1/2. At the point where the stitches join the fabric, change to straight stitch, then back to zigzag again, zigzagging several stitches over both threads to hold them together. Then travel on over the next thread. Stitch down to the tape, then back over both threads with a few stitches before zigzagging over the next thread to the other side of the tape (Fig. 5.6B). Complete the area. Then stitch the righthand loop the same way.

To finish the last loop, stitch from where the two tapes cross, up to the center of the loop (Fig. 5.6C). Zigzag back to the starting point. Change to straight stitch and follow the side of the tape to the first dot. Stitch across it to the dot on the other side. Then stitch back across with a zigzag. Straight stitch to the next dot, stitch across the center to the other side and come back as you did previously. Continue until the section is completed. When you complete the last cross, anchor your thread in the tape.

The remaining large area is worked much the same way. First, lay in the long center thread from the top point down and across to the last loop you embroidered. This is an extremely long area so you may want to leave the stabilizer in place as you stitch. (This will give the section a slightly different appearance from the other areas when completed.) Zigzag your return.

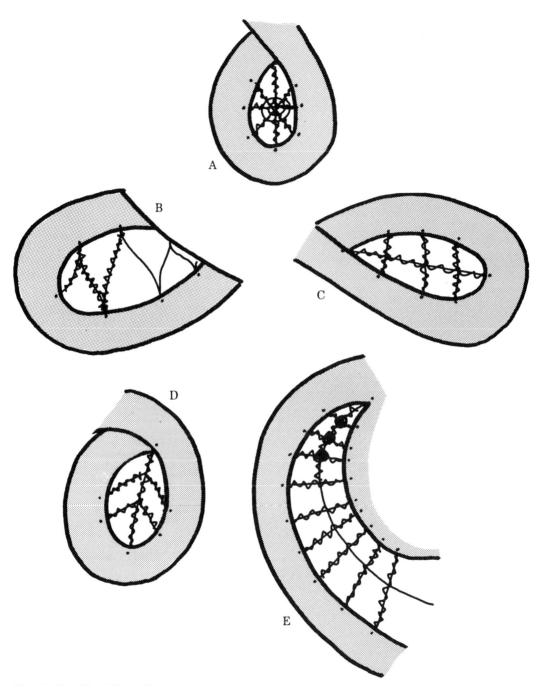

Fig. 5.6 Details of Battenberg stitching. A. Circles are stitched very closely together in this spiderweb. B. This fill-in stitch is referred to as Point d'Alençon when done by hand. C. Stitch from where tapes cross to top of loop, then stitch across from side to side to lay in a grid pattern. D. This area is filled in with Sorrento bars. E. A grid is stitched inside the long curved area, with circles stitched at the crossed threads.

Change to straight stitching and stitch at the edge of the tape to the first bar. Stitch across to the other side, but on the return zigzag, stop when you reach the center, change to straight stitching and stitch a small circle around the crossed threads. Continue zigzagging to the other side. Change to straight stitches, travel to the next point, stitch across the open area to the other side and continue as you did for the first bar, until the area has been completed (Fig. 5.6E).

Now stitch the tape ends and crossed tapes in place. Wherever the tapes cross, straight stitch all four sides, as shown in Fig. 5.5. You may attach the tape ends in one of two ways. The traditional way is to fold the ends back between the tapes and then zigzag at both edges. This produces a strong, clean join, but it is bulky. I find that I can live with merely crossing the tapes and stitching a narrow zigzag at both sides, then cutting back the ends that are protruding. You may want to zigzag all four edges to make it stronger.

After the lace is stitched, wash out the stabilizer and place the Battenberg between layers of toweling to press.

Lesson 15. Hemstitching

Hemstitching is used on garments and table linens whenever a delicate, feminine look is desired. The technique looks complicated and difficult, but it is surprisingly easy to accomplish using both double- and single-winged needles.

Before you begin to stitch the bonnet, practice on two layers of cotton organdy.

Set up your machine.

Stitch width: 0 to no wider than the throat plate opening when using a double needle (use special function button on 1100 machines)
Stitch length: varies
Needle position: center
Needle: single and double hemstitching needles; double needles to match sizes of pintuck feet
Feed dogs: up
Presser foot: #147 (#20) open embroidery foot, pintuck feet
Tension: *top*, normal; *bobbin*, normal
Fabric: crisp fabric, such as organdy or linen
Thread: cotton machine embroidery

To thread two needles, treat both threads as one until you reach the tension disk. Divide the threads so they lie on either side of the disk, then continue to thread with the threads together until you reach the guide just above the needle. One thread will be left out of that loop. Thread the needles. That's all there is to it. Remember to always thread your machine with the presser foot up.

Try hemstitching as described in your Bernina manual. Start with the single-winged needle and use a zigzag. Stitch a row of hemstitching. At the end of the first run, leave the needle in the hole at left, turn and return, poking into the same holes as on the first run.

You can make an all-over design, covering a large area with hemstitches. This is usually worked on the bias, then appliquéd to something else.

Now practice with the double hemstitch needle. Set up your machine in this way:

Stitch width: 1 3/4
Stitch length: 1 3/4
Needle position: center
Feed dogs: up
Presser foot: #147 (#20) open embroidery foot

Make one pass, ending to the left. Lift the presser foot, turn the fabric and stitch the second pass.

Try this blind hemstitch.

Stitch width: 1 3/4
Stitch length: 1 3/4
Needle position: center
Feed dogs: up
Presser foot: #147 (#20) open embroidery
    foot
Built-in stitch: blind hem stitch

Turn your hemstitching into shadow work as well. Cut back the piece of organdy underneath, clipping out both sides of the double fabric on either side of the blind hemstitches.

On the 1130 machine, the following stitches lend themselves beautifully to hemstitching: #15, #17, #18, #27. The 1120 machine includes #27. Experiment with other stitches. Combine practical stitches, such as the blind stitch, and sew one row. Turn the fabric and go back, cutting into the same holes your wing needle cut on the first pass.

Project
Infant's Bonnet

I've combined hemstitching with built-in stitches and double needles to make the infant's bonnet shown in Fig. 5.7. Also included is a line of ribbon sewing. This can be made in the time it would take you to shop for a baby gift.

Nora Lou Kampe of LaGrange, Illinois, made this bonnet using embroidered eyelet fabric with a scalloped border–a way to make a baby gift in no more than an hour's time. I used her bonnet idea, but took the long-cut and embroidered the bonnet myself; it fits a newborn and you could make one for a christening. A gown can be done in the same hemstitching technique.

The finished bonnet is 13″ × 5¾″ (33.0cm × 14.6cm). Add to both width and length if you're adapting it for an older baby.

Stitch width: varies
Stitch length: varies
Needle position: center, right
Needle: 1.6 twin needle; single and double
    hemstitching needles
Feed dogs: up
Presser foot: #147 (#20) open embroidery
    foot; 5-groove pintuck foot; 560 (#1)
    multi-motion foot (optional)
Tension: *top,* normal; *bobbin,* normal
Fabric suggestion: white cotton organdy
Thread: light-blue, fine machine-embroidery
    thread; #5 light-blue pearl cotton; white
    cordonnet
Other supplies: two pearl beads (optional);
    ⅛″ (3.2mm) double-faced satin ribbon,
    approximately 1 yard (91.4cm); ¼″
    (6.4mm) double-faced satin ribbon, ½
    yard (45.7cm); ½″ (12.7mm) double-
    faced satin ribbon, approximately 1½
    yards (137.1cm)

Begin with two pieces of organdy, each 18″ × 9″ (45.7cm × 22.9cm). I start with a much larger area than I need because I practice on the margin—running the decorative stitches so they will match when I do a mirror image. If you have the 1130 model, you will push a button to begin a perfect mirror image.

Wash and iron the organdy. Mark the top fabric lengthwise, using a water-erasable marker (Fig. 5.8). Start by marking lines 1″ (2.5cm) apart from the front edge. Use a T-square for accuracy. Draw six lines. Then mark a line ½″ (12.7mm) from the last line, and another ½″ (12.7mm) from that one; 7″ × 13″ (17.8cm × 33.0cm) is marked. Pin the two pieces of fabric together at the top of the lines.

Once you have learned how to hemstitch, the decoration is up to you. The following is only a suggestion: Thread the double-wing needle with light-blue thread. The first line of blind hemstitches are stitched 1″ (2.5cm) from the front edge.

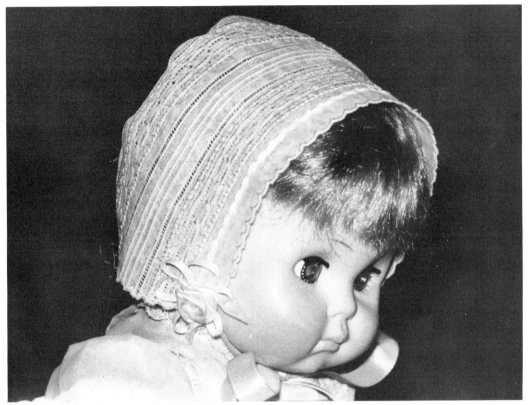

Fig. 5.7 Hemstitching, pintucking, and embroidery decorate the organdy bonnet for an infant or a doll.

Use the blue line as your guide and stitch on top of it. When you reach the end, turn and go back, cutting into the same hole you stitched on the first run. Sew slowly. If the needle does not hit exactly in the right place, stop and move the fabric by one or two threads. Continue.

Spread the fabric apart. The pintucking is done between the blue lines on the top piece only.

Change to the 1.6mm double needle. Use the 5-groove pintuck foot, light-blue #5 pearl cotton, feed dogs up, stitch length 2. Thread the hole in the throat plate with pearl cotton.

There are three lines of pintucking, so stitch the first line exactly in the middle, between the blue marker lines. Stitch the others on either side of this one, using the grooves in the pintuck foot as guides.

If you wish, stitch all four groups of pintucks between the blue lines at one time, then go back, take the pearl cotton out of the throat plate, change to the hemstitching needle, and continue to hemstitch on the blue lines with the blind hemstitch. Remember, when you pintuck, work on one layer of fabric, but hemstitch on both layers.

Complete 4½″ (11.4cm) of the bonnet (shaded area on Fig. 5.8) by filling in the empty spaces between the hemstitched

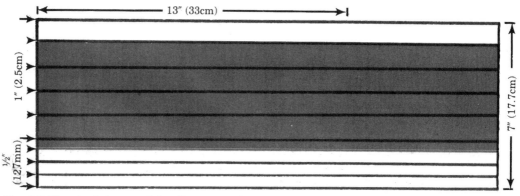

Fig. 5.8 The shaded area of the diagram indicates the portions to be embroidered.

blind hem pattern and the pintucks. Use the open effect of the single-wing needle, sewing in a straight line. Remember to come back again, punching holes in the same places where the first ones were.

Should you still want more decoration, use a built-in stitch of your choice. Sew down the sides of the lines of blind hemstitches. When you have decorated the fabric enough, straight stitch around the edge of the bonnet rectangle. Cut back to the stitching line. Put the piece you've practiced on into your notebook.

Fold the bonnet rectangle in half (Fig. 5.9). The fold will be the top of the bonnet. Pin the fabric together, matching decorative stitches so it is exact. Round off the front corners where the rosettes will be sewn (see Fig. 5.12). Open up and stitch 1/8" (3.2mm) in from the edges of the bottom and front.

Change to the scallop design to stitch the front edge and the sides of the bonnet. Use the #030 (#6) embroidery foot, size #80/12 needle, stitch width 4, stitch length 1/2 (or whatever works best for you to cover cord smoothly). Do a sample first.

Thread cordonnet through the hole in the foot. Place the foot with the thread hole on the line of stitching. Hold the cord up slightly as you cover it with stitches. When the scallops are completed, clip fab-

ric back from the edge to the stitching, but not too close to the scallops.

Stitch down on the line 1/2" (12.7mm) from the edge (back of bonnet) and stitch another 1/2" (12.7mm) from that line. Fold the back under 1/2" (12.7mm), then again another 1/2" (12.7mm). Stitch across the first fold to make the ribbon casing.

Next, wind the bobbin with 1/8" (3.2mm) double-faced satin ribbon. Tape the end onto the bobbin and begin winding by hand. Finish by winding slowly on the machine. Don't thread it through the spring when full. Instead, feed the end up through the square hole and into the two

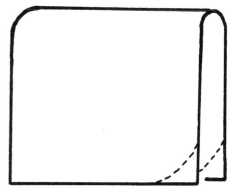

Fig. 5.9 When stitching is completed, fold the rectangle in half and round off the front corners, as shown.

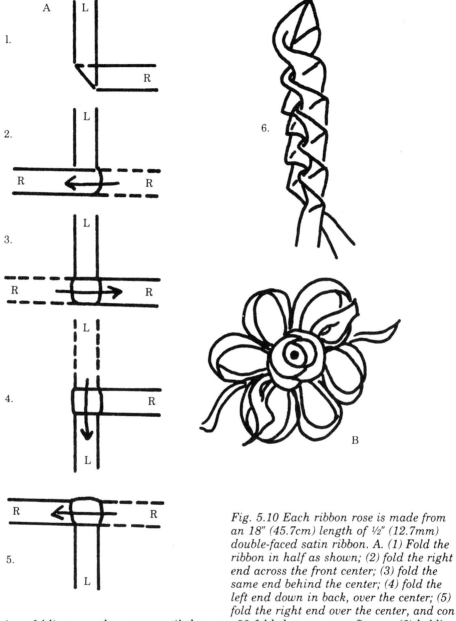

Fig. 5.10 Each ribbon rose is made from an 18" (45.7cm) length of ½" (12.7mm) double-faced satin ribbon. A. (1) Fold the ribbon in half as shown; (2) fold the right end across the front center; (3) fold the same end behind the center; (4) fold the left end down in back, over the center; (5) fold the right end over the center, and con-
tinue folding over the center until there are 30 folds between your fingers; (6) holding the last fold between your thumb and forefinger, release the rest of the ribbon, then pull on the ribbon end under the last fold to create the rose. B. By hand, stitch from the back to the center and back again to keep the rose from unwinding. Leave ½" (12.7mm) ends and cut each on a slant. Hold the loops in place with a small ribbon rose or tie small bows at the centers.

teeth on the bobbin case. Insert the bobbin into the machine and bring the ribbon to the top. Pull out at least 8″ (20.3cm) of ribbon before beginning to sew. Set the machine for topstitching if you have a 900, 1000, or 1100 model machine. Use the 4 stitch length on machines that do not have a topstitch setting.

Use the #000 (#0) foot, tension turned up to 10, and needle position to the right. Place the bonnet front on the bed of the machine. The ribbon will be stitched from underneath, ½″ (12.7mm) from the front edge. When you finish stitching, pull out 8″ (20.3cm) of ribbon and cut off.

Instead of the previous method, try this alternate idea to attach ribbon ½″ (12.7cm) from the front edge of the bonnet. Using stitch #15 and multi-motion foot #1, stitch across on the line you've drawn. Then thread ⅛″ (3.2mm) blue ribbon through the stitching.

Cut two ½″ (12.7mm) satin ribbons, each 12″ (30.5cm) long, for the bonnet ties and attach by stitching several zigzag stitches in one place at the rounded corners under the ⅛″ (3.2mm) ribbon.

Make six loops from the 8″ (20.3cm) of ⅛″ (3.2mm) ribbon. Tack them by hand at the center on top of the ribbon ties. Make ribbon roses as shown in Fig. 5.10A, or tiny bows from the ½″ (12.7mm) ribbon and attach these over the loops by hand (Fig. 5.10B). Use double thread. Poke the needle up from the inside of the bonnet,

Fig. 5.11 Pull on each end of the back ribbon and tie into a bow to shape the crown of the bonnet.

through the ribbon ties, loops, and the center of the flower and a pearl bead. Then poke the needle back through the flower, loops, ribbon tie and bonnet. Do this several times. It's not necessary to go through the bead each time. Anchor the thread underneath.

Thread 18″ (45.7cm) of ¼″ (6.4mm) ribbon through the back casing on the bonnet and pull up to tie into a bow at the back (Fig. 5.11). Cut off at the length you prefer. There you have it—a priceless gift.

Lesson 16. Stitching in rings

Stitching in rings is like making needlelace (Fig. 5.12). Instead of fabric surrounding a space, in this lesson the thread is attached to narrow gold rings about 2½″ (6.4cm) in diameter. See Sources of Supplies for ordering these rings. They are available in copper, silver, and several metallic colors.

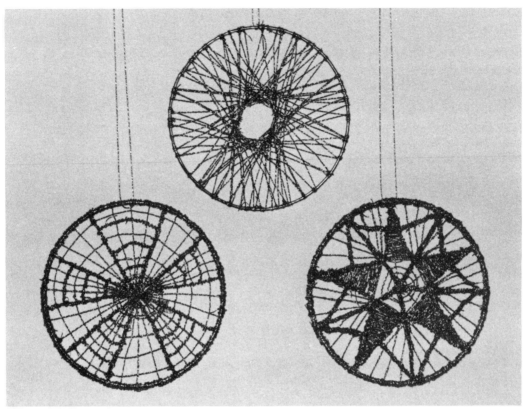

Fig. 5.12 Christmas ornaments stitched in gold rings.

Project
Christmas
Ornaments

A stabilizer isn't needed when you sew in space with a Bernina. You can stitch without fear of your thread knotting and snarling. I used to make these Christmas ornaments without a stabilizer and it worked beautifully. But with water-soluble stabilizer underneath, you can stitch more intricate designs, and the thread will stay in one place, as if you were stitching on fabric.

Set up your machine.

Stitch width: 0–4
Stitch length: 0
Needle position: center
Needle: #80/12
Feed dogs: lowered
Presser foot: bare needle
Tension: *top*, slightly loosened; *bobbin*, normal
Thread: gold metallic on top and bobbin
Accessories: 2½″ (6.4cm) gold ring; 7″ (17.8cm) spring hoop; permanent white marker
Stabilizer: water-soluble

Double the stabilizer and put it into the hoop. Place the gold ring in the center. Draw a design in the ring.

Dip the needle down at the side of the ring and bring the bobbin thread to the top. Hold the threads to one side. Anchor the ring by hand-walking the needle from the outside to the inside of it. Stitch from one side to the other several times. Hold onto the ring and stitch across to the other side. The chain of stitches will be tighter if you sew fast but move the hoop slowly. Anchor the thread on the other side by sewing over and back on the ring as you did at first.

Work back across and anchor on the other side. Keep doing this until you have laid in the spokes of the design. After the last anchoring stitches, go back into the ring and finish the piece. It can be symmetrical or not. I feel that the lighter the look, the better. Stitching it too densely will be a detraction.

Anchor the last stitches and take the ring out of the hoop. Cut back the stabilizer, then dissolve it by holding the ring under running water. Hang it from your Christmas tree with a cord.

Lesson 17. Making Alençon lace

Alençon lace took its name from the French town. The lace was developed there and was so expensive it was rarely seen, except in shops with a wealthy clientele, where it was sold as yardage and used as trimming for lingerie, dresses, and household items.

On the fine, mesh net background is a heavy design, so closely woven it is almost clothlike. Characteristic of Alençon lace is the heavy thread that outlines the design.

Project
Alençon Pincushion

Our Alençon is made on a single layer of bridal veiling. The design is freely embroidered by machine, then outlined with pearl cotton or cordonnet (Fig. 5.13).

Stitch width: 0–4
Stitch length: 0–2
Needle position: center
Needle: #80/12
Feed dogs: lowered
Presser feet: #285 (#9) darning foot, #24 freehand embroidery foot, #147 (#20) open embroidery foot, #030 (#6) embroidery foot
Tension: *top*, slightly loosened; *bobbin*, normal
Fabric suggestion: bridal veil, 36″ × 5″ (91.4cm × 12.7cm); blue linen, 4½″ × 11″ (11.4cm × 28.0cm)
Thread: #100 or #120 fine white sewing thread; #8 pearl cotton or cordonnet on bobbin to match
Accessories: 7″ (17.8cm) spring hoop; permanent white marker; 2 cups of sawdust
Stabilizer: tear-away and water-soluble

Prepare a sample of your stitching to be sure it looks like you want it to. I like a slight bubbly look to the pearl cotton, but you may want a tighter or even looser stitch. If so, tighten or loosen the top tension.

Put the water-soluble stabilizer in the hoop. Place it over the design and copy it with the permanent marker (Fig. 5.14). Then place the veiling over the stabilizer in the hoop.

Thread with fine thread in the top and bobbin. Bring the bobbin thread to the top and hold both threads to one side. After stitching a few stitches, clip these ends off. I don't anchor the threads as they will be sewn in anyway.

Fig. 5.13 Alençon lace pincushion.

Begin by filling in your design with rows of freely stitched lines that follow the pattern in Fig. 5.14. Sew a line next to the outline, then another within that and another, and so on until you have filled it in. If some of the lines overlap, don't despair, as this will happen. Just try to keep from building up heavy stitching lines.

Go from one side of the design to the other, filling in flowers as well as leaves. If the vine threatens to become too heavily stitched with the numerous passes you'll make, stop, clip the thread on top and begin again where you wish to continue. There's no need to bring up the bobbin

thread again, as long as it is still connected to the fabric.

If there are any long threads to be brought to the back, do so when finished stitching. If you wish, dot with Fray-Check on the back and clip close to the work. Actually, a project such as this will not receive the wear a collar will and you can forego the Fray-Check, as it is not necessary when the lace is backed with another fabric.

Change the bobbin to the one containing pearl cotton. Take the veiling out of the hoop and turn it over. The topside of the lace will be underneath. Double check the

Fig. 5.14 Lace pincushion design.

tensions by sewing on another piece of veiling in another hoop. The pearl cotton should lay flat underneath without pulling; yct it should not be so loose it looks loopy.

Dip the needle into the veil and bring the pearl to the top. Hold it to one side as you begin: Don't anchor it. Outline the design. It is very important to keep from going over lines too many times. You want it to be thick, but not ugly.

When you complete outlining, cut off the pearl cotton, bringing any long ends to the back. Work those under a few stitches on back by hand and clip them off. Put your lace, still in the hoop, under the faucet to wash out the stabilizer.

Measure the top of the pincushion. The finished size will be 4″ × 5″ (10.2cm × 12.7cm) so add ½″ (12.7mm) to each measurement; 4½″ × 5½″ (11.4cm × 14.0cm). Cut two pieces of blue linen this size.

But first, a helpful hint! When I sew two pieces of fabric together, as I am doing with the blue linen, I cut out only one, the top piece, to the size I want. I leave the second piece several inches larger for a reason: It's easier to stitch the two pieces together and have them fit beautifully if I use the larger piece underneath the one that is cut exactly to size.

This hint is especially helpful when the fabric has lace or cording at the edges or is a bulky fabric. By the way, I back all my tote bag squares this way, too, then I trim off the excess fabric after I've straight stitched around it (joining the top and backing). To finish, I satin-stitch the edge. But back to the pincushion.

Stitch the lace to the top piece. Seam allowance is ¼" (6.3mm). Cut a piece of veiling 45" (114.3cm) long (2½ times the perimeter of the pincushion), and 5" (12.7cm) wide. Cut a piece of tear-away stabilizer the same length and 2" (5.1cm) wide. Pin the cut edges of the veiling together to hold it in place. Slip tear-away under the fold. Set your machine to the scallop stitch (refer to your manual).

Turn feed dogs up. With the right edge of the #147 (#20) foot placed just within the edge of the fold, stitch width 4, length at 1/2 (or whatever would give you an attractive scallop), stitch down the length of the veiling and cut back to the stitching.

To gather the ruffle, use the #030 (#6) foot with cordonnet threaded through the hole. Zigzag the length of the cut edges (stitch length 2, stitch width 1). Use the cord to gather the ruffle.

Join the two ends of the ruffle by placing one end over the other about ½" (12.7mm). Using a 2 stitch width, and 1/2 length, satin stitch down the width of the piece of veiling. Cut back to the line of stitching on both sides.

Gather the ruffle, placing the seam at a corner. Corners should be heavily gathered to make sure they lay beautifully when completed. Distribute the ruffles around the edge of the pincushion. Remember that the scalloped edge will be toward the *center* of the pincushion. Stitch in place. It's not necessary to remove the cordonnet.

The last step is to sew the back of the pincushion to the lace. Place right sides together, and work all the net ruffles inside as you pin around the edge.

Sew within the stitching line on front. Trim and clip corners diagonally. Leave a large enough opening so you can turn the pincushion to the outside. When turned, fill it very tightly with sawdust. Stitch the opening shut by hand.

I've made appliqués on bridal veil the same way as I made Alençon lace. The only difference is that I filled in the design more heavily with the lines of free-machined straight stitches. With pearl cotton I also stitched around the outlines, as well as inside the appliqué flowers and leaves. In other words, the design was thicker and heavier, although net could still be seen in areas inside the flowers. When completed, I took the appliqué out of the hoop and placed it on the satin background I'd chosen. With my machine set on a narrow zigzag (stitch width 1) I freely attached the lace to the fabric — inside and at the edge of the design.

Once attached, I cut off all the veiling around the motif, added seed pearls, and it went to a wedding.

Do you like making lace? Try other variations by using built-in stitches, satin-stitch star flowers, or bands of intertwined cordonnet at the edges.

CHAPTER 6

Drawing Threads Out of Your Fabric

■ **Lesson 18. Needleweaving**

To create an area of free, lacy openwork called needleweaving, first draw threads out of a fabric, then stitch over the remaining threads. On this long-cut, I used exactly the same color thread on the top and bobbin as that of the dress; I'm constantly being asked how it was stitched. The solution to the mystery follows.

Lesson 18. Needleweaving

Because needleweaving is worked in a straight line, I chose to decorate the sleeves of a summer dress (Fig. 6.1). I knew this dress would be washed many times, so I chose a polyester sewing thread for durability. I matched it perfectly, both spool and bobbin, with the fabric.

First do a small sample of needleweaving for your notebook. The openwork is 1″ (2.5cm) wide. Pull out a horizontal thread at the top and the bottom where the openwork will be. Straight stitch across those lines using thread a shade lighter or darker than the color you've chosen for your embroidery. These are guidelines for stitching that you will use later. Then pull out the horizontal or weft threads in that space.

Project Openwork on Sleeves

You will machine stitch over the vertical or warp threads, drawing them together as you zigzag (Fig. 6.2).

Stitch width: 0 – 4
Stitch length: 0 – 2
Needle position: center
Needle: #80/12
Feed dogs: lowered, up
Presser foot: #147 (#20) open embroidery foot, no presser foot
Tension: *top,* normal, loosened; *bobbin,* normal
Fabric suggestion: loosely woven
Thread: Metrosene polyester
Stabilizer: tear-away, or construction paper to match thread

Take off the regular presser foot and use a bare needle. Try working without a hoop on this project. The stitching goes fast and a hoop would only slow you down. Prepare your machine for embroidery by lowering the feed dogs. Be sure the presser bar is down before you start to stitch. Dip the needle down and bring the bobbin thread to the top. Anchor the threads. Set the machine at stitch width 4 and normal tension.

Using both hands, grasp the top and bottom of the fabric between your fingers, stretching it slightly as you stitch. Keep

110

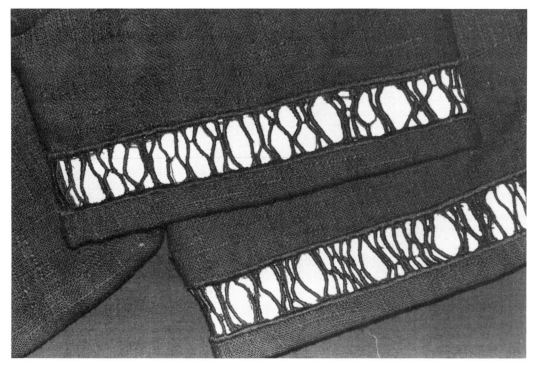

Fig. 6.1 Needleweaving decorates the sleeves on a summer dress.

Fig. 6.2 Pull out warp threads from the fabric and zigzag freely over the remaining wefts. Then finish the edges on each side with satin stitching.

the fabric as close as you can to the needle-plate, and keep tension on the warp threads.

Begin to move from just below the stitched line at the bottom to just over the stitched line on top. Move the fabric slowly, but sew at a comfortable speed, catching several warp threads together as you zigzag to the top.

When you reach the top, move sideways to the next several warp threads and begin stitching those together. About halfway down, move the fabric to the side and catch a few stitches into the previous group of zigzagged threads. Then move back and continue to the bottom of the threads. Finish all the warp threads in the same manner, satin stitching up and down, while at the same time catching threads from the previous run in one or two places. This adds interest and strength to your open-work and is an integral part of your needleweaving.

On a piece of stabilizer, draw two horizontal lines 1″ (2.5cm) apart, the same length as your stitching. Place the stitching on the piece of stabilizer and adjust the embroidery so it lies flat. Place the guidelines you stitched on the lines you've drawn. Dampen and press it if necessary, but be careful not to stretch it out of shape.

Set up your machine for straight stitch-ing with feed dogs up and the open embroidery foot on. Sew a line of straight stitches across the top and bottom on the same guidelines you stitched at the beginning. This will hold the needlelace in place and stabilize it for the final stitching.

Set the machine to a wide zigzag, feed dogs still up, stitch length 1/2 (or whatever will result in a perfect satin stitch). Loosen tension slightly and satin stitch over those lines. The stitching will fall just to one side of the fabric and will catch the fabric on the other side to neatly finish the edge of the needlelace. Tear off the stabilizer and steam press the embroidery carefully.

If the stabilizer can still be seen behind the stitches, it may be possible to remove it by dampening it, then using a tweezers to remove it. Or use this trick: if you can find a permanent marker the same color as the thread, dab in the color where necessary.

Try needleweaving across the yoke or pocket of a blouse, or down the middle of sleeves, or combine two rows of this with lacy spiderweb circles scattered between.

If you don't like the see-through look, or if you want to add another color, back the open area with another fabric.

You are more than halfway through *Know Your Bernina*. Do you know your Bernina?

CHAPTER **7**

Layering Fabrics: Quilting

- Lesson 19. **Quilting with feed dogs up**
- Lesson 20. **Quilting with feed dogs lowered**
- Lesson 21. **Trapunto**
- Lesson 22. **Italian cording**

I've always taken time to make handmade gifts for special people. But if I make a crib quilt, for example, I'd like to know that the baby won't be twice as long as the quilt by the time the gift is presented. If I'm sewing clothes, I'm realistic: I want the garment to be in style when the recipient opens the box.

So, although I love hand quilting and hand sewing, they often take too long. Machine quilting, on the other hand, is speedy and sturdy. You can use heavy fabrics like corduroy, as well as thick batts, and you will have no trouble stitching them together. If machine quilting is done properly, it can be as fine as handwork.

In this chapter I've included quilting with the feed dogs lowered and in place, trapunto, and Italian cording. You'll soon know that your Bernina does them all effortlessly.

Remember several things when doing any type of quilting. The first is to pre-shrink all fabrics. I usually use cotton polyester blends for my quilts so they stay new-looking for a long time. Sheets are excellent backing materials. They come in a myriad of colors and prints, can be of excellent quality, and they won't have to be pieced. When I make a quilt, I use a sheet that is larger than the top.

I usually quilt with a polyester sewing thread. Most brands come in a wealth of colors. Should I want to emphasize the stitching line, I will double the thread. But when I sew on a patterned material or a fabric that changes color throughout, I choose a monofilament. I may or may not use monofilament on the bobbin, depending upon the samples I do first.

Using safety pins instead of hand basting is my favorite method of holding the fabrics and batt together before I quilt. I don't use dressmaker's pins because many of them fall out before the quilt is completed—and those that don't usually stab me.

Lesson 19. Quilting with feed dogs up

Instead of a regular presser foot, I usually use an even-feed or walking foot when I sew lines of straight quilting stitches. It minimizes puckering on the backing fabric, as the top and bottom fabrics are fed through at the same speed with no slipping.

Before I had one of those helpful attachments, I grasped the quilt in both hands and kept it taut as it fed through the ma-

113

chine. As I progressed, I stopped and looked underneath to be sure I had a smooth lining. I must admit I became an expert at sewing without puckers. It may take a little longer, but the lack of a walking foot should not deter you from starting your first quilt experiment.

Can you imagine how fast you could make a quilt using striped fabric or a striped sheet for the top? Use the stripes as quilting lines. If you use stripes for garments, keep in mind that the more rows of quilting, the smaller the piece becomes. I either quilt the fabric first and then cut out the pattern, or I cut my pattern larger than necessary, do the quilting and then lay the pattern back on it when finished. I recut the pattern where necessary.

If you piece a quilt and decide to machine quilt it by using stitch-in-a-ditch, you may prefer using the #492 (#10) edge foot. Stitch-in-a-ditch is done on top of the quilt by stitching in the seam lines (the ditches). With this presser foot, it is easy to stitch exactly in the ditch because you have the black bar guide and the needle positioning dial for accuracy.

Know your Bernina and quilt any fabric or thickness without a skipped stitch.

Project
Tote Bag Square (Appliqué and Quilting)

This quilted sample can be used as a square for the tote bag in Chapter 12. It includes appliqué and satin stitches (Fig. 7.1; see also color section).

Stitch width: 0–3
Stitch length: 0–2
Needle position: center
Feed dogs: up

Presser foot: #030 (#6) embroidery or #147 (#20) open embroidery
Needle: #90/14
Tension: *top,* normal; *bobbin,* finger threaded—or *top,* slightly loosened; *bobbin,* normal
Thread: red cotton machine embroidery
Fabric: two 9″ (22.9cm) squares of lightweight red cotton fabric; yellow, royal blue and green scraps—check design for sizes; 10″ (25.4cm) square of fleece
Accessories: water-erasable marker, tracing paper and pencil, dressmaker's carbon and empty ballpoint pen, fusible webbing, quilting pins
Stabilizer: freezer paper

Back all the fabrics except red and the fleece with fusible webbing. Trace the pattern from Fig. 7.1, using the tracing paper and pencil. Transfer this to your red square by using dressmaker's carbon and the empty ballpoint pen. This will be your guide.

After it has been transferred, cut apart the design elements from the tracing paper and, using these as guides, cut out the designs from the fabrics.

Place the appliqués on the background fabric in the appropriate places and fuse in place. Press a piece of freezer paper to the underside of the red fabric. Satin stitch the edges of the appliqués with red machine embroidery thread. I stitch in two passes to emphasize the satin stitching and make it a part of the design. The first pass will be at stitch width 2 3/4, stitch length 3/4, the second, stitch width 3, stitch length—satin stitch. This, of course, varies with each machine. The satin stitches should be close together, but not so close that they keep the fabric from moving smoothly. When completed, tear off the freezer paper.

Layer the appliquéd fabric over the fleece. I quilted these two layers together without fabric under the fleece, but you may choose to back the fleece with another square of fabric. Pin this quilt sandwich

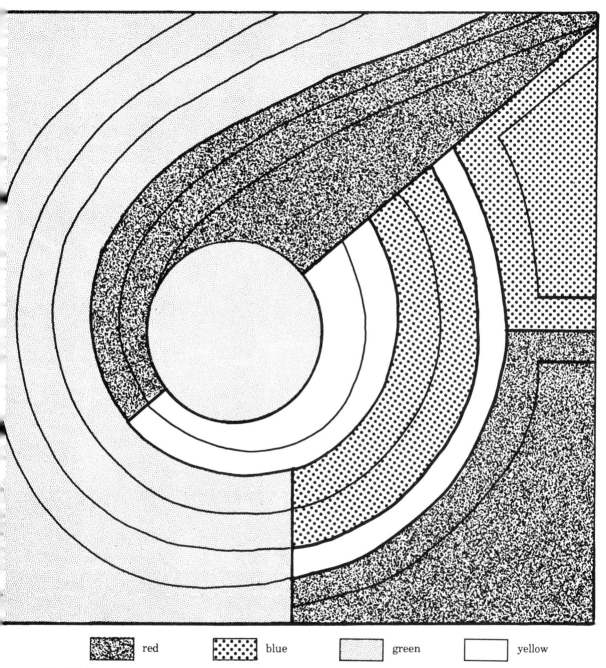

Fig. 7.1 Tote bag square.

| | red | | blue | | green | | yellow |

together to keep the fabrics from shifting while you sew. (Remember to pull the pins out of the fabric before stitching over them.) Change machine settings to stitch length 2 and sew at the sides of the satin stitches, which quilts your square. Go back to the places indicated on the design and stitch the lines of echo quilting.

After the quilting is completed, back the square with the other square of red fabric. Straight stitch carefully around the outside edge of the square. Trim to 6¾″. With the layers held together firmly, satin stitching the edges is easier. Then finish the square as described in Chapter 12.

Project
Cathy's Quilt

I made this scrap quilt—shown in the color insert—from the mountainous collection of old blue jeans I'd saved for years, knowing they had possibilities.

But before you begin to make one of these quilts, be warned that they are so heavy your children may need help getting out from underneath. I'm lucky that my family loves heavy bedding. They want to feel a quilt's snugness, but they don't like the puffy lightweights. Jeans quilts are tailor-made for them.

Stitch width: 0
Stitch length: 2
Needle position: center
Needle: #90/14 or #100/16 jeans needle
Feed dogs: up
Presser foot: #000 (#0) zigzag or #145 (#8) jeans
Tension: *top*, normal; *bobbin*, normal
Fabric suggestion: blue denim scraps, strips of old fabric, quilt batting, backing sheet, long denim strips for binding
Thread: medium-blue polyester or monofilament
Accessories: Olfa cutter and board, fabric shears

You will need dozens of jeans—I don't know exactly how many. It depends on what is salvageable and the size of your quilt. (Of course you can buy denim, but if you do, then remember to wash and dry it a couple of times before you make the quilt.) I cut out all the usable fabric in dozens of pairs of pants and skirts with no thought to size, length or width. Then I arranged them according to width, or the short sides. I had five or six piles of denim from the palest blue to almost black. All pieces were not perfect rectangles or even squares—remember bell-bottoms? You know about torn knees? But those are not problems with these quilts. Just keep cutting off the thick seams and the belts, pockets and hems and trim off any worn, thin areas.

The next step is to find some old fabric you hate but can't throw away. Or use an old sheet or muslin.

Let's say that one of the denim stacks has pieces 6″ (15.2cm) in width. Tear a muslin strip that width, and as long as the muslin will allow. Later you'll tear up many of these strips for the denim you'll apply, but tear them as you need them; there's no way to know what size and how many you'll require to finish the quilt. The design and layout of mine is shown in Fig. 7.2.

If the scraps are larger than 4″ (10.2cm) to 6″ (15.2cm) wide, cut off the excess. Cut them off straight across, but vary them—don't cut all of them the same width, and if one or both of the other sides slope, leave it that way to match with another sloped piece when attaching them. Also, be sure those sides are straight for stitching. The rotary cutter and board makes trimming a breeze.

Place one of the denim stacks at the side of your Bernina. Mix up the colors making sure you don't sew two pieces together that are the same shade. You can use the backs of the fabrics, as well as the fronts, for color changes.

Fig. 7.2 Units of denim scraps were assembled for this quilt.

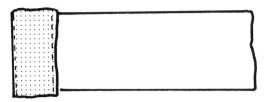

Fig. 7.3 Sew down both sides of the first scrap to a strip of backing fabric.

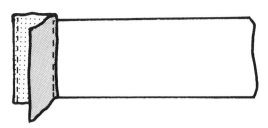

Fig. 7.4 Place the next strip, right sides together with the first, and stitch down the edge to attach the second strip.

Place the first denim piece with topside up at one end of the strip of muslin. With the zigzag or jeans presser foot on, use blue polyester thread or monofilament to sew down both sides of the denim patch. Leave the top and bottom edges open (Fig. 7.3). The side of the presser foot can be your guide; place it at the edge of the scrap when you stitch it down. I don't anchor the thread at the beginning and the end of each strip because it's not necessary and it saves time not to do it.

Place the next strip, right side together with the first, and line up the righthand edges. Stitch through the two pieces of denim and the backing (Fig. 7.4). Flip the piece you just sewed to the front and smooth in place. Sew down the other edge. Place the next strip on and sew it down, then the next until you get to the end of the fabric strip.

If the strips become too heavy, cut them apart from the backing strip and start a new strip of scraps. This is probably the most casual quilt ever made.

When handling irregular pieces, match them with others so they will end up traveling across the backing strip as straight as possible. The backing will be your guide. If this is not feasible in some instances, then cut the width or slope to fit the patch before it. When you finish the long strip of scraps, turn it over and press it. I also press as I go if I find a piece of recalcitrant denim that won't fold back easily. The last step is to stitch, from the back, the length of your strip, keeping the same width seam allowance as on the scraps. Then cut off all the ends of the denim that are beyond the edge of the fabric strip (Fig. 7.5) You will have made a long piece of denim fabric for your quilt.

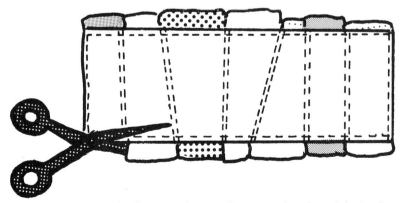

Fig. 7.5 Cut off all the denim ends extending past the edge of the backing fabric.

Fig. 7.6 Stitch three of these kaleidoscope squares, beginning each in the center, using the log cabin method of applying irregularly shaped strips.

Continue making denim strips with your denim pieces and strips of fabric. When you calculate that you probably have enough for the size quilt you are making, put them aside and stitch up three kaleidoscopes (Fig. 7.6).

You will make these by cutting three dif-

ferent sized squares from your old fabric. I used 12″ (30.5cm), 16″ (40.6cm) and 18″ (45.7cm). See Fig. 7.2.

To begin the kaleidoscope, stitch a small patch of denim in the center of the large backing square. The patch must have four sides, but it doesn't have to be square. Af-

119

ter that patch is in place, add a strip of denim face to face with it, one edge lined up with an edge of the center patch. Stitch and fold back. Clip out any extra denim fabric underneath. Add another strip next to it, face to face with the center patch and also covering the end of the previous strip. Then go to the third side of the center patch, then the fourth. Keep going in the same direction, either clockwise or counterclockwise, as if you were making a log cabin quilt square in the dark. Here is a good place to use the denim scraps you were going to throw out as these pieces should all be different shapes and sizes. Sometimes the strips are triangles or trapezoids, and sometimes they are narrow, sometimes wide. Check the illustration if you are not familiar with this type of quilt square. No two kaleidoscopes are ever the same. Work till you are out to the edges of the squares. Stitch around at the edge and trim the denim back to the muslin strip.

When you finish this part, you will be ready to put your quilt top together. Lay the three squares on the floor within the area you've decided to use for the quilt (Fig. 7.2). Now lay the fabric strips around them. It takes time to arrange and rearrange, but this is the fun part. Some strips will be put down lengthwise, some across the quilt. You may have to cut strips shorter or add to them.

Next, take the strips off the floor and sew them together to make your quilt top. Press open all your seams. You'll eliminate bulk this way.

I backed my quilt with a sheet because sheets don't have to be pieced.

The next step—putting the backing, batting, and quilt top together—should not be done on carpeting, as there is too much shifting of layers. Instead, follow this helpful method taught to me by my friend, Ruth Drosen of Pleasanton, California. Find a floor (or Ping Pong table) where you can tape down the fabrics. Place the backing on the floor, underside up, smooth it

out and tape it to the floor with masking tape. Be sure the corners are square. Do the same with the batting. Next, place the quilt top over them and, starting at the top, pin with safety pins all across the top of the quilt to hold the three layers together. Smooth the quilt down from the top and out from the center as you work your way down while pin-basting it. I basted the sheet, batting and top together with safety pins about every six inches. I always choose a sheet and batt that are larger than the quilt top and I don't cut them off till I've finished quilting.

I used the #492 (#10) edge foot to quilt stitch-in-a-ditch. My starting point was at the top of the right side. I first rolled the quilt tightly and pinned the roll down the length of it. I kept unrolling and repinning as I progressed. At the same time, I rolled up what I had completed as I went along. Another alternative is to roll up the quilt on both sides so you can start at the middle. Then after completing one side, turn it around, and from the bottom up this time, stitchdown all the other seams until you get to the other edge. This is a thick, heavy quilt so you may want to quilt with the jeans foot and needle.

I quilted with monofilament on top and bobbin, but you may prefer a thread that matches your fabric. All the long seams were stitched first and then I did those going the width, removing the basting pins as I came to them. It is not hard to keep puckers from forming on the back of your quilt if you learn to keep smoothing the lining as you go along. Eventually you will get the rhythm of it and it is quite easily accomplished. But do whatever is easiest for you. Be sure you have a large board supporting the quilt as you work, or work on a large table. I've even enlisted the aid of children ("It's your quilt, for Pete's sake!") to stand on the other side of the dining room table to help guide these huge masses of fabric and batting through the machine.

Go back then and stitch around the kaleidoscopes and stitch down in every ditch between every patch. Yes, this takes time, but try my method. Set aside an hour every morning and work only that hour. It goes much faster this way—or you think it does. Or stitch only the long seams one day, the width the next, etc.

When finished, sew completely around the quilt with a straight stitch right at the edge. Cut off the sheet and any extra batting sticking out.

Check again to see that the quilt is straight and has square corners. You probably have your own method of checking if your quilt is square, but I will explain how I square any large quilt I sew. I spread the quilt out on the floor and use two pieces of ⅛" (3.2mm) Masonite, each about 24" × 36" (61cm × 91.4cm), as T-squares to help me square it. I place each piece of Masonite on top of the quilt at a top corner and across the top edge of the quilt. The boards stretch over most of the quilt edge and it's easy to mark the new edge, then to square off corners and trim the excess fabric by either cutting with a scissors or placing the Olfa mat under it and cutting with the rotary cutter. I do the same at the sides and bottom of the quilt.

After it is squared, I finish the edges with a French binding. If I want a 1" (2.5cm) binding to show, I add a 1" (2.5cm) seam allowance as well and, because this is doubled, I'll need to cut 6" (15.2cm) wide strips on the straight of my fabric. Measure the length and width of your quilt to determine how long your strips must be. Then fold one of the side strips in half lengthwise, wrong sides together, and stitch down 1" (2.5cm) from the long side (raw edges).

Place the binding on the topside of your quilt with the raw edges of the binding on the raw edges of the quilt. Pin it in place, then sew it down, following the stitched line on your binding, 1" (2.5cm) from the edge. Do the other side the same way. Cut off any binding that extends past the top or bottom of the quilt. Next, wrap each side binding around the edge to the back of the quilt and catch the fold to the stitched line with hand stitches. You can sew it by machine, but you will like the look of invisible stitching better—trust me.

Then bind the top and bottom of the quilt. Tuck in the corners before you start to stitch and pin in place. When you have finished attaching the binding, hand tack the opening at each corner. The binding is strong and durable. Also, it's much easier stitching down a fold than contending with single raw edges on a binding.

I love this quilt because, in among the generic blue denim, I can pick out Steve's fishing overalls, or Chip's funny pinstripes, Cathy's beloved bell-bottoms, remembrances of past adventures, sewing disasters—a family history.

Lesson 20. Quilting with feed dogs lowered

As you can tell from the lesson title, this will be free-machine quilting. The machine setting will not control the length of the stitches; you will. If you move the fabric fast, the stitches will be longer than if you move it slowly. Not working in a hoop, you must use a darning foot to prevent skipped stitches. And no hoop means you must hold the fabric taut while stitching.

Stitch width: 0
Stitch length: 0
Needle position: center
Needle: #90/14
Feed dogs: lowered
Presser foot: #285 (#9) darning foot or #24 free-hand embroidery foot
Tension: *top*, slightly loosened; *bottom*, normal

121

Fabric suggestion: medium-weight cotton; fleece or quilt batting
Thread: machine embroidery
Accessories: water-erasable marker

One of the easiest ways to learn free quilting and to practice control at the same time is to quilt around the motifs of a printed fabric as shown in Fig. 7.7. Even the underside looks terrific: you may like the looks of the lining better than the printed side. If so, it makes for a stunning reversible jacket.

When quilting any fabrics with feed dogs lowered, don't place the stitching lines too closely together, unless you want to emphasize the area that *isn't* stitched. Closely stitched, it will be too stiff and you'll lose the contrast of light and dark shadowing that makes this type of machining so effective.

Fig. 7.7 Cotton print, batting and velveteen are quilted together by stitching the butterfly design.

Lesson 21. Trapunto

In trapunto, two pieces of fabric are stitched together, following a design. Then the quilter selects the areas of the design to be stuffed with fiberfill. Usually trapunto is done from underneath the fabrics.

Layer two pieces of material together and use the design in Fig. 4.6. Stitch in all the lines with straight stitches. Make small slits in the backing fabric behind the sections you wish to pad. Add fiberfill, poking it in with a tool that is not sharply pointed. Whip stitch the slits closed by hand.

You can trapunto from the top by appliquéing on top of a base fabric. Slip filling inside the appliqué before you've attached it all the way around. You may want more stitching over the appliqué to hold the stuffing firmly and to add to the design.

Lesson 22. Italian cording

Italian cording is often mistaken for trapunto. The difference is that the area to be stuffed in Italian cording will be the space between two stitching lines. Instead of using fiberfill, thread a cord of appropriate size through the double lines of stitching.

122

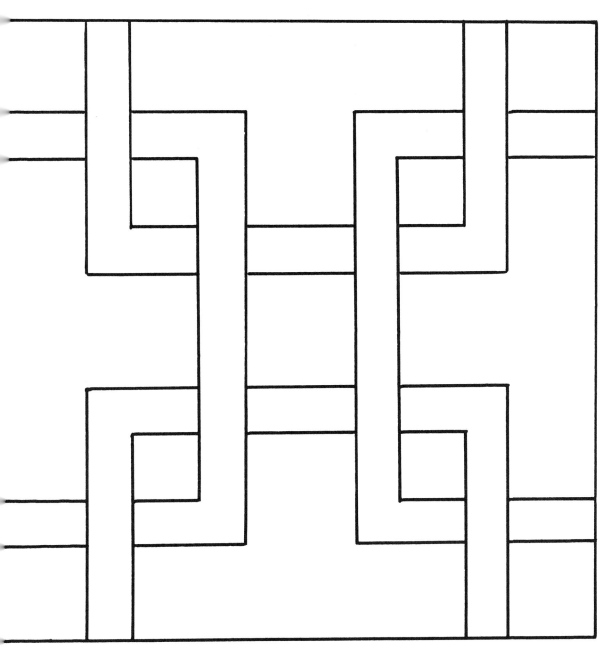

Fig. 7.8 Italian cording tote bag square.

It's also possible to create the look of Italian cording in one pass of the machine, on one layer of fabric when stitching with a double needle. Thread gimp or pearl cotton through the needle plate of your machine and it will be caught between the lines of stitching by the bobbin thread.

Project
Tote Bag Square (Italian Cording)

This square (Fig. 7.8) was done using a single needle.

Stitch width: 0
Stitch length: 3
Needle position: center
Needle: #90/14
Feed dogs: up
Presser foot: #147 (#20) open embroidery foot
Tension: *top,* normal; *bobbin,* normal
Fabric suggestions: lightweight cotton for top; stiffer cotton for backing
Thread: shiny rayon or machine embroidery cotton to match or contrast
Cord: appropriate-size acrylic yarn or cable cord
Accessories: hand-sewing needle; large-eyed hand-sewing needle such as ball-tipped plastic needle or bodkin to thread cord through the design; water-erasable marker

Draw your design on the fabric with a water-erasable marker, indicating where the lines will cross and which one crosses over, which under.

When you are stitching the lines, don't anchor threads when the lines cross. Instead, pull several inches of thread out of the needle. Hold the thread to one side. Skip over the intersection; then begin stitching again. When finished, go back and clip the threads in the middle. Thread up a sewing needle and poke all the top threads through to the back and work them in.

Finish up by working the cord through the design by hand. It's difficult to turn corners with cording and make those corners look sharp. Poke the needle out of the back fabric at a corner, and then back in again in the same place, leaving a small loop of the cord out in back.

To cross over a cord when threading through a channel, poke the needle out through the lining when you reach the first line of stitching, cross over the stitching line, cord, and line of stitches on the other side of the channel. Poke your needle back into the lining at this place and continue threading the cord through the channel.

When working with a double needle, turn corners in three steps. Stitch to the corner. Stop. Needles should be grazing the fabric. Lift the presser foot. Here is where the knee lift becomes all-important. Half-turn the fabric. Lower the presser foot and turn the wheel by hand to make one stitch. Raise the needles and again bring the needle points down to barely touch the top of the fabric. Lift the presser foot again and complete the turn. Lower the presser foot and continue stitching.

Look for inspirations for Italian cording in books on Celtic designs or bargello borders.

CHAPTER 8

Adding Interesting Seams to Your Fabric

- **Lesson 23. French handsewing by machine**
- **Lesson 24. Seaming with feed dogs up and lowered**

In previous chapters, the emphasis was on decorative stitchery. In Chapters 8 and 9, the focus is on sewing. The chapters are so closely related that at times they even overlap. The most important thing to learn in these two chapters is that your Bernina is dependable. It will sew lace, but it will also sew canvas—and all types of fabrics in between. Knowing your Bernina is a joy, isn't it?

Included in Chapters 8 and 9 are many of the sewing long-cuts I mentioned in the Preface and Chapter 1. But now, instead of decorating a garment by embroidering or appliquéing on it, you'll learn to make the garment unique by changing the seams, hems and edges.

Let's face it: seams are not always interesting. Most of them are hidden and it's not necessary that they do anything but hold two pieces of fabric together. On the other hand, seams can be the focal point of your creation. This chapter includes seams for the finest lace to the heaviest canvas—seams purely practical and those that combine decoration with practicality. Stitch up samples of all of them for your notebook.

The project in this chapter is a wedding handkerchief (Fig. 8.1). After learning how to accomplish French handsewing on the machine, work this project. It can also be used as a pillow top.

Fig. 8.1 French hand-sewn wedding handkerchief stitched on my Bernina.

Lesson 23. French handsewing by machine

When I first heard about the type of clothing construction called French handsewing, I thought it was something new–until Marcia Strickland, a friend from Birmingham, Alabama, showed me her daughters' dresses. They were made of laces, with pintucks and embroidery, entredeaux and hemstitching, and looked like our family's christening gown. I knew French handsewing; I just hadn't been acquainted with the term. We'd always called it "sewing by hand" and I had agonized over it years ago, when I was sure I'd be struck blind by the tiny stitches before I made it through junior high school. It was hard for me to believe that I could accomplish the perfection of Marcia's clothing on my sewing machine (called "French handsewing by machine" or "French machine sewing").

It's possible to find lace and tucked blouses, skirts and dresses in any department store today. Because this feminine look is expensive in ready-to-wear, if you learn the following hand-sewing techniques by machine and sew them yourself, you will save money and have a lot of fun besides.

First, I had to learn basics before I could stitch collars or dresses. Marcia taught me that if I apply fabric to lace, one of the rules of French handsewing is that I must always have entredeaux between.

Entredeaux literally means "between two." It is purchased by the yard in fabric shops. The fabric on either side of the ladderlike strip down the center is trimmed off before it is attached. I also learned that the holes in entredeaux are never evenly spaced, no matter how expensive it is.

Marcia suggested size 100 pure cotton thread and #70/10 needle for sewing. She uses an extra-fine thread because the batiste fabric used is extremely lightweight, and stitches are visible when attaching lace and entredeaux or stitching pintucks. And she suggests using cotton thread for heirlooms because it will last a long time.

When handsewing, Marcia chooses cotton batiste because it is easier to roll and whip the edges of cotton. Polyester or cotton/polyester blends have minds of their own. It's hard to roll them as they keep unrolling while you try to whip them in place.

But French machine sewing can easily be done on blends, so I often choose a cotton/polyester for fabric (and thread), as it doesn't wrinkle like pure cotton.

I learned so much from Marcia, I filled a notebook with samples, ideas, and shortcuts. When you stitch up samples for your own notebook, if a technique can be done several ways, do them all and then decide which works best for you. The following techniques are all you need to learn for French machine sewing.

Sewing French seams

French seams are used on lightweight, transparent fabrics to finish the seams beautifully, disguising raw edges. They are also found on smocked garments as a fine finish.

The seams are accomplished in two different operations (Fig. 8.2). Begin with fabric pieces, wrong sides facing. Stitch the seam, using a #70/10 needle and fine sewing thread. Open and press seam to one side. Cut back the seam allowance evenly, to ⅛" (3.2mm). Turn the fabric back over the raw edges, press again (the seam will be at the edge), pin, and stitch again, enclosing the ⅛" (3.2mm) seam allowance.

The Cut'n'Sew accessory produces an exceptionally clean French seam. As you sew the seam on the first pass, the fabric is also trimmed to ⅛" (3.2mm), without the uneven edge that sometimes occurs when

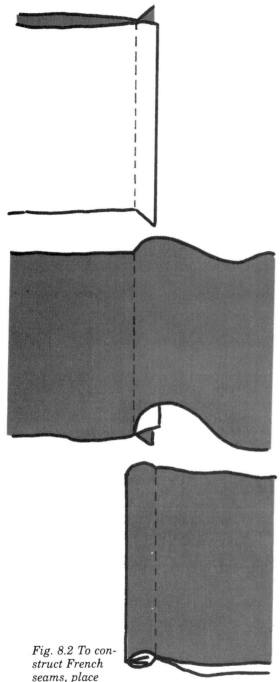

you cut by hand. When the fabric is folded back over the seam allowance, no maddening wispy threads poke out to ruin the perfect French seam.

Stitching rolled and whipped edges

Rolled and whipped edges (Fig. 8.3) are always used in conjunction with French handsewing because each piece of fabric must have a finished edge before it is attached to lace or to entredeaux. When working by machine, sometimes you can finish the edge at the same time you attach it to the lace. These edges can be worked several ways and everyone seems to have her own favorite. This is my favorite way, using the #452 (#3) buttonhole foot:

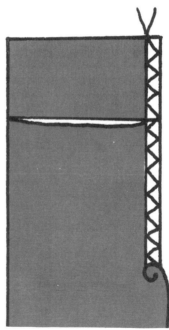

Fig. 8.2 To construct French seams, place fabrics wrong sides together, stitch the seam, trim to ⅛" (3.2mm), then fold the fabric back over the seam allowance and stitch down outside the allowance.

Fig. 8.3 Rolled and whipped edges, started by stitching first on a piece of scrap fabric, then placing the good fabric directly in front of the scrap to begin the roll and whip at the edge.

127

Stitch width: 2 1/2
Stitch length: 1
Needle position: far left
Needle: #70/10
Feed dogs: up
Tension: *top,* normal; *bobbin,* finger threaded
Fabric: batiste
Thread: #100 cotton

Start the edge so even the first thread in the fabric will be rolled and whipped: Feed a small piece of scrap fabric—about 2″ (5.1cm) long—under the foot. Use the same fabric as you will be using to sew. The edge should be placed to the right of the middle extension on the buttonhole foot.

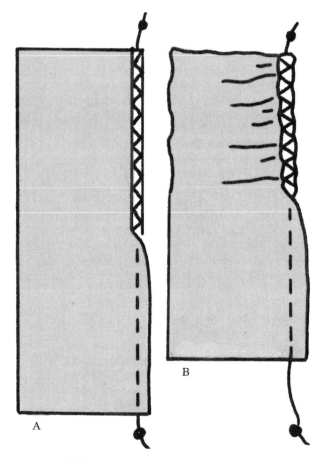

A

B

Stitch, holding the threads from the top and bobbin until the fabric begins to roll. As it rolls and as you approach the end of the scrap fabric, butt the good fabric up to it (see Fig. 8.3). It will also roll, beginning exactly at the edge. Later you will cut off the scrap fabric.

I also like working a rolled and whipped edge with the Cut'n'Sew accessory.

Stitch width: 4
Stitch length: 1
Needle position: right
Tension *top,* 10; *bobbin,* normal
Fabric: batiste, work on wrong side
Presser foot: remove pin from Cut'n'Sew foot

To start the fabric when using this attachment, first cut a notch in the fabric by clipping from the top down the cutting line ⅜″ (9.5mm). Tuck this piece to the right of the knife or cut it off. Slip the fabric into the Cut'n'Sew and sew a few stitches. Hold onto the threads to guide the fabric through.

Gathering rolled and whipped edges

Before you roll and whip, stitch (stitch length 2) along the edge of the fabric. Instead of anchoring your threads, leave several inches of thread at the beginning and end of the stitching. Starting at the top again, overcast the edge as you did before rolling and whipping (Fig. 8.4A). The straight stitching must not be caught in these zigzags.

Hold the thread ends at the beginning of your line of straight stitching to keep them from slipping through as you gather. Pull on the top thread at the other end of the

Fig. 8.4 Gathering a rolled and whipped edge. A. Sew a line of straight stitches along the edge of the fabric, then roll and whip over the line of stitching. B. Gather the material by pulling on the top thread from the line of straight stitches.

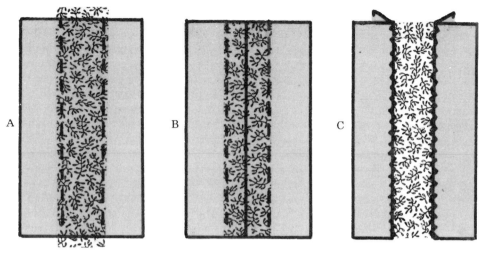

Fig. 8.5 A. Sew lace insert to fabric by straight stitching down each side of the lace. B. Cut through the fabric behind the lace from top to bottom. C. Turn back the seam allowances on both sides and zigzag down the edges of the insertion. Trim the seam allowances back to the stitching.

line of straight stitches and evenly distribute the ruffling (Fig. 8.4B).

Applying insertion

Insertion is lace with two straight sides. It is easily applied by machine (Fig. 8.5). Draw two lines the width of the lace on the fabric. Pin the lace inside the lines. Machine straight stitch down both sides of the lace to hold it in place. Cut straight down the fabric behind the lace, creating seam allowance on both sides. Fold the seam allowances back and press.

Then zigzag on top (stitch width 1 1/2, stitch length 1) over the edges of the lace and the straight stitching to attach the lace and finish the edges simultaneously. Cut the seam allowances back to the stitching.

Apply scalloped lace as an insertion by placing it on the fabric and basting it down both sides. Using the previous settings, zigzag closely over the edge, following the scallop. Cut away the fabric underneath. This method can also be used for straight-edge insertion, but the join will not be as strong as folding back the seam allowance and stitching over the doubled fabric.

Joining scalloped lace

Find the most heavily patterned place in the design to join scalloped lace. Overlap two identical patterns, and stitch a fine zigzag (stitch width 1 1/2, stitch length 3/4) with feed dogs up. Follow the edge of the design as shown in Fig. 8.6. Trim back to the line of stitching.

Using entredeaux

Entredeaux is used between fabric and lace. Only the ladderlike strip of stitching down the center of the entredeaux is attached.

Stitch width: 2 or adjust
Stitch length: 1–1 1/4
Needle position: center
Needle: #70/10
Feed dogs: up
Presser foot: #452 (#3) or #000 (#0)

Fig. 8.6 *Join two pieces of lace together by overlapping the design at each end, zigzagging the "seam," then cutting back the surplus lace to the stitches.*

Tension: *top,* normal; *bobbin,* normal
Fabric suggestions: batiste
Thread: #100

Measure the length of entredeaux you will need and cut off the fabric on only one side. Attach that side. Place the topside of the entredeaux to the topside of the rolled and whipped edge, the entredeaux on top, as shown at left in Fig. 8.7. Be sure the edges touch. Hand walk the machine through the first couple of stitches to be sure the needle is clearing the edge on the right side and falls into the holes of the entredeaux on the left (Fig. 8.7). Don't worry if the needle skips a hole in the

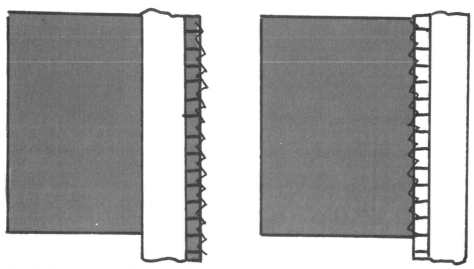

Fig. 8.7 *To apply entredeaux to rolled and whipped edges, place it on the fabric, right sides together. Zigzag into each hole and off the edges. Then press open.*

entredeaux once in awhile, because it won't show. Sew with the machine set on moderate speed. When finished, pull the entredeaux to the side away from the fabric and press (at right in Fig. 8.7). Repeat for the other side.

Gathering lace edging

There are several threads at the edges of lace. Use a pin to find the one that gathers the lace and then pull up the thread. Hold onto both ends of this thread, or you might pull it all the way through when gathering the lace. Evenly space the gathers.

Attaching straight-edged lace to rolled and whipped edges

Place the topside of the lace against the topside of the fabric (Fig. 8.8). Be sure the edges are even. Use a zigzag at a setting of stitch width 2 1/2 and length 1. The needle should stitch within the edges of lace and fabric on the left, and stitch off of them on the right swing (Fig. 8.8). Flatten out and press.

Attaching entredeaux to lace insertion

Stitch width: 2, or adjust
Stitch length: 1, or adjust
Presser foot: #452 (#3) buttonhole; or #000 (#0) zigzag; or #492 (#10) edge foot

Trim fabric from one side of the entredeaux. With topsides up, place the trimmed edge of the entredeaux up next to the edge of the lace.

Zigzag the edges together so the needle barely catches the lace and goes into each hole of the entredeaux (Fig. 8.9). Start by using a 2 stitch width and 1 stitch length, but make adjustments in these figures if you find they are needed.

You can use the #492 (#10) edge foot, too. Put entredeaux on one side of the black bar extension, the lace on the other. Set the stitch width to catch both sides as you stitch. The extension on the edging

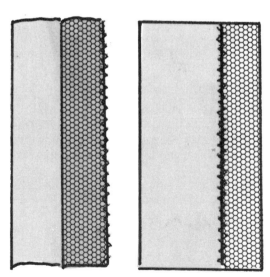

Fig. 8.8 Place insertion on top of a rolled and whipped edge; zigzag to attach. Press open.

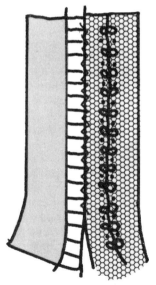

Fig. 8.9 To attach entredeaux to lace insertion, place edges next to each other and zigzag together.

131

foot helps keep the entredeaux and lace apart until stitched.

Sewing lace to lace

Stitch width: 2 1/2
Stitch length: 1
Presser foot: #492 (#10) edge foot or #000 (#0) zigzag

Put a strip of straight-edged lace on each side of the #492 (#10) edging foot. Stitch between the lace pieces. This foot will keep the lace separated until stitched, so one will not overlap the other.

If you don't have the edging foot, you can use the #000 (#0) zigzag foot and butt the edges of the two laces. Use stitch width 3, stitch length 2. Sew the length of the lace.

Fagoting

There are times when we need different detailing on a bodice, sleeve or skirt. It may not be called for in the pattern, but it's a way to make that garment our own, so we choose to take a long-cut and add a creative touch of our choosing to the original pattern.

Fagoting is one way to change a seam or add one. With your Bernina, you need only a #419 (#7) tailor tacking foot.

Stitch width: 2
Stitch length: 1/2
Presser foot: #419 (#7) tailor tacking; #147 (#20) open embroidery

Make a sample first. Set up your machine by taking your thread out of tension. To do this, thread the machine correctly, then go back and pull the top thread out of the tension and thread guide and loop it over the selector lever on the top of the machine. On the 1000 and 1100 machines, dial down the top tension.

Place two pieces of fabric together, with right sides facing. Stitch along the seam line. When the line is completed, pull the seam open to reveal the stitches. Fold back

seam allowances and press. Change to an embroidery foot and put stabilizer underneath your work. Choose a decorative stitch with a straight edge or even straight stitch to sew each side of the fabric close to the fold. Remove stabilizer.

Go even further with fagoting and bundle the stitches: Sew down the center of the openwork over four stitches with a free-machine straight stitch, back up, and go forward again, stitching past the first bundle and four more stitches (Fig. 8.10). Back up over those four stitches, then stitch forward and over four more stitches. Continue like this until you finish bundling all the stitches.

If you have a model with a triple straight stitch, use this stitch to bundle. Set up your machine with feed dogs up, stitch length 4. The backward-and-forward

Fig. 8.10 Fagoting and bundling stitches for an open seam.

stitching will bundle the middle section automatically.

Use fagoting above the hem of a skirt or around a sleeve or square collar.

Project
Wedding
Handkerchief

Many of the techniques you have learned for French machine sewing will be used to make the handkerchief (see Fig. 8.1). You will need: 5″ (12.7cm) square of fine batiste; ½″ (12.7mm) lace insertion; 1″ (2.5cm) beading; entredeaux; lace edging; ⅛″ (3.2mm) double-face satin ribbon, about 6 yards (5.5m); a ruler and water-erasable marker.

How to figure exact amounts of lace and entredeaux is included in the directions below; the width of your lace will determine the length you will need. Use a #70/10 needle and #100 sewing thread.

For the center of this handkerchief (Fig. 8.11), I rolled and whipped a 5″ (12.7cm) square of batiste. Use the method you prefer. Entredeaux was added to the edges; do one side of entredeaux at a time, cut and overlap the openings of the entredeaux at the corners.

Stitch the beading (the lace with holes for threaded ribbon) and lace strip together before attaching them to the entredeaux. Together, the strip of lace is 1½″ (3.8cm) wide.

Estimate how much lace you'll need for your wedding handkerchief by first measuring around the center square of batiste and entredeaux; the example is approximately 20″ (50.8cm).

Double the width measurement of the strip of lace you've made when you stitched the beading to the lace insertion: 1½″ × 2 = 3″ (3.8cm × 2 = 7.6cm).

Multiply 3″ × 4 = 12″ (7.6cm × 4 = 30.5cm) to arrive at the number of inches (cm) needed for the corner miters.

Add the distance around the center square (20″ or 50.8cm) to the corner miters (12″ or 30.5cm). Exact measurement of the lace needed is 32″ (81.3cm). Add 2″ (5.1cm) more for safety.

Leave 2″ (5.1cm) of lace at the corner before you begin attaching lace to the entredeaux (Fig. 8.12). Trim the entredeaux. Place the edge of the lace strip next to the entredeaux so the edges touch (see Fig. 8.12A). Stitch along the first side, ending with needle down at the corner, extending the lace 1½″ (3.8cm) beyond the corner (this is the width measurement of the strip of lace I used). Raise the presser foot. Fold the lace back on itself by the same measurement, 1½″ (3.8cm) or the width of your lace. Pin the lace together at the corner and then fold the lace so it will lie at the edge of the entredeaux on the next side you will stitch (Fig. 8.12B). Turn your work to continue stitching, and put the presser foot down. Hand-walk the first stitch to be sure it catches the lace. Continue stitching slowly to the next corner. Attach lace to the other sides as you did the first.

After the strip of lace has been attached, go back to each corner and fold the lace diagonally to miter it. Check carefully that the corners will lie flat. Pin each one. Mark with a ruler and water-erasable pen where the line of stitching will be (Fig. 8.12B). Sew down the line with a straight stitch before cutting back, leaving enough lace to roll and whip by machine (Fig. 8.12C).

Attach entredeaux to the edge of the lace, overlapping the holes of each piece at the corners, as done previously.

Measure around the outside edge. Double this for the gathered lace measurement. Sew the ends of the lace together by overlapping and at the same time, matching the designs top and bottom. Sew a narrow zigzag along the design and cut back to the line. Place this seam in a corner.

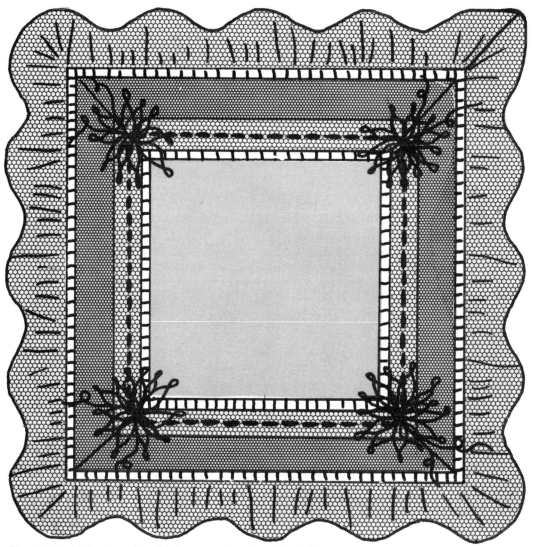

Fig. 8.11 Wedding handkerchief pattern (see also Fig. 8.1)

Gather the lace edging by pulling the correct thread and attaching it to the entredeaux. Pin the gathered lace to the entredeaux first to adjust the gathers. Keep the corners of the lace ruffle quite full. Next, stitch the lace to the entredeaux. This can be done in two ways: (1) Place entredeaux on top of the gathered lace, topsides together. Line up the edges and proceed as if attaching the entredeaux to rolled and whipped edges; or (2) Place gathered lace next to the entredeaux,

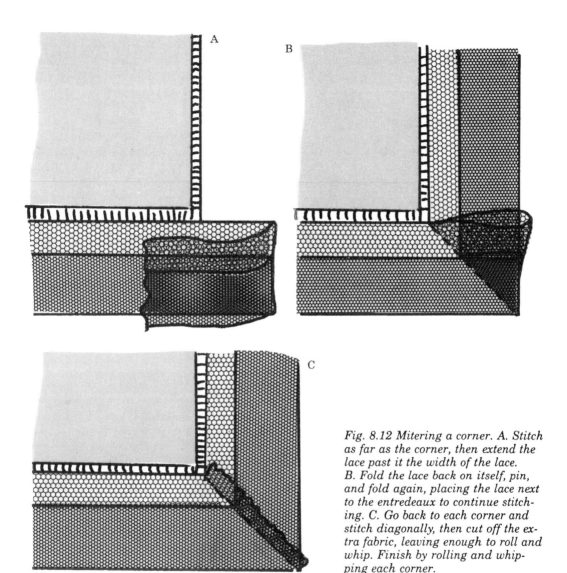

Fig. 8.12 Mitering a corner. A. Stitch as far as the corner, then extend the lace past it the width of the lace. B. Fold the lace back on itself, pin, and fold again, placing the lace next to the entredeaux to continue stitching. C. Go back to each corner and stitch diagonally, then cut off the extra fabric, leaving enough to roll and whip. Finish by rolling and whipping each corner.

topsides up, and zigzag stitch as you did in "Attaching Entredeaux to Lace Insertion."

Thread ⅛" (3.2mm) double-faced satin ribbon through each of the four sides. Leave 3" (7.6cm) tails at each end. Tie overhand knots at the ends. Stitch the tails in place by hand to keep the ribbon in place.

Make rosettes for each corner (Fig. 8.13). First tie an overhand knot every 2½" (6.4cm) along a length of ribbon until you

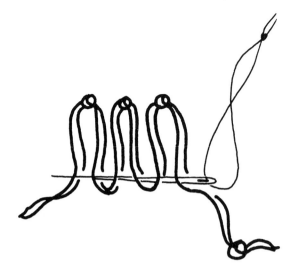

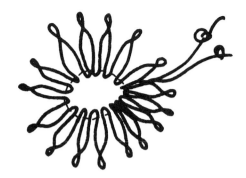

Fig. 8.13 To make a rosette, tie overhand knots in the ribbon every 2½" (6.4cm). Fold the ribbon into loops with knots at the tops. Sew through each loop, then pull into a rosette.

have 16 knots. Leave long ends. Use a double-threaded needle. Make loops on the needle by arranging the ribbon with knots at the top (Fig. 8.13). Sew back through all of the loops again. Pull up and attach the rosettes to the corners of the handkerchief. Tie knots at the ends of the ribbons.

Lesson 24. Seaming with feed dogs up and lowered

Using a #174 lapped hemmer

Why is the #174 (#70) foot called a hemmer when it is really a seamer? And why is it so infrequently used? It sews seams that are used for strength and decoration. Using the feller, another name for it, makes a seam that looks good on both sides (Fig. 8.14).

Use the #174 (#70) for shirt-weight material. The seam will be 4mm. If you want a wider seam for denim weights, then buy the #178 for an 8mm seam.

To use the narrow hemmer, pin two pieces of fabric together so the fabric underneath projects ⅛" (3.2mm) beyond the top piece (Fig. 8.14A). Fold the ⅛" (3.2mm) over the top piece and sew a few stitches (8.14B). Leave the needle in the fabric. Lift the hemmer so you can slide the fabric into it. Stitch the seam. Guide the fabric carefully so it feeds evenly.

Iron the seam. Open up the fabric. Again put it into the hemmer. Pull gently away from the seam on both sides as you guide the seam through the presser foot for the second time. The second line of stitching finishes the seam so it will lie flat (Fig. 8.14C).

For a wider seam, let the bottom layer of fabric project ¼" (6.3mm) beyond the top piece.

Sewing a fake lapped hem

If you don't have the felling foot, then sew a ⅝" (15.9mm) seam and press the fabric to the left (Fig. 8.15A, B).

Using the #492 (#10) edging foot or #016 (#5) blind stitch foot, place the black

136

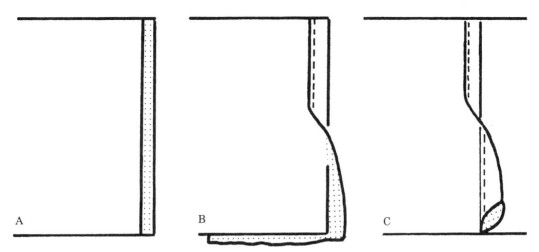

Fig. 8.14 Constructing a lapped hem. A. Place two pieces of fabric together, with the underneath fabric extending beyond the top. B. Use the lap hemmer to stitch the first seam, overlapping the top fabric. C. Open the fabric for the second pass, which will hold the seam in place.

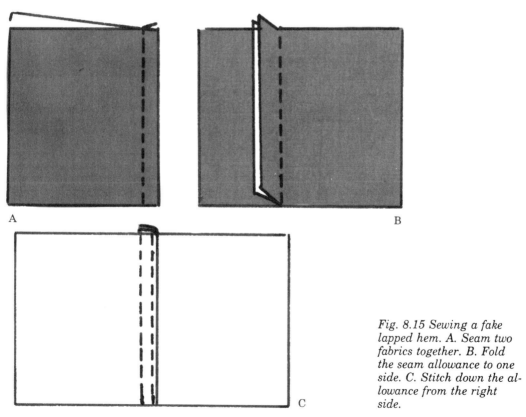

Fig. 8.15 Sewing a fake lapped hem. A. Seam two fabrics together. B. Fold the seam allowance to one side. C. Stitch down the allowance from the right side.

bar in the ditch or seam line, needle position to the near left. It will be about 1/8″ (3.2mm) from the ditch. Stitch.

For the second run, place the guide on the first stitched line, needle to the far left, and sew a fake-felled seam (Fig. 8.15C). Or use a 4.0mm double needle with the zigzag foot to stitch in one pass. Remember, that means the distance between the needles is 4mm and that will be the distance between the stitching. Trim fabric back to the stitching when completed.

Seaming with the Cut'n'Sew

The Cut'n'Sew is wonderful for cutting fabric and overcasting it in one operation. I didn't think I needed one until it was given to me as a gift. Now I use it constantly. You'll want to use it with many of the practical stitches, such as vari-overlock, double overlock and zigzag. One limitation is the type of fabric it will accept. I could not sew the canvas tote bag with it — it doesn't like tough, tightly woven fabrics.

Stitching over thread on knits

No more stretched-out seams on knits and jerseys when you use this method.

Stitch width: 2
Stitch length: 1
Needle position: center
Needle: #80/12
Feed dogs: up
Presser foot: #030 (#6) embroidery
Tension: *top*, normal; *bobbin*, normal
Thread: polyester sewing

With a separate spool of thread, thread polyester through the hole in the presser foot from front to back and tie a knot at the end. Zigzag stitch over the thread, pulling on it gently as you stitch.

Imitating hand piecing on quilts

Here is a seam shown to me by a quilter. After stitching two quilt pieces together,

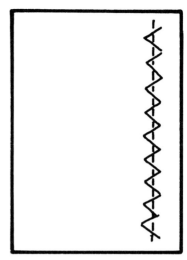

Fig. 8.16 To create the look of hand piecing, zigzag over a seam of straight stitches. Then press the seam open.

run a narrow zigzag over this line of straight stitches (Fig. 8.16). When the seam is pressed open, it gives the impression of perfect hand piecing. Why not skip the first step of straight stitching? Because the two passes will make the quilt seams sturdier, and the line of straight stitching is an excellent guideline for the zigzagging.

Joining veiling with a scallop stitch

What kind of a seam can be used on veiling? In Lesson 17, a straight seam is stitched on Alençon lace, using a close zigzag stitch. A more decorative seam is stitched with the built-in scallop stitch. Overlap the edges, stitch, then cut back excess material on each side to the scallop.

Using built-in stitches

Don't overlook the built-in jersey and honeycomb stitches on your Bernina. They are sewn from the top of the fabric. You may have avoided using them when sewing ribbing onto sweatshirts or for top decora-

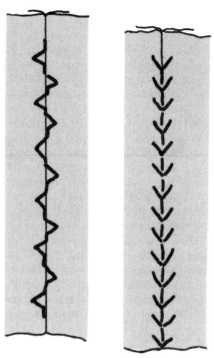

Fig. 8.17 Decorate and stitch a seam with either the gathering stitch (left) or feather stitch.

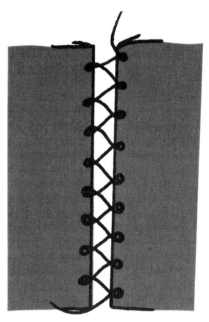

Fig. 8.18 Stitching a decorative seam using free machining.

tion if you experimented on thick fabric and had an uneven look to your stitches. But now you can balance the stitches if you have an 1100 model. Using a sample of the same fabrics, use the balance pushbuttons (+ and −) to find the correct setting for a perfect decorative stitch.

Built-in stitches can be sewn between two pieces of fabric to create an open, interesting seam (Fig. 8.17). The gathering stitch on the 930 and 1130 is one that works beautifully, as well as the feather stitch on the 1100 machines. The feather stitch is one of my favorites—I've been waiting for Bernina to add that one for years. I use the feather stitch on quilt tops to stitch the layers together.

I also used the gathering stitch on a leather and Ultrasuede belt I made from scraps (see Chapter 11).

Creating seams with feed dogs lowered

If you use a similar seam with fabric instead of Ultrasuede, fold under seam allowances at least 5/8″ (15.9mm) and press. Move the two pieces of fabric about 1/8″ (3.2mm) apart, topsides down. Use thick cord in the bobbin. Lower the feed dogs and use the #285 (#9) darning foot or free-machining foot (#24). Sew freely from one side of the fabric to the other, making loops as you enter and leave it (Fig. 8.18). When you finish, change to regular bobbin thread. Turn your fabric over and stitch down along the folds again. Then cut back underneath to the stitching.

These techniques only scratch the surface of interesting seams for your fabric. New seams are introduced every time a new utility or decorative stitch is incorporated into a machine. They are welcome, of course, but in the meantime there is no lack of beautiful and practical work you can do.

CHAPTER 9

Adding Hems and Edges

I remember when "good clothes" didn't mean "clean jeans." There were puffed sleeves, sweetheart necklines—always braided, piped, or embroidered in some way. We wanted to dress like movie stars. Dresses were molded to them and then decorated creatively. Designers always took many long-cuts.

The more you know about your machine, the more inventive you can become: no more boring clothes! You may not think you'll ever use all the decorative hems and edgings in this chapter, but make samples for your notebook anyway. You may be surprised.

With the range of fabrics and styles now available, and the variety of effects we want to achieve, choosing the appropriate hem or edge is not always easy. Before sewing a hem or decorative edge on anything, ask yourself these questions: What type of fabric? What type of garment? Who is the garment for? Will it be worn forever? How decorative is it to be?

I have my favorite ways to hem and finish edges. I've also learned hems and edges I will never do again. What makes the difference? Appearance, of course, and ease of stitching. I think I have tried every imaginable variation, and those that follow are the ones I prefer because they are useful and good-looking.

Stitch samples of each and put the results in your notebook for reference. Include your own favorites as well. Write the machine settings on each one, along with comments such as what fabrics work well, where you would use them, whether they were long-cuts with happy endings or more trouble than they were worth.

Lesson 25. Turning hems once

I used to cringe at the thought of hems turned only once — all those raw edges! But I have changed my way of thinking.

Using double needles on knits

My favorite hem for T-shirts and other casual knits is turned once and stitched in place with a double needle. The two stitching lines share one bobbin thread, giving the stitches the stretch they need.

Stitch width: 0
Stitch length: 2
Needle position: center
Needle: double, at least 2mm
Tension: *top,* normal; *bobbin,* normal
Fabric: knit
Presser foot: pintuck or embroidery foot
Thread: polyester
Stabilizer: tear-away (optional)

It is simple to fold up the hem and sew with a double needle from the topside of the fabric.

When finished, trim the fabric back to the stitching underneath. The sewn-out zigzag can be used for variation. Handwalk the needle through the first few stitches to be sure the zigzag will clear the needle plate opening. On the 1130 model, press the double needle button.

Hemming with a double needle on sheers

Use a double needle for sheer fabrics, too. When a narrow hem would not be suitable or attractive, fold up a 4″ (10.2cm) hem on lightweight fabrics and sew across. Lightweight garments hang better with the weight of a deep hem and it's also more attractive when the hem of the underskirt isn't visible underneath.

Of course you can add more rows of stitching, evenly spaced from the first. Cut back to the top of the stitching.

Hemming with built-in stitches on front

The next hem for delicate fabrics is much the same, but uses a single needle and the built-in scallop stitch.

Stitch width: 4
Stitch length: satin stitch
Needle position: center
Presser foot: #030 (#6) embroidery foot

To hem heavy, canvas-type fabrics on the 930, or 1000 or 1100 series, first find the correct width and length by practicing on a piece of the same fabric you will use for the finished article. Set up the machine for a triple zigzag or triple straight stitch.

Stitch width: varies
Stitch length: varies
Needle position: center
Needle: #110/18 jeans
Presser foot: #560 Red Dot or #1 multi-motion foot
Thread: polyester or heavy duty cotton

This is an extremely strong stitch. Use it for anything from deck furniture canvas to jeans.

Refer back to the stitch samples you did in Chapter 2. You may prefer other decorative built-in stitches to those mentioned here. Experiment with different fabrics and built-in stitches, keeping all your samples in your notebook.

Quilting a hem

Another single-fold hem can be done on heavy materials such as wool or velveteen. Use a walking foot. Allow about 8″ (20.3cm) for the hem of the skirt. Put light batting, such as flannel sheeting, inside and pin in place. Sew four or five rows of straight stitches, one line at a time, to quilt the hem (Fig. 9.1). Space the lines of

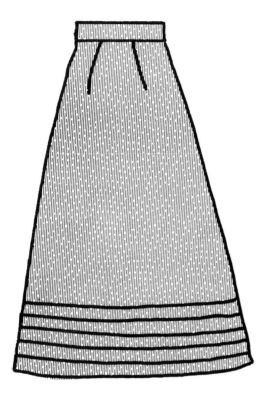

stitching as you wish. Try quilting a long Christmas skirt using metallic thread.

Use a double needle for a different look. Or turn the skirt inside out and put pearl cotton on the bobbin to contrast with the skirt. The topside will be against the bed of the machine. Stitch rows, then cut back to the last line of stitching. This can be done around sleeve bands or down jacket facings as well.

Fig. 9.1 Use light flannel between hem and skirt, then quilt the hem with lines of straight stitching.

Lesson 26. Blind hemming

I remember when most of the hems I put in garments were blind hems worked by hand. Times have changed, but that doesn't mean I've given up blind hems. The only difference is that I do them more quickly now—by machine.

To begin the hem, decide first if you can live with a raw edge. If you can, then leave it as it is, but if you hate that unfinished edge, then attach a lace edging over it or stitch around the edge with the sewn-out zigzag stitch before you proceed.

Turn up the hem 1½" to 2" (3.8cm to 5.1cm) and pin very closely around it,

about an inch from the top. If the fabric slips, the hem will be a mess, so don't try to save time by not pinning a lot.

Tami Durand, a sewing specialist for Bernina, uses this method: Baste the hem about ¼" (6.4mm) from the edge, using the fast and easy basting button, long stitch, or straight stitch set at a long stitch length (it will depend on which machine you use).

Set your machine up for blind hem. The 1100 series sets up automatically for the blind hem when you press the blind stitch button. You can change the settings if you wish.

Stitch width: 2 1/4–2 1/2
Stitch length: 2
Needle position: right
Feed dogs: up
Presser foot: #016 (#5) blind stitch
Built-in stitch: blind hem
Tension: *top,* loosened; *bobbin,* normal
Thread: sewing
Accessories: dressmakers' pins

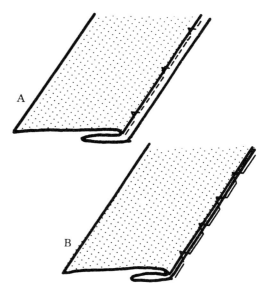

Fold the garment back on itself, leaving ⅛″ (3.2mm) of hem at the edge to stitch on (Fig. 9.2A). Put the fold of the fabric against the left side of the black middle extension. Stitch on the edge of the fabric and let the needle catch about 2 threads of the fold. Check the settings on scrap fabric first to determine the correct stitch width and length. Thick fabrics will require different settings than lightweight fabrics.

I made a fine batiste bishop dress with yards of blind hemming, but the stitching pulled too tightly. Despite the fine thread, loosened tension, and a #60/8 needle, I didn't like the looks of it. The answer? I sewed from off the fabric. I folded the fabric back so the fold met the edge exactly. Then I stitched outside the fabric and the left bite held it together with no pulling (Fig. 9.2B). I've tried it on other weights of fabric as well, and it works beautifully.

Fig. 9.2 Blind hemming. A. Fold over the hem, then fold the skirt back, letting ⅛″ (3.2mm) show beyond the edge; stitch on the edge of the fabric. B. Or fold the garment back even with the edge, and stitch off the fabric, the left swing stitching the fold.

Still hesitant about stitching in space? Then place water-soluble stabilizer under your stitching.

Lesson 27. Sewing narrow hems

Next to hemstitching needles, the most unused accessories are the hemming presser feet. I think I know why: few stitchers ever take time to practice with them. They're great time savers, but I had to learn to use them, too. Now after yards of hem samples, I can't do without them.

Set up your machine, read the directions, and reread as you work. Before you begin to hem a garment with one of the hemmers, cut back the seam allowances that have to be sewn over. Then learn to start the fabric. I hated starting a hem because of those first problem inches until I tried Gail Brown's method, which follows.

Straight stitching

Practice with the #003 (#64) hemmer because it produces twice as wide a hem as

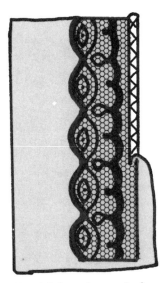

Fig. 9.3 Lace is attached with a finished edge in one step.

mer, the hem is being sewn down starting on the first thread of the fabric.

Guide the fabric by holding it taut and lifting it slightly as it rolls through the foot. The edge of the fabric must be vertical. As long as you pay attention, guiding and holding the fabric correctly, the machine does the rest.

Sewing on lace

This method is simple and it does save time.

Stitch width: 3 – 4
Stitch length: 1 – 1 1/2
Needle position: left
Presser foot: #452 (#3) buttonhole
Fabric: lightweight cotton, lace edging
Thread: fine sewing thread to match

Place the lace on top of the fabric, topsides together, the edge of the lace 1/8" (3.2mm) from the edge of the fabric.

The fabric is placed to the right of the middle extension of the presser foot. As you sew, it will roll and be whipped over the heading of the lace (Fig. 9.3).

See other methods of sewing lace to fabric in Lesson 25, "French handsewing."

Attaching scalloped lace

Apply scalloped lace to fabric, topsides up, by overlapping it to make a hem (Fig.

the #168 (#68) and is easier to use when first learning. Also needed are lightweight cotton to hem and a 3" (7.6cm) square of tear-away stabilizer.

Overlap the piece of tear-away stabilizer with the fabric about 1/4" (6.3mm) and sew them together. Start rolling the stabilizer into the scroll of the hemming foot. By the time the fabric is introduced into the hem-

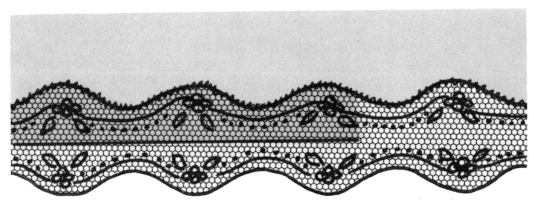

Fig. 9.4 Attach scalloped lace to fabric by overlapping it, zigzagging along the scalloped edge, then cutting the fabric back to the stitching line.

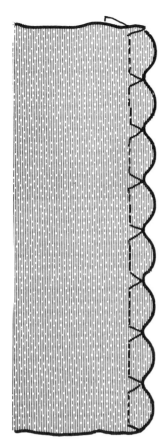

Fig. 9.5 A shell edge on tricot, stitched with the blind-hem stitch.

9.4). Let the fabric extend well past the curve on top of the lace. Baste lace to fabric. Zigzag along the edge, following the scallop. Cut back the fabric underneath to the stitching line.

Stitching shell edging

This is a good hem and edging for lingerie (Fig. 9.5). Or use it to decorate ribbon and tucks.

Set up your machine:

Stitch width: 4
Stitch length: 1
Needle position: center

Feed dogs: up
Presser foot: #000 (#0)
Built-in stitch: blind stitch pattern

If you are going to cross a seam when hemming, then cut back the seam allowances that will be sewn over.

The foot rests on the fabric for this one; you do not feed fabric into the foot. Fold the fabric under ½″ (12.7mm) and place the folded edge to the left. Stitch, letting the left swing of the needle sew over the edge, creating the shell pattern. At the end, cut back to the stitching underneath.

Mirror the blind hem stitch if your machine has this capability and if it is easier for you to sew with the bulk of the fabric to the left of the needle.

Roll and shell hemming

The #168 (#68) hemmer not only makes a narrow, straight-stitch hem, but it also rolls and shells as shown in Fig. 9.6, if the machine is set on zigzag. Usually it's the finish of choice when hemming tricot, as it decorates and hems in one operation. It's impossible to turn square corners on these hems, so round off any corners before you begin to stitch. Because tricot rolls to one side, hem with the right side up. If you will stitch over a seam while hemming, first cut back the seam allowances you'll cross so the fabric will feed in without a problem. As the fabric is rolled into the foot, it will curl and be sewn into a narrow, puffy roll.

Stitch width: 4
Stitch length: 2 1/2
Needle position: center
Feed dogs: up
Presser foot: #168 (#68) roll-and-shell hemmer

It's important to keep the fabric straight ahead of the presser foot and raise it a bit to keep it feeding easily. The needle goes into the fabric at the left, then off the edge of the fabric at the right.

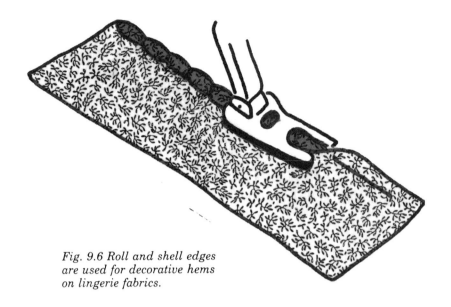

Fig. 9.6 Roll and shell edges are used for decorative hems on lingerie fabrics.

Lesson 28. Using bias tape

I must admit, I equate bias tape with the edges of Grandma's apron, but now that I can apply it so easily, I'm finding new ways to use it. I especially like it for toddlers' sunsuits and dresses.

This is the only method I use; what I like best about it is that the tape is sewn on almost invisibly. You don't need the bias binder accessory.

Stitch width: 0
Stitch length: 2
Feed dogs: up
Presser foot: #492 (#10) edge foot
Needle: #80/12
Needle position: center
Thread: monofilament
Fabric: lightweight cotton, double-fold bias tape
Accessories: glue stick, pins

Look at the bias tape: One side is wider than the other. The wide side will be on the back of your work. Open the bias tape and place the narrow side on top, the cut edge of the tape along the cut edge of the fabric. If there is a 5/8" (15.9mm) seam, cut it back to fit the width of the bias. Pin in place.

Stitch along the crease with the needle centered, the black extension of the presser foot in the crease.

Fold the tape over the edge. I sometimes dab the underside with glue stick between tape and fabric. Pin if you wish, or baste by hand.

Press the bias and check that the underside of the bias extends slightly beyond the seam line on the topside.

From the topside, stitch in the ditch of the seam, needle still centered. The black bar of the foot should be placed in the seam to guide you as you stitch. The stitching catches the edge of the bias underneath. I've decided I can't sew without the edging foot.

Lesson 29. Zigzagging a narrow edge

This is only one of several methods to produce a strong, finished hem or edge of tiny, tight zigzag stitches. Use it to finish ruffles, napkins and scarves.

Stitch width: 1 1/2
Stitch length: satin stitch
Needle position: center
Presser foot: #030 (#6) embroidery

Fold the fabric under about ½" (12.7mm) and guide the fold of the fabric directly under the hole of the embroidery foot (I often use the hole in the #030 (#6) foot for a guide). Stitch on the fabric with the left swing of the needle, the right swing stitching just off the right side of it (Fig. 9.7). After stitching is completed, cut the fabric back to the stitched edge, as partially done below.

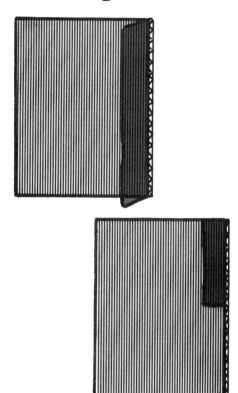

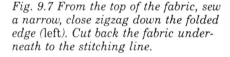

Fig. 9.7 From the top of the fabric, sew a narrow, close zigzag down the folded edge (left). Cut back the fabric underneath to the stitching line.

Lesson 30. Covering wire for shaped edges

In a bridal shop I saw yard goods that included nylon filament at the edges of chiffon and organdy ruffles. It was an attractive finish for the ruffles that can be applied to skirt and sleeve hems or across the drop-shoulders of wedding gowns and formal wear.

A case displayed dozens of headpieces using the same nylon filament to keep bows perky and ribbons from wilting. You are invited to create your own, combining filament and sheer fabrics, beads and silk flowers.

I could also see many Halloween cos-tume possibilities here. Use the filament at the bottom edge of a long, filmy skirt or, if you want to make an angel costume, use heavy gauge filament for floppy wings.

Nylon filament is available by the yard at stores that sell bridal lace and fabrics. But I found that it is much easier to buy 25-pound-test fishing line in a sporting goods store. Cheaper, too. I've used both and I don't think there's a difference. There are different weights to fishing lines, which means they come in different thicknesses.

For super-thick costume fabric, you can

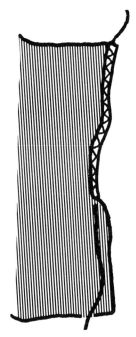

Fig. 9.8 Rolling fabric over nylon filament or wire creates a rigid, finished edge.

use weed-trimmer line. It comes in a 50-foot length and the diameter to use is .05mm. This fits in the groove of the #033 (#27) foot. Use the same foot and the same method to apply any of the nylon filament mentioned.

Stitch width: 4
Stitch length: 1
Presser foot: #033 (#27)

I placed the filament about ¼″ (6.4mm) from the edge of the fabric (the needle should stitch off the edge of the material on the right swing). As you sew, the edge of the fabric will roll over and enclose the line (Fig. 9.8).

Milliner's wire or florist's wire is available already covered with thread. Both of these can be stitched into the edge of fabric in the same way as nylon filament. They both come in different gauges. Unlike the nylon edge, the wire can be bent into shapes. Buy milliner's wire at bridal shops and florist's wire at craft shops. Make flower petals and leaves using wire.

Lesson 31. Cording edges

Covering cords

Covered cord produces one of the finest, prettiest edges to use on table linens, on scarves, collars, wherever you want a delicate but very strong edge.

Stitch width: 2, 4
Stitch length: 1/2
Needle position: center
Presser foot: #030 (#6) embroidery; #033
   (#27) non-auto buttonhole
Thread: machine-embroidery or sewing
   thread; #5 pearl cotton

Fold the fabric under about ½″ (12.7mm) and press. Thread pearl cotton through the hole in the embroidery foot. Place the hole at the edge of the fabric and

stitch (Fig. 9.9). Cut back to the stitching underneath when it's completed.

To create a thicker edge, go back over the first line of stitching with the #033 (#27) foot. Place the edge you've completed in the slot to the left and another cord of pearl cotton between the toes of the presser foot to hold it in place. Change to stitch width 4.

If you use this method to finish the edge of a collar, first place wrong sides of upper and under collar together to eliminate the bulk of a turned-in seam allowance. Stitch cording on the seam line around the outside edge of the collar. Trim seam allowance back to the cord. Then stitch down the second cable cord as you did previously.

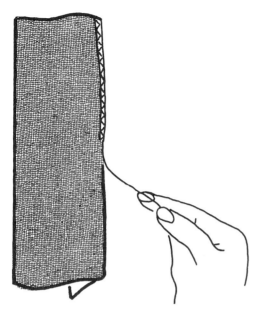

Fig. 9.9 Zigzagging over cord produces a strong corded edge.

To make a delicate edging for a bridal veil, cord the edge.

Stitch width: 2
Stitch length: 1/2–3/4 (not too tight)
Needle position: center
Presser foot: #030 (#6) embroidery
Thread: fine sewing thread to match veil; #8 pearl cotton to match veil

Without folding the veiling, place it so the edge extends past the presser foot on the right. Slip #8 pearl cotton in the hole of the embroidery foot. Sew over the pearl. Cut back to the pearl for a fine finished edge. (Try a corded scallop stitch, too.)

Creating crocheted edges

This decorative edge is used to finish shirt plackets and collars. It's a delicate, lacelike finish that lends itself to feminine clothes and baby items.

Instead of threading pearl cotton or gimp through the presser foot, this time it is threaded up through the needle plate on the bed of the machine.

Stitch width: 4
Stitch length: almost 0
Presser foot: #030 (#6) embroidery foot
Built-in stitch: scallop
Fabric: medium-weight cotton
Thread: color to contrast with fabric; gimp or #5 pearl cotton the same color as the thread
Accessories: tear-away stabilizer or colored paper to match thread

Use the embroidery foot and pearl cotton to do a corded edge using the scallop stitch. Place stabilizer underneath and far enough to the right to be under the stitches, as shown in Fig. 9.10. The fabric should

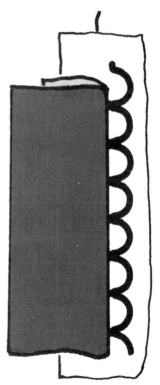

Fig. 9.10 Make a crocheted edge with the built-in scallop stitch.

be doubled; the fold is placed just to the left of the hole in front of the presser foot. Stitch at the edge. The scallops will catch the fabric, but most of the stitches will be off the edge onto the stabilizer (Fig. 9.10). Carefully tear off the stabilizer when you finish.

Try other decorative stitches at the edges of fabrics. I like the small, undulating scallop, too. Use it on the edges of plackets or sleeves and decorate collars with it. Sew on doubled fabric, then cut back to the stitching. The edge of the baby bonnet in Fig. 5.10 was worked this way.

Reshaping knits with elastic

Elastic can be used to keep stretchy edges in shape, or to reshape them.

Stitch width: 2
Stitch length: 2 or your preference
Presser foot: #030 (#6)

Thread the elastic though the hole in the embroidery foot. Keep the elastic at the edge of the knit and sew down the fold (Fig. 9.11).

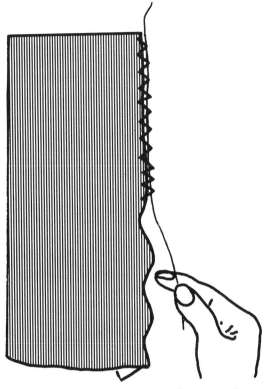

Fig. 9.11 Keep knits from stretching out of shape by stitching in an elastic thread.

Lesson 32. Making thread fringe

How many machine owners use a tailor-tacking foot for tailor tacking? I can't find one. Most of the time the #419 (#7) foot is used for fringing (Fig. 9.12), fagoting, or for sewing on buttons.

To make thread fringe, you'll need one piece of fabric, folded over at least 1″ (2.5cm) at the edge where you want the fringe to be sewn. Press the fold line (Fig. 9.12A), then open up the fabric so you can stitch on that pressed line.

Stitch width: 2
Stitch length: satin-stitch
Presser foot: #419 (#7) tailor tacking, #147 (#20) open embroidery

Needle position: center
Tension: *top*, loosened; *bobbin*, normal
Stabilizer: tear-away

Stitch on a single thickness of fabric; no stabilizer is needed for this. Be sure the stitches are as close together as you can make them and still have the fabric move easily under the presser foot (Fig. 9.12B).

When stitching is completed, refold on the line, then clip and smooth the fringe in place (Fig. 9.12C). Press, then choose a decorative stitch or use a straight stitch to hold the fringe in place (Fig. 9.12D). Remember the 1130 mirror image button. If

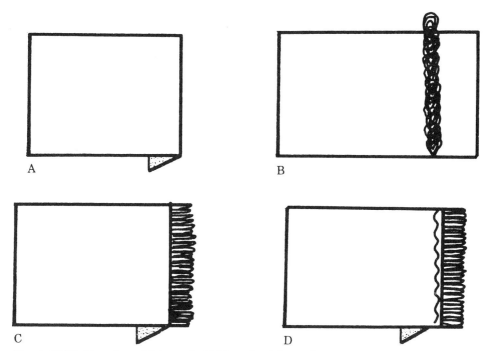

Fig. 9.12 Making thread fringe. A. Fold under fabric edge 1" (2.5cm). B. Open fabric and use closely stitched tailor tacking along the crease. C. Fold fabric edge under again and smooth down fringe. D. Stitch close to fold to hold fringe in place.

you find a stitch, but it is facing the wrong way for your convenience, turn it around. Slip stabilizer under your work and use the embroidery foot as you stitch. I may place a strip of paper over the fringe as I stitch, so it can't possibly get tangled up in the presser foot. Cut back underneath to your

stitching and clip the fringe loops if you wish.

If you look closely at the eyelashes of the denim doll in Fig. 3.17, you will see thread fringe. Know your machine and use it on the simplest of tasks to make them simpler.

Lesson 33. Piping edges

Miniature piping is especially pretty and colorful on the edges of children's clothing. Use a #3 or #5 pearl cotton and a piece of bias fabric twice the width of the seam allowance. I may not use bias fabric at all. It seems to make little difference, and though held sacrilegious, you can save fab-

ric by cutting on the straight, so try it for yourself. Or cover the pearl with purchased bias tape.

Both the #181 (#23) clear appliqué foot and the #033 (#27) non-automatic buttonholer work well. So does the invisible zipper foot. Each has a groove in which to fit the covered pearl while stitching it. Adjust the needle position to sew at the edge of the cord.

To cover thick cord for upholstery, use the #528 (#12) bulky overlock foot. Forget what you've learned about always using a zipper foot for this procedure. The wrapped cord fits into the groove of the overlock foot and never slips. I sewed over 100 yards of that one day and it couldn't have been easier. Attaching covered cording to a pillow is also a breeze with this foot.

Lesson 34. Topstitching

There is nothing richer-looking on a coat or suit than an even line of topstitching.

When you need a narrowly spaced double line, use a double needle. For topstitching a heavy fabric, I use a topstitching needle with two sewing threads, eliminating the fraying of buttonhole twist. Sew the second line of stitching in the same direction as the first.

When topstitching on lapels, the roll line indicates where the top threads will go to the underside. For this reason, if you use two threads on top, you must use two threads on the bobbin as well. Wind the bobbin with two threads at one time instead of using only one. Then treat the threads as if they were one.

Instead of anchoring threads, leave a long enough thread at the beginning and the end to work in later invisibly by hand.

If you have a machine with the triple straight stitch, experiment with it. Use orange thread and stitch on denim to create the look of commercial topstitching on jeans.

Don't forget the obvious — the long stitch or topstitching button. Use this stitch for a professional look every time. It is set to stitch every other stitch. (There are more uses for this stitch in Chapter 11). Borrow a trick from Sashiko (Chapter 3) and topstitch with a contrasting color from the fabric. Use the same color as the fabric in the bobbin. (Remember, this can't be used on a rolled lapel.)

How can you keep topstitching straight? You have several choices. Use tape along the edge of the fabric and sew next to it. Use the Cut'n'Sew foot (width is limited). Again, using the #492 (#10) edging foot is my first choice because the width can be set with needle positioning. With the black bar up against the garment edge, it is simple to sew a perfectly straight line of topstitching.

If using lightweight material, set the machine for 10–12 stitches per inch. If using medium-weight fabric, a longer stitch looks better. Stitch samples on scraps of the same material to see what stitch length setting you prefer.

I think there is hope for more decorative dressing. Have you noticed how Joan Crawford's clothes don't look so funny anymore?

CHAPTER 10

Machine Tricks: Adding Threads to Threads

- **Lesson 35. Making cord**
- **Lesson 36. Making tassels**

For nine chapters, we've used fabric and thread for sewing and embroidering. I'll bet you know your Bernina pretty well by now, but there's more: In this chapter, I'll show you how to make cords using your machine. Some will be used for practical purposes, such as belt loops and hangers for pendants, but we'll make other cords for decoration, bunching them together into tassels.

Lesson 35. Making cord

Twisting monk's cord

Monk's cord is made from several strands of thread or yarn held together and twisted to make a thick cord. The cord may be used in many ways—as a finish around pillows, as a handle for handbags, and as thick fringe in tassels.

On the machine, monk's cord is made using the bobbin winder and a cord such as #8 pearl cotton. (If it is too thick, it will not seat properly on the winder, so the size you can use is limited.) However, there is a way to get around this. You can tie dental floss—it doesn't slip—around the center of a thick cord, leaving long enough ends to seat the floss into the middle of the bobbin. Then you are able to wind monk's cord of any thickness.

Start with a length of pearl cotton about 2 yards (1.8m) long. Fold this in half, knot the two ends together, and slip the knot down through the center of a bobbin. Let

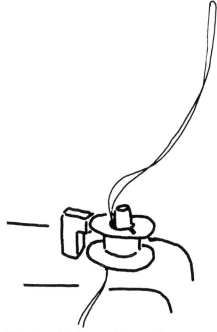

Fig. 10.1 Make monk's cord by slipping a doubled pearl cotton thread down inside the bobbin and activating the bobbin winder.

153

an inch or two (2.5 – 5.1cm) of cord extend beyond the bobbin.

Next, push the bobbin down into place on the pin (Fig. 10.1). When clicked into place, the bobbin will hold the cord securely. Put your index finger or a pencil in the loop of the cord at the other end and stand over the bobbin mechanism, stretching the cord upward to keep tension on it. Activate the bobbin mechanism.

If you are using the 1000 or 1100 series, instead of the foot pedal used to activate the bobbin, you must move the engaging lever to the left. It's not as hard as it sounds, although working with a partner helps. After you have the cord seated, your index finger in the loop, hold onto the cord with your other hand, about 12″ (30.5cm) from the bobbin. Stretch the cord to keep tension on it for this 12″ (30.5cm). Click the mechanism to start the bobbin with the hand that is holding the end of the cord. As soon as it starts to wind, let go with the hand closest to the bobbin, but keep the cord taut with the other hand by moving back away from the machine.

Keep winding the cord until it is so tight the blood supply to your finger is threatened. If you've used a pencil in the loop, how can you tell if the cord is wound tightly enough? Stop winding, but keep tension on the cord. Take hold of the cord about 6″ (15.2cm) from the pencil. Don't let loose of the entire cord, only the 6″ (15.2cm) between hand and pencil to see if it will twist tightly. If it does, then take the pencil out of the loop, find the middle of the cord with your free hand and, still keeping tension on the cord, place the loop on the spool pin. Don't let go of the cord, but from the end,

Fig. 10.2 Machine-made monk's cord is used to make this tassel.

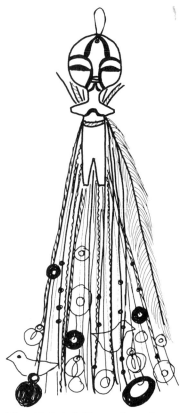

Fig. 10.3 A doll tassel made with monk's cord.

154

work down the twists with both hands to keep the cord smooth.

When it is twisted as tightly as it will go, take it out of the bobbin and off the thread-holder spool pin. Tie an overhand knot to hold the two ends together until you actually use it. (Yes, you really need three hands.)

I use this cord to make the thick fringe in tassels, sometimes slipping washers, bells, beads or spacers to the middle of the cord after I have twisted it and before I double it and make the final twists (Figs. 10.2 and 10.3).

These quick cords can be used for belt loops, button loops, ties for clothing. Or twist up a batch to tie small packages.

Stitching belt and button loops

Belt loop cords can be made by pulling out the bobbin and top threads and folding them over to make about six strands (or as many as will go through the hole in the #030 (#6) embroidery foot). Use a stitch width 4 and stitch length 2 1/2, with a center needle position. Hold the threads tightly, front and back, as you stitch.

If you find it too difficult to coax these through the hole in the foot, set your machine for free machining, with feed dogs down. Take the presser foot off. Fold up your threads and hold them as before. Using the same zigzag setting, stitch over them. The difference is that you, not the feed dogs, feed the threads under the needle and determine the stitch length. These tiny cords work well for corded buttonholes.

You can also zigzag over thicker cords to hold them together. If you add a contrasting thread color, you can make interesting tassels (see the next lesson).

Lesson 36. Making tassels

I'm drawn to tassels. I sketch them when I see them in museums or books, and I have a notebook full of ideas cut from magazines. I've labored over a few myself, using hand embroidery, even tiny macramé knots. Sometimes they look like fetish dolls—another weakness—and so I play them that way.

How can my sewing machine help me make tassels? First of all, I make monk's cord using the bobbin winder. I combine those with other cords, sometimes stringing beads or bells on them (Figs. 10.4 and 10.5).

I can also use the #189 (#21) braiding foot or #147 (#20) open embroidery foot to make colorful cord. Holding several pearl cotton cords together, I place them in the groove on the bottom of the presser foot and zigzag stitch over the pearl with a contrasting color. I choose a stitch width 4 to enclose the cords, and a stitch length 1 to let some of the cord show through.

Project
Tassel Collar

Several ways to make tassels by machine involve using water-soluble stabilizer. The first method is for a collar of stitched cords to wrap around the main tassel cords.

Stitch width: 4
Stitch length: satin stitch
Needle position: center
Needle: #80/12
Presser foot: #147 (#20) open embroidery
Feed dogs: up
Tension: *top*, normal; *bobbin*, normal
Cord: 16 yards (14.5m) rayon cord (available at fabric shops) for the collar; #5 pearl cotton to match cord; many yards of string, thread or yarn for main part of tassel (the more yarn used, the plumper and more attractive the tassel), cut into 16″ (40.6cm) lengths

Thread: rayon embroidery to match rayon cord

Accessories: water-soluble stabilizer

First fold the 16″ (40.6cm) lengths of yarn in half to find their centers. Use one yarn piece to tie the lengths together there. Knot tightly. Then tie an overhand knot with the ends of that cord to make a hanger for the tassel.

Cut six dozen 8″ (20.3cm) lengths of purchased rayon cord. Place a piece of water-soluble stabilizer on the bed of the machine and lay these cords next to each other across the stabilizer (in horizontal rows as you are looking at them). Starting ½″ (12.7mm) in from the right side, place a strand of #5 pearl cotton perpendicular to and crossing all the cords (Fig. 10.6). Satin stitch over the pearl cotton and the rayon

Fig. 10.5 More tassels stitched by machine.

cords. Sew down several more rows of pearl, lining up each pearl cord next to the one stitched before it. When completed, cut off the ½″ (12.7mm) rayon threads protruding from the top of the collar. Zigzag over the edge, which will give the top a smooth finish.

Wrap the collar, inside-out, 1½″ (3.8cm) down from the fold of the tassel cords. Pin the collar tightly around the cords. Remove it from the tassel and machine stitch the ends of the collar together. Cut back to the stitching line and zigzag over the edge. Turn right side out, then pull the yarn tassel cords from the bottom through the collar to complete it. The collar should fit snugly.

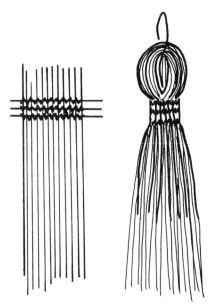

Fig. 10.6 Make a collar for the tassel by placing cords next to each other, then zigzagging over cords laid at right angles across them.

Fig. 10.7 Cover milliner's wire with stitches and twist the wire around cords to make a tassel.

Project
Covered Wire Tassel

Cover 18″ (45.7cm) of milliner's wire with stitches for the next tassel (Fig. 10.7).

Stitch width: 4
Stitch length: satin stitch
Needle position: center
Needle: #80/12
Feed dogs: up
Presser foot: #147 (#20) open embroidery foot
Tension: *top*, normal; *bobbin*, normal
Thread: rayon embroidery
Accessories: tweezers

Set up your machine and sew over the wire. If the wire doesn't feed well, then use a longer length stitch and go over it twice.

The milliner's wire is covered with thread and this keeps the rayon stitches from slipping.

Make 45 thick cords for the tassel by zigzagging over two 12″ (30.5cm) strands of #5 pearl cotton for each one. *Hint:* Stitch two 15-yard-long (13.7m-long) cords together and cut them into 12″ (30.5cm) pieces.

To use the wire for the tassel, first fold the 12″ (30.5cm) long cords in half. Slip an end of the wire through the fold, extending it past the cord 2″ (5.1cm). Bend the wire back 1″ (2.5cm) at the end and twist it around itself to make a loop for hanging (the loop will enclose the cords).

With the other end of the wire, wrap the tassel around and around till you reach halfway down the length of it. Hold the end of the wire with the tweezers. Wrap it around the point of the tweezers to make a decorative coil at the end (Fig. 10.7).

Project
Doll Tassel

The fertility doll tassel is a combination of several dozen 10″ (25.4cm) cords, including linen, jute and monk's cords (see Fig. 10.3) all tied to a small African doll. I placed the bundle of cords on the bed of the machine, letting it extend 1″ (2.5cm) to the right of the presser foot and flattening it with my fingers to allow me to stitch over the cords. The machine was set up for free-machining, with feed dogs lowered and a darning foot in place. Using the widest zig-zag, I stitched forward and back across the cords. When I finished, I spread glue from a glue stick across the stitching on one side of the bundle and placed this at the back of the doll, wrapping and tying it in place with a linen cord.

To decorate the tassel, I slipped a long feather under the linen wrapping cord, and strung some of the tassel cords with beads, brass bells and metal washers. Overhand knots held the objects in place at different heights on the cords. There's a hole in the top of the doll, so I added a loop of cord there to hang the tassel.

Project
Making
Two Tassel Tops
by Machine

For the following tassels shown in Fig. 10.8C and 10.9, the tops are made on the sewing machine. Put a 7″ (17.8cm) square of felt in a 5″ (12.7cm) spring hoop. Draw half a circle and embroider this using decorative, built-in machine stitches. Take it out of the hoop and cut out the half-circle (Fig. 10.8A). Cut out a wedge from the side of the half-circle (Fig. 10.8B). Fold the

larger piece in half, topsides together. Straight stitch the cut edges. Turn to the right side.

Cut six tassel cords, each 18″ (45.7cm) in length, from rayon cord or machine-made monk's cord. Find the center and tie them together at the middle with a cord 8″ (20.3cm) long. Thread that cord through a large-eyed needle and push it up from in-

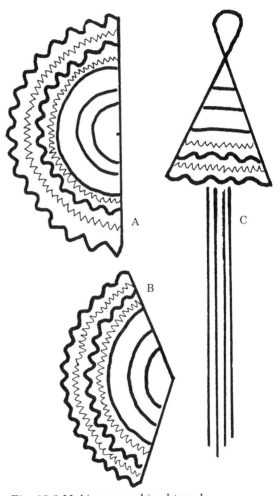

Fig. 10.8 Making a machined tassel.
A. Embroider a half-circle of felt.
B. Cut a wedge from it, and sew up the sides to form a cone. C. The cone becomes the top of the tassel.

159

side through the top of the cone. Tie a knot at the end and hang the tassel.

The second tassel is also made of felt, with a machine-stitched top (Fig. 10.9).

Stitch width: widest
Stitch length: varies
Needle position: center
Needle: #90/14, topstitch
Feed dogs: up
Presser foot: #470 (#2) vari-overlock, #030 (#6) embroidery
Tension: *top*, normal; *bobbin*, finger threaded
Fabric suggestion: 9″ (22.9cm) square of felt (tassel top will be completely covered with stitches)
Thread: rayon machine embroidery–I chose red, yellow and blue; #8 red pearl cotton; #5 blue pearl cotton (optional)
Accessories: 7″ (17.8cm) spring hoop, small bells, glue stick, fine-point marker
Stabilizer: tear-away

The finished size of the tassel top is 2″ × 2″ (5.1cm × 5.1cm). I worked with a 9″ (22.9cm) piece of felt so it would fit in the 7″ (17.8cm) spring hoop. This allows enough room for the presser foot without hitting the edge of the hoop, as you will stitch both sides of the tassel top − 2″ × 4″ (5.1cm × 10.2cm) area − at once.

Trace the pattern from Fig. 10.9. Cut around the tracing and lay this on the felt. Draw around the pattern with a marker (it won't show when tassel is completed).

Begin by carefully stretching the felt in the hoop. Use the #470 (#2) vari-overlock foot for this top or use corded (#5 pearl cotton) satin stitches with the #030 (#6) embroidery foot. Starting on the right side, place one line of close, smooth satin stitches. Add another row, next to the first and continue, changing colors as you wish. Now sew between the satin stitches, using a contrasting color and the triple stitch if your machine has that capability. You can also use double thread in a topstitching needle, with a straight stitch for other models.

Fig. 10.9 A tassel made of satin stitches on felt.

Cut out the stitched design; then cut it in half. Place wrong sides together.

Cut about five dozen lengths of pearl cotton, each 12″ (30.5cm) long. Fold them in half. Place the folds inside the felt pieces along the straight edge. Pin the felt together or use a dot of glue stick to hold everything in place as you stitch. Zigzag across the straight edge of the felt to keep the pearl cotton in place. Zigzag around the curve as well. Then go back with a satin

160

stitch and stitch around it again with stitch width at the widest, stitch length 1/2. Add bells to each side and a hanger at the top.

I agree, making tassels is a nutty thing to do (but it's fun). Use them to decorate your tote bag, for key chains, zipper pulls, decorations on clothing, curtain tiebacks. I confess that I hang them all over my sewing room.

CHAPTER 11

Decorative Stitches

- **Lesson 37: Fantasy Stitches**
- **Lesson 38: Stitches to wear**
- **Lesson 39: Stitches to give**

Decorative stitches often play a major role in the selection of a new machine. But numbers of stitches on a display panel never tell the whole story. For example, instead of only the 34 stitches on the panel of the Bernina 1130, the machine actually contains many more waiting for discovery. In this chapter I'll show you how to invent new stitches by combining the 35 (34 plus buttonhole) stitches already built into the machine with the general and special function buttons. To inspire you, I've included a chart of Fantasy Stitches already discovered by June Florey of Dayton, Virginia; Diana Schlumpf of Ogden, Utah; Bernina of America; and my own experiments.

In this chapter, we'll change the face of fabrics with decorative stitches, sometimes combining the decorative stitches with techniques taught in previous chapters. If you have a model different from the 1130, this chapter is for you, too, with eight projects included that are sewn with built-in stitches.

Lesson 37. Fantasy Stitches

Bernina divides up its practical and decorative stitches on the 1130 into six categories: utility, or practical, stitches are #1–#14; hand-look stitches are #15–#18; compact stitches, #19–#22; edge stitches, #23–#26; pearl stitches, #27–#30; floral stitches, #30–#34. The buttonhole is considered a decorative stitch, too—and not, as you might expect, a zigzag stitch. When you combine these 35 stitches with general and special functions, you create Fantasy Stitches.

In order to know your 1130 to its full potential, you need to understand what each of these function buttons accomplishes. Look on the panel below the 14 practical stitches to find general function buttons

(Fig. 11.2). The first one, needle down, keeps fabric from shifting when you stop stitching and helps in pattern matching.

The next button is for ½ speed. The 1130 sews 1050 perfect stitches a minute at full speed, both forward and in reverse, but we don't always want to go full tilt when we sew. Use ½ speed to limit yourself to a slower pace when carefully matching patterns, embroidering, or striving for precision in any sewing situation.

Unlike the securing stitch control, which is used for anchoring threads, the reverse sewing button, when depressed, stays depressed until you clear that function. It sews stitches backward without distortion. You'll find many uses for it in

Fig. 11.1 Jean Kottke's original drawing utilizes many Fantasy Stitches to look like blackwork.

combination with the balancing buttons when creating Fantasy Stitches.

The pattern begin button is the favorite of everyone who loves decorative stitches. When this button is pushed, the stitch you've chosen starts exactly on the first stitch.

The next button, long stitch, is used for basting and topstitching. When it's pushed, the machine sews every other stitch, producing a stitch as long as ⅜″ (9.5mm). But I'm more excited about its use with Fantasy Stitches. The simple combination of a built-in stitch with the long stitch creates brand-new stitches. If you have the 1120 or 1130 machine, make a sample of built-in stitches combined with the long stitch. Some will be throwaways, but others are wonderful. Mark the Fantasy Stitches you like, and put the sample in your notebook.

The basting button sews every sixth stitch, so you can get a stitch over 1″ (2.5cm) long. It, too, can be combined with other stitches, but doesn't produce nifty combinations as does the long-stitch button.

The balancing buttons can be pushed at

163

CHART 11.1

Fantasy Stitches

1.	1	M	M	M	M	27	M				
2.	6	/-5	[buttonhole]								
3.	6	/+5	[double stitch]								
4.	7	M	[single pattern]	M	/-9	[buttonhole]					
5.	11	/-2	[long stitch]	[buttonhole]							
6.	11	/-3	[double stitch]	[buttonhole]							
7.	11	/-4	[double stitch]								
8.	11	/-6	[long stitch]								
9.	11	/-11	SL 3								
10.	11	+3/	[long stitch]	[double stitch]							
11.	11	+4/	[long stitch]	[buttonhole]							
12.	11	[long stitch]	[double needle]								
13.	11	M	[single pattern]	M							
14.	11	M	[single pattern]	M	/-3	[long stitch]	[double needle]				
15.	11	M	[single pattern]	M	/-4	[long stitch]	[double stitch]	[double needle]			
16.	11	M	[single pattern]	M	/-8	[long stitch]					
17.	11	M	[single pattern]	M	/-8	[long stitch]	[double needle]				
18.	11	M	M	[single pattern]	M	M	[long stitch]				
19.	11	M	26	M	11	[single pattern]	M	26	M	/-8	[long stitch]
20.	11	M	26	M	11	[single pattern]	M	26	M	/-10	[long stitch]

Legend

[icon]	Buttonhole
[icon]	Pattern begin
D	Single pattern
R	Mirror image
[icon]	Double stitch pattern
[icon]	Double needle limitation
U	Reverse sewing button
¦	Long stitch
+/−	Balance
M	Memory
SW	Stitch width
SL	Stitch length

164

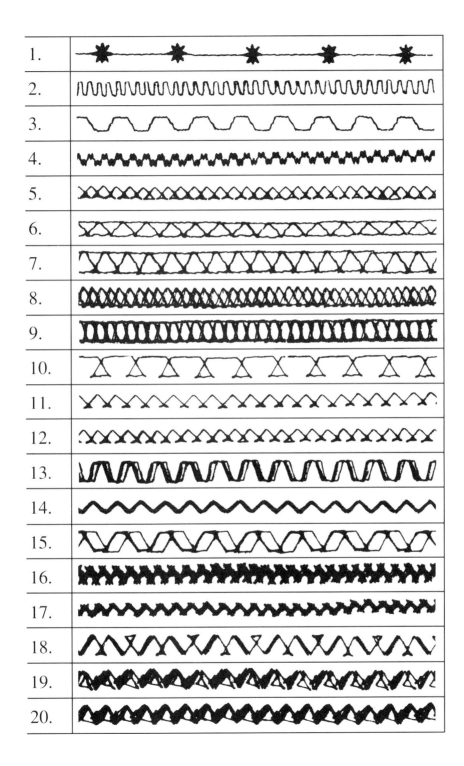

#										
21.	12	Balance −4								
22.	12	Balance +26	Reverse sewing							
23.	12	Long stitch								
24.	12	M	Pattern begin	M	Double needle					
25.	12	M	Pattern begin	M	Balance −5					
26.	12	M	Pattern begin	M	Balance +26	Reverse sewing				
27.	12	M	Pattern begin	M	Balance −1	Long stitch	Double stitch pattern			
28.	12	M	Pattern begin	M	Balance +5	Long stitch	Double stitch pattern			
29.	12	M	Pattern begin	M	Balance −5	Long stitch				
30.	12	M	30	M	12	Pattern begin	M	30	Pattern begin	M
31.	13	Balance −7	Double stitch pattern							
32.	13	Balance −12	SL 4							
33.	13	Balance −12	SL 4	Double needle						
34.	13	Balance +26	Reverse sewing							
35.	13	M	Pattern begin	M	Long stitch					
36.	13	M	Pattern begin	M	Balance +26	Reverse sewing				
37.	13	M	30	M	Balance +27	Reverse sewing				
38.	14	M	Pattern begin	M	Double needle					
39.	14	M	Pattern begin	M	Balance −5					
40.	14	M	Pattern begin	M	Balance +5					

Legend:

(buttonhole)	Buttonhole
(pattern begin)	Pattern begin
D	Single pattern
(mirror)	Mirror image
(double)	Double stitch pattern
(double needle)	Double needle limitation
U	Reverse sewing button
|	Long stitch
+/−	Balance
M	Memory
SW	Stitch width
SL	Stitch length

166

21.	
22.	
23.	
24.	
25.	
26.	
27.	
28.	
29.	
30.	
31.	
32.	
33.	
34.	
35.	
36.	
37.	
38.	
39.	
40.	

41.	15	⫼ (long stitch)						
42.	15	M	▷ (pattern begin)	M				
43.	15	M	▷ (pattern begin)	M	⫼ (long stitch)			
44.	16	/-2 (balance)	⇅▷ (double stitch)					
45.	16	/-10 (balance)						
46.	16	/-12 (balance)	$\frac{SW}{2\frac{1}{2}}$	⇅▷ (double stitch)				
47.	16	+14/ (balance)						
48.	16	M	14	M				
49.	16	M	27	M	/-2 (balance)	⇅▷ (double stitch)		
50.	16	M	▷ (pattern begin)	M	⇅▷ (double stitch)			
51.	17	+7/ (balance)						
52.	17	⫼ (long stitch)						
53.	17	M	▷ (pattern begin)	M				
54.	17	M	1	M	M			
55.	18	+9/ (balance)	↺ (reverse sewing)					
56.	18	+9/ (balance)	↺ (reverse sewing)	⇅▷ (double stitch)				
57.	18	⫼ (long stitch)	/-2 (balance)					
58.	18	D◀ (single pattern)	▷ (pattern begin)					
59.	18	M	1	M	/-2 (balance)			
60.	18	M	1	M	⫼ (long stitch)	/-2 (balance)		

Legend:

🔲	Buttonhole
▷	Pattern begin
◁	Single pattern
ꟿ	Mirror image
⇅▷	Double stitch pattern
⫼	Double needle limitation
↺	Reverse sewing button
⫼	Long stitch
+/−	Balance
M	Memory
SW	Stitch width
SL	Stitch length

41.	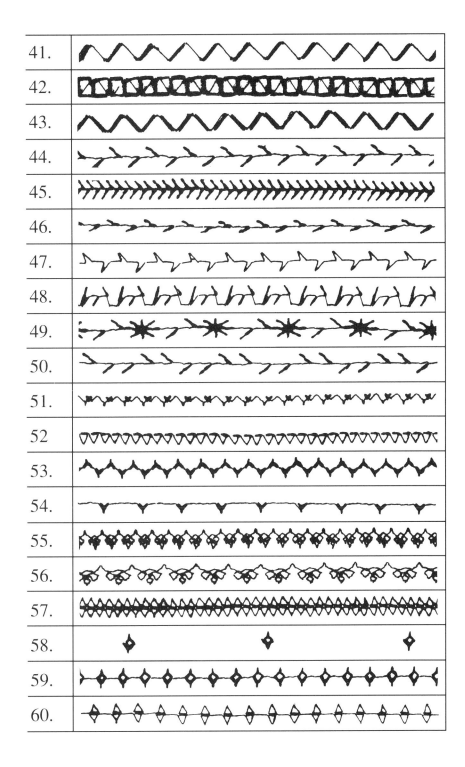
42.	
43.	
44.	
45.	
46.	
47.	
48.	
49.	
50.	
51.	
52	
53.	
54.	
55.	
56.	
57.	
58.	
59.	
60.	

61.	21	/-5	D←	D←						
62.	21	/-5	D←	D←	(buttonhole)					
63.	23	M	D:	M	/-6					
64.	23	M	D:	M	/-6	(long stitch)				
65.	24	(double stitch)								
66.	24	+6/	(double needle)							
67.	26	(long stitch)								
68.	26	SL/4	(double stitch)							
69.	26	(double needle)								
70.	26	M	1	M						
71.	27	/-4	(double stitch)							
72.	27	D←	D←							
73.	28	/-2								
74.	28	+6/								
75.	28	+12/	(reverse)	(double stitch)						
76.	28	+20/	(reverse)	(double stitch)						
77.	28	M	D:	M	(double needle)					
78.	28	M	D:	M	+5/					
79.	28	M	D:	M	+15/	(reverse)				
80.	28	M	M	D:	M	M	+1/			

Legend:

(buttonhole)	Buttonhole
D:	Pattern begin
D←	Single pattern
D:	Mirror image
(double stitch)	Double stitch pattern
(double needle)	Double needle limitation
(reverse)	Reverse sewing button
(long stitch)	Long stitch
+/−	Balance
M	Memory
SW	Stitch width
SL	Stitch length

170

61.	
62.	
63.	
64.	
65.	
66.	
67.	
68.	
69.	
70.	
71.	
72	
73.	
74.	
75.	
76.	
77.	
78.	
79.	
80.	

#	Col1	Col2	Col3	Col4	Col5	Col6	Col7	Col8	Col9
81.	29	/−9 (balance)	Double needle limitation						
82.	29	+15	Reverse sewing	Double stitch pattern					
83.	29	+26	Reverse sewing	Double stitch pattern					
84.	30	/−4 (balance)	SW/2	SL/1					
85.	30	+1	SL/1	Double needle limitation					
86.	30	+4	SW/4	SL/1					
87.	30	+21	Reverse sewing						
88.	30	+24							
89.	30	M	Mirror image	M	+24				
90.	30	M	Mirror image	M	+30	Reverse sewing			
91.	30	+30	Reverse sewing						
92.	30	M	Mirror image	M	+10				
93.	30	M	M	Mirror image	M	M	+1		
94.	30	M	M	Mirror image	M	M	+21	Reverse sewing	
95.	30	M	Mirror image	M	+21	Reverse sewing			
96.	31	/−2 (balance)							
97.	Buttonhole	SL/1½	Double stitch pattern						
98.	Buttonhole	M	Mirror image	M	SL/1½	Double stitch pattern			
99.	Buttonhole	M	Mirror image	M	/−10 (balance)				
100.	Buttonhole	M	Mirror image	M	1	M	1	M	Double stitch pattern

Legend:

(buttonhole icon)	Buttonhole
(pattern begin icon)	Pattern begin
D (single pattern icon)	Single pattern
R (mirror icon)	Mirror image
(double stitch icon)	Double stitch pattern
(double needle icon)	Double needle limitation
U (reverse icon)	Reverse sewing button
I	Long stitch
+/−	Balance
M	Memory
SW	Stitch width
SL	Stitch length

81.	
82.	
83.	
84.	
85.	
86.	
87.	
88.	
89.	
90.	
91.	
92.	
93.	
94.	
95.	
96.	
97.	
98.	
99.	
100.	

Fig. 11.2 Stitch and function button panel of the Bernina 1130.

least 30 times each to open out (+) or close up (−) stitches. Use them in practical sewing to keep stitches shaped perfectly no matter what fabric you're using, or when stitching buttonholes — stitch length affects the first bead of a buttonhole while the balancing buttons adjust the second bead. In Fantasy Stitches, the balancing buttons shorten or lengthen the stitches within the built-in stitch.

The last button on the panel clears the function buttons. By pressing the clear button once, the memory is cancelled.

Press twice, the clear button cancels reverse, balance, single pattern, mirror and double stitch. It will not clear needle down, ½ speed or double needle limitation. If you want to cancel those, press the button you want cleared or turn off the machine.

On the panel under the decorative stitches, you'll find special functions. The first button is single pattern. To stitch one pattern and stop on exactly the last stitch, then press this button. It's also useful when turning the fabric around and returning, combining the first row of pattern with the second row—exactly stitching point to point. If you have more than one stitch in memory and press this button, the machine will stitch through all the stitches in memory before it comes to a stop after the last stitch of the last pattern.

Mirror image is next. It's helpful to make up a sampler of practical and decorative stitches, first placing a stitch in memory, then its mirror image in memory, then stitching a row of pattern. Look at the stitches. It won't change some of them, but the ones it will change are usually those facing in one direction. Using the mirror image in combination with a built-in stitch makes the Fantasy Stitch symmetrical. Also use mirror image for convenience. It's always more comfortable to keep bulky fabric to the left of the presser foot when you sew, but if that is impossible because the stitch faces the wrong way, press mirror image to reverse it. For example, when I stitch at the edge of an appliqué with stitch #26, which looks like a hand-made buttonhole stitch, I sometimes mirror image the stitch so I can keep the bulk of the fabric to the left, or I might find it easier to use a mirror image in certain areas of my appliqué so I don't have to keep turning my fabric around.

The next button, double stitch, is pressed to sew a stitch twice as long as the original one without losing any of the density.

Double needle limitation, the next special function, is used to narrow the stitch width to 3mm, so the needles won't hit the edges of the opening in the needle plate. Whether you actually use a double needle or not, this function is useful when you want narrowed stitches in the memory. Otherwise, stitch width in memory is always the machine's basic setting; the only way you can narrow it is to use the double needle function. Also use the double needle limitation in clothing construction—to narrow buttonholes on fine fabrics, doll and baby clothes. I used it on the baby shoes later in this chapter.

The last button is memory. Combinations of up to five stitches plus alterations (except stitch width and length) can be placed in memory. Without the memory, you can combine one stitch with function buttons, including stitch width and stitch length.

To invent your own Fantasy Stitches, remember that only the order in which built-in stitches and mirror images are entered is important, because only the mirror image function affects individual stitches in the memory. All the other function buttons affect every stitch in memory so they can be pushed at any time—in any order—before or after the memory is put in. That is why you see directions for Fantasy Stitches written in so many ways. To bring order to the directions and to my mind, I construct and record each Fantasy Stitch by following the same progression.

Here is an example of that progression: First, I push in a built-in stitch. Do I want the stitch as shown? If so, then I press the memory button to lock in the stitch. Or do I prefer a mirror image of the stitch? If so, then after pressing the stitch button, I press mirror image, and finally press memory. To repeat mirror image, I press memory again. To add another stitch, I press the appropriate stitch and memory button. To repeat the last stitch, memory is pressed again. When all the stitches are entered, then I modify the selection by general and special function buttons. Now you have all the tools to build your own Fantasy Stitches.

I suggest you stitch up several of the Fantasy Stitches provided in the chart before you begin experimenting on your own because my directions will become much clearer to you after you have become familiar with the stitch, general and special function buttons—and you've seen the results.

Project
Fantasy Stitch Doll

This rag doll, shown in the color section, takes Fantasy Stitches out of your notebook to become a colorful record of your favorites. If you prefer, use the striped fabric and colorful Fantasy Stitches to create a tote-bag square.

I used medium-weight cotton/polyester striped fabric for the doll. The white stripes, on which I stitched, are ¼" (6.4mm) wide, which is a perfect width for my decorative stitches; the bright blue stripes between them are a narrow ⅛" (3.2mm) wide.

Stitch width: use machine settings
Needle: #90/14; #100/16 jeans
Feed dogs: up
Presser foot: #030 (#6) embroidery; #560 (#1) multi-motion
Tension: *top*, normal; *bobbin*, normal
Fabric suggestion: 24" × 10" (61cm × 25.4cm) royal-blue-and-white-striped medium-weight fabric (make short side parallel to stripes)
Thread: blue sewing thread; red, yellow, purple, green, and orange machine-embroidery cotton for top and bobbins (or use white basting thread in bobbin throughout)
Accessories: nine 6" lengths of ¼"-wide (15.2cm × 6.4mm) grosgrain ribbon — red, orange, green, yellow; wooden, large-holed beads in same colors; fiberfill or quilt batting; rotary cutter and mat; 6" × 24" (15.2cm × 61cm) ruler
Stabilizer: iron-on, crisp tear-away

First, back the 24" × 10" (61cm × 25.4cm) piece of striped fabric with iron-on, crisp tear-away stabilizer. The doll is created from fabric stitched with *my* favorite Fantasy Stitches, but of course you'll use the ones you prefer. Using green machine-embroidery cotton and the multi-motion or embroidery foot, stitch down the first white stripe at the edge, then every fifth white stripe with a Fantasy Stitch. Change to orange thread and stitch in the second stripe, then every fifth stripe, with more Fantasy Stitches. Continue in the same manner using red, purple, and yellow thread. After the stripes are all filled in with Fantasy Stitches, use the ruler, rotary cutter and mat to trim the rectangle ½" (12.7mm) at both long sides. This will cut off the threads and clean up the edges. Change to blue sewing thread and sew a guideline of straight stitches 1" (2.5cm) from the bottom edge, across the 24" (61cm) width. (It's easier and more accurate to fold under fabric on a guideline of stitches — which you'll do later). Leave the stabilizer in place (it's impossible to remove). Cut the embellished fabric (always cut on a blue stripe) into six rectangles, each 4" × 9" (10.2cm × 22.9cm). Place right sides of two rectangles together, with the line of blue straight-stitches at the bottom. Cut out the head and shoulders of the doll, following the pattern (Fig. 11.3).

Fold each piece of grosgrain ribbon in half and, following the diagram in Fig. 11.4, place ribbon folds on the raw edge of one side of the doll's head. Pin as shown, then machine baste the ribbons ⅛" (3.2mm) from the edge of the head. Place right sides of the doll (head and body) together and stitch around the outside (except for the bottom), using a ¼" (6.4mm) seam allowance. Turn right-side-out. Fold the bottom edge up and inside on the line of straight-stitching and press in place.

Arms and legs are each made from one rectangle. To make an arm, fold a rectangle in half the long way so right sides are together and the line of straight-stitching is at the top. At the bottom, draw a hand shape as shown in Fig. 11.3, stitch around three sides, leaving the top open, and turn to the right side.

To shape the foot, machine stitch small darts at the ankles as shown in Fig. 11.5.

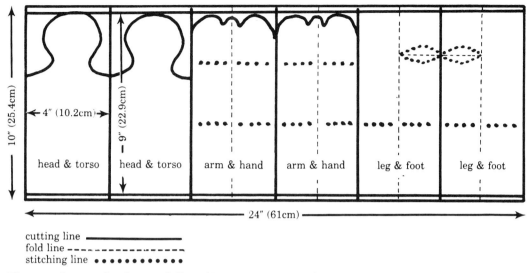

head & torso	head & torso	arm & hand	arm & hand	leg & foot	leg & foot

10" (25.4cm)

4" (10.2cm)

9" (22.9cm)

24" (61cm)

cutting line ─────────
fold line ─ ─ ─ ─ ─ ─ ─ ─
stitching line ● ● ● ● ● ● ● ● ● ●

Fig. 11.3 Pattern for the rag doll, indicating cutting, folding, and stitching lines.

Then fold each of the two rectangles in half the long way, right sides together, with straight-stitching at the top. Stitch around each leg, except for the top, and turn right-side-out.

Stuff the head and body of the doll tightly with fiberfill or batting so the neck will not bend. (I use a 10″ long stuffing tool, which is a dowel, ½″ in diameter,

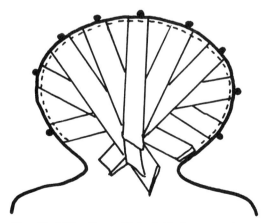

Fig. 11.4 Pin, then stitch, folded grosgrain ribbon to the head of the doll.

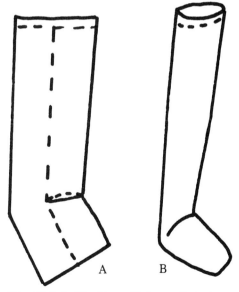

A   B

Fig. 11.5 A. Machine stitch small dart to create the foot. B. Stitch down the side and across the foot end to make each leg. Turn right-side-out.

sharpened to a blunt point on one end and a chisel shape on the other end. The handle of a wooden spoon works well, too).

Arms and legs are next. Determine where you'll stitch joints on the arms and legs and use less batting in those areas when you stuff them, because you'll straight stitch across the fabric and batting at each joint. Change to the jeans needle to straight-stitch from one side of the joints to the other and then back again with bright blue thread.

Fold in the tops of the arms and legs at the lines of straight stitching by pushing down the fabric edges to the insides. With a hand needle and thread, whip together the tops of the arms at the fold line.

To assemble the doll (Fig. 11.6), slip the legs inside the bottom opening, pin, then stitch in place by hand, poking the needle from front to back through all the layers, catching the edges of the folds of the bottom with every stitch. You can machine stitch, using invisible thread and a jeans needle, and attach the legs by stitching across at the bottom edge of the doll, but I think hand stitching, in this case, looks more professional.

Fold one arm in half at the top and slip the shoulder of the doll into the fold (Fig. 11.6). Hand-stitch through the folds of the arm, and through the shoulder, stitching from front to back across the top edge of the arm to attach it.

Thread each doubled ribbon through a wooden bead, as shown, then push the beads down to within ⅜" (9.5mm) of the seam.

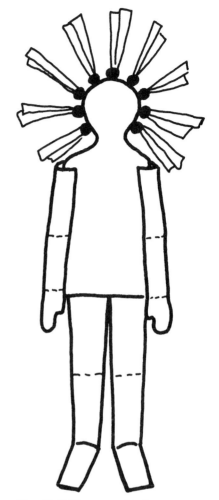

Fig. 11.6 The assembled doll, with joints and darts stitched, will look like this.

Lesson 38. Stitches to wear

Although not advertised as such, practical stitches can be decorative, too. They often cross over the line, depending on whether you use them in practical ways like overcasting seams, or creatively in embroideries and lacemaking. Likewise, decorative stitches can be practical — sew hems in linings with decorative, built-in stitches, use them to quilt, or to sew fabrics together.

When decorative stitches are used in this chapter, I often use the machine's basic settings for stitch width and stitch length. If so, I'll indicate that and, if needed, I'll also give settings for models other than the 1130. Built-in stitches used in the projects are numbered (1130) or named for use with other models. Not all models contain the same built-in stitches so I'll suggest alternate stitches.

Project
Child's Pleated Blouse

This pleated blouse is made from a green cotton/polyester blend, decorated with three pleats that are manipulated to lay flat on one side and flip up on the other side (Fig. 11.7). The flipped-up edges reveal a polka dot fabric. Holding the edges of the pleats together is feather stitch #16, though you can substitute a favorite open embroidery stitch. I chose yellow thread for the top, and red for the bobbin; yellow thread is visible when the pleats are pressed down, but red thread shows when the pleats are turned up.

Stitch width: 1–3
Stitch length: 1–2 1/2
Needle position: center
Needle: #80/12
Feed dogs: up
Presser foot: #147 (#20) open embroidery
or #560 (#1) multi-motion

Fig. 11.7 Child's pleated blouse.

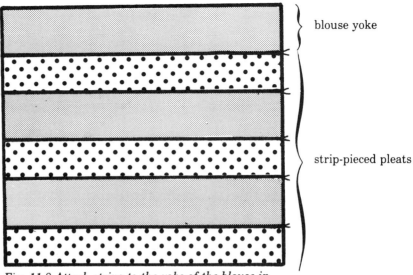

Fig. 11.8 Attach strips to the yoke of the blouse in this order.

Built-in stitch: #16 (double needle limitation, double stitch pattern)
Tension: *top,* normal; *bobbin,* normal
Fabric suggestions: green cotton/polyester blend; red, green, yellow, blue polka dot fabric for pleats
Thread: yellow and red machine-embroidery cotton; green sewing thread
Accessories: rotary cutter and mat; 6″ × 24″ (15.2cm × 61cm) plastic ruler; commercial blouse pattern

Use the following method to attach pleats and keep the inside of the blouse neat. First, using the ruler and rotary cutter, cut three polka dot strips, each 1½″ (3.8cm) deep by chest pattern width. Next cut two green strips, each 2½″ deep (6.4cm) and chest pattern width.

Check the front of the blouse pattern. Where should the pleats be inserted? Draw a line across, adding a ¼″ (6.4mm) seam allowance at this place. Lay the pattern on the green fabric. Cut out only the blouse yoke above the line you've drawn. Put aside the rest of the blouse fabric.

Next, strip-piece the polka dot and green fabric strips together. Using ¼″ (6.4mm) seam allowances, sew a polka dot strip to the blouse top. Next, sew one of the green strips to the polka dot strip you attached (Fig. 11.8). Then sew on another polka dot strip, and so on, until you've pieced togeth-

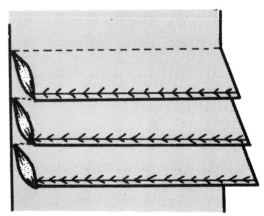

Fig. 11.9 Use decorative stitches along the edge of the pleats to hold them together.

er three polka dot strips and two green strips to the top of the blouse.

Next, cut a piece of green fabric for the bottom of the blouse. It will be a rectangle as wide as a polka dot strip (slightly more than chest width) and length needed (including hem and the seam allowances). Sew this, right sides together, to the top of the blouse.

Press open all the seams. Then press the pleats on the seam lines so only the blouse color shows, with the polka dots hidden underneath. Place the pattern over this and finish cutting out the blouse. Then, one by one, hold the outside pleat folds together and stitch, using #16 (double needle limitation, double stitch pattern) close to the fold of each pleat (Fig. 11.9). To keep the pleats from opening like an accordion and at the same time to neaten the underside of the blouse, press the seam allowances toward the inside of the pleats and pin them together. With green thread the exact color of the blouse, stitch-in-a-ditch across the bottom of each polka dot strip and through the green fabric, too, to permanently stitch the pleats in place (Fig. 11.10).

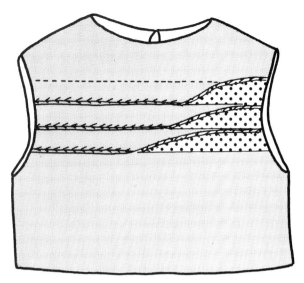

Fig. 11.11 Blouse with three turned-up pleats.

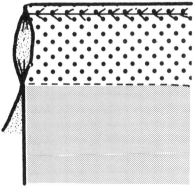

Fig. 11.10 Stitch-in-the-ditch across the bottom of each polka dot strip and through the green fabric underneath to hold the pleats in place.

Press down the pleats at the right side of the blouse and pin them in place. Finger press them *up* at the left side and pin (Fig. 11.11).

On the top pleat, 1″ (2.5cm) to the right of center front, tack the pleat down at the front edge with green thread and several anchoring stitches (Fig. 11.11). On the pleat under that, tack at center front. The third pleat is tacked, too, 1″ (2.5cm) to the left of center. Baste the pleats in place at the edges to keep them from shifting as you finish constructing the blouse.

Project
Bias Tape Collar

This collar design has its origins in the 30s, when white piqué bias strips were linked by hand embroidery. Our bias tape collar, shown in Fig. 11.12, can be made quickly and easily by machine, using one package of white double-fold bias tape.

Fig. 11.12 A 1930s look-alike collar.

Stitch width: 0–5
Stitch length: 2 1/2
Needle position: center
Needle: #70/10
Feed dogs: up
Presser foot: #000 (#0) zigzag; #492 (#10) edge
Built-in stitch: long stitch, #16 feather stitch or zigzag
Tension: *top,* normal; *bobbin,* normal
Fabric suggestions: one package double-fold white bias tape; purchased white lace trim for edge
Thread: wash-away basting thread (optional); white basting or sewing thread; white machine-embroidery cotton
Accessories: dressmaker's pins, pearl button, collar pattern, pencil, white permanent marker
Stabilizer: crisp tear-away, water-soluble

Choose a Peter Pan collar pattern that fits you comfortably and copy it onto a sheet of crisp tear-away stabilizer. Place two layers of water-soluble stabilizer over this, pin in place, and then transfer the outline of the collar to the water-soluble stabilizer with the white marking pen. You may want to leave the tear-away pinned in place for stability as you lay down the strips of bias tape, first pinning, then basting them in place (the tear-away should be cut away before you stitch the collar together or you will spend hours later picking stabilizer out of stitches with a tweezers). If you use this first method, baste with sewing thread (otherwise, the basting stitches may pull out when the tear-away is removed).

A second method is to pin the bias tape onto the water-soluble stabilizer and tear-away, but then carefully lift the water-soluble stabilizer and bias tape from the tear-away, removing pins and repinning to only the water-soluble stabilizer before you baste the tape in place with wash-away basting thread. I prefer a third method: pinning the bias directly to the two layers of water-soluble stabilizer, using wash-away basting thread to machine or hand bast the bias tape in place.

Whichever method you use, pin the first strip of bias tape to the neck edge of the collar, open edge of the tape at top. Following the diagram in Fig. 11.13, always extend both ends of each strip of tape about ½" (12.7mm) past the edge of the collar at center fronts. Trim the bias tape to the length you need as you progress, not before you begin.

The second line of tape is pinned in place about ¹⁄₁₆" (1.6mm) from the first strip. Continue laying down tape and pinning until you get to the last strip. Begin that tape at the center front neck edge, leaving ½" (12.7mm) at the top beyond the starting point to fold in later (Fig. 11.13). *Don't pin down this last piece of tape* until you reach the bottom corner. Begin pinning at the bottom of the collar and continue on to the corner at the other side. Leave enough

tape free to extend around the corner and up past the top center front ½" (12.7mm). Cut the tape.

Either baste by hand or set your machine for the long stitch at the longest setting if you have it, or the longest straight-stitch setting. Baste down the tape with white basting or sewing thread or wash-away basting thread, depending on which method you chose earlier. Remove the pins as you progress and, when finished basting, carefully cut away the crisp tear-away (if you've used it).

Place the edge foot on the machine. Use stitch #16, stitch width 5, stitch length 2 1/2 or zigzag to stitch the tapes together. Keep the black bar of the edge foot between the tapes, but riding on the left edge (where bias is open) to stitch it closed and the tapes together.

When all but the last tape have been attached, clip off all the center-front tape ends at the pattern edge. At the top of the collar, clip off all but ¼" (6.4mm) of the two tape ends and fold them inside (Fig. 11.14). Then slip all the other tape ends in-

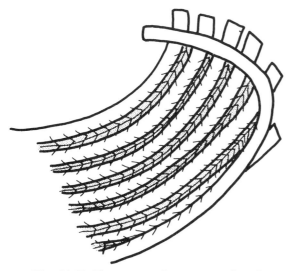

Fig. 11.13 Always extend tapes past the edge of the collar, but move edge tape away from center front before stitching tapes together with feather stitch #16.

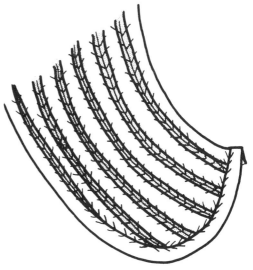

Fig. 11.14 Clip tapes off and slip them inside the edge of the last tape laid in place.

side the last strip of bias tape and pin the tapes in place. Fold the collar in half to check on the shape of it. Now is the time to change the rounded corners, if needed, to make them both the same.

Attach the last strip of bias by sewing from one corner, across to the other corner, up to the center front on one side. Go back, start at the corner again and stitch up the other side so the feather stitches face in the same direction in the center front. Clip basting threads or dissolve them when you remove the water-soluble stabilizer. To do this, first trim off as much of the stabilizer as you can before immersing the collar in water. Then when the stabilizer and threads are removed, dry the collar on a towel, gently patting it into shape. Press the collar carefully. Although you've used the feather stitch, as soon as the stabilizer is removed, it becomes a wide zigzag stitch.

The trim I used for edging has a straight edge on one side, to hold the flower shapes together. By hand, I stitched the straight edge of the trim under the edge of the collar and hand-stitched the bias tape closed at the neck edge as well. The last step is to attach a small pearl button at the top center of the left side, and make a button loop by hand on the other side.

Project
Leather and Ultrasuede Belt

Over the years I've collected Ultrasuede scraps—leftovers from clothing and accessories or purchased scraps from fabric stores and mail-order companies. This belt project (Fig. 11.15) introduces you to sewing leather and Ultrasuede; even if you need no introduction, this patternless idea is a simple way to make a comfortable, affordable, smashing designer belt.

Backed by Ultrasuede, the belt front combines Ultrasuede and leather scraps. The scraps I chose have been dyed interesting colors and many have been stamped with designs that give them wonderful textures. One of the multicolored, stamped pieces includes fuchsia, cornflower blue, light and dark gray, black, and mustard, so I used it as a guide when I chose other colored scraps from the bin at the fabric store and combined them all into a scrap belt.

Stitch width: 0–5
Stitch length: 1/2
Needle position: center, near left
Needle: #100/16 jeans needle
Feed dogs: up
Presser foot: #142 (#52) Teflon
Built-in stitch: #7 gathering, or use zigzag
Tension: *top,* normal; *bobbin,* normal
Fabric suggestion: Ultrasuede and leather scraps in assorted colors; black Ultrasuede 3″ (7.6cm) wide by waist length + 3½″ (8.9cm)—this can be pieced; one strip of black Ultrasuede 1″ (2.5cm) by twice as long as the belt + 7″ (17.8cm), which can be pieced; heavy black interfacing as long and wide as the belt
Thread: black polyester sewing thread
Accessories: rotary cutter and mat; 6″ × 24″ (15.2 × 61cm) see-through plastic ruler; 3″ (7.6cm) strip of black Velcro; sliver of soap; glue stick

Cut the heavy black interfacing to belt length and width: 3″ wide (7.6cm) by waist

Fig. 11.15 Use this layout for a belt of leather and Ultrasuede scraps.

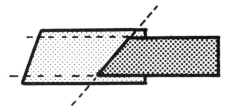

Fig. 11.16 Match edges before stitching by placing scraps right-sides-up. Overlap the edges of the leather you wish to match with the piece you are matching, then with ruler and rotary cutter, cut to match.

length + 3½″ (8.9cm). Beginning with the multicolored leather scrap, cut, using the rotary cutter and mat, a 3″ × 5″ (7.6cm × 12.7cm) piece to fit the belt. Instead of a perfect rectangle, slant one or both of the sides. Place this in the center of the interfacing and begin to add pieces of leather and Ultrasuede — first to one side, then the other. Don't cut any more yet; you are arranging for color and texture only. Vary the sizes of the scraps to make it visually more interesting, and repeat the colors or textures at least once.

When you're pleased with your arrangement, use the rotary cutter and mat to cut each piece into the size and shape you need. Edges will be butted, so it's important they meet perfectly. For accuracy when matching, overlap the edge of the second patch with the one you're matching, both with right sides up; with ruler placed on the top edge, use the rotary cutter to cut the exact slant of the first scrap (Fig. 11.16). When you have covered the interfacing, stand away from it and look to see if the combinations of colors and textures are pleasing. Adjust where necessary and, when you are satisfied, glue each piece in place on the interfacing. With the gathering stitch (#7) and Teflon foot, stitch down the centers between the leather patches or use a symmetrical, open embroidery stitch of your choice. Try a zigzag,

feather stitch, running stitch or sewn-out zigzag. Be careful to keep the stitches far enough apart so they don't cut the leathers.

When stitching is finished, use the ruler and rotary cutter to even the edges. Then place both belt ends together and round off the corners.

Apply the 1″ strip of black Ultrasuede next. If you must piece the strip, seam it first, then fold back the seam allowances and glue them down with the glue stick. With right sides together, place the 1″ (2.5cm) strip of edge-binding on the front edge of the belt (Fig. 11.17A). Place the right toe of the presser foot off the edge of the belt and, with needle position near left, stitch ⅛″ (3.2mm) from the edge. If you proceed slowly and accurately, there's no need to pin or glue beforehand, but you may want to use the ½ speed button. When you get 1″ (2.5cm) from the end, join the two ends, and trim them. Again, glue down the seam allowances, and continue stitching the strip to the belt.

Fold the Ultrasuede strip around the edge and glue it in place on the back of the interfacing (Fig. 11.17B). Stitch-in-a-ditch from the front to hold it in place.

Next, place one half of the Velcro strip on top of the belt at one end, centered and parallel to the sides. Straight stitch around the strip. The other half will be attached to

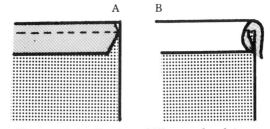

Fig. 11.17 Application of Ultrasuede edging strip. A. Stitch right sides of strip and belt together at edge. B. Fold the strip over the edge of the belt, glue, then stitch-in-the-ditch to hold it in place.

the opposite end—stitched to the Ultrasuede lining only. With a sliver of soap, mark the lining for placement of the Velcro strip. Then strengthen the Ultrasuede by backing it with a strip of interfacing before attaching the Velcro.

With glue stick, dot the back of the lining and press interfacing and back side of the lining together. Finish the belt by sewing stitch-in-a-ditch again around the edge, then cut back the Ultrasuede lining to the stitching to clean the edges.

Lesson 39. Stitches to give

Project Baby Shoes

Crazy as it sounds, originally this pattern began as a nut-cup at a baby shower. Then Sharon Knudson, a Bernina sewing specialist, showed me a tiny pair of baby shoes she had decorated with Fantasy Stitches for an expected grandchild. I was inspired to find my old pattern, modify it to fit feet instead of mints, change the strap and construction method and use it for this project (see color section). You can make the shoes larger or smaller by changing the length of the sole and adding or eliminating fabric at the back seam. If you'll notice, the shoe top is longer than needed to fit the sole. I did this for a reason: when the top is at least 1″ (2.5cm) longer, I don't have to fit and fudge the top and sole together on each side. I stitch one to the other and then cut off the excess fabric.

Stitch width: 0–5
Stitch length: 0–2
Needle position: center
Needle: #90/14
Feed dogs: up, lowered
Presser foot: #147 (#20) open embroidery,
    #24 freehand embroidery, or #285 (#9)
    darning
Built-in stitch: #21, #27 daisy, buttonhole,
    #17, #10 triple straight-stitch
Tension: *top,* normal, slightly loosened; *bobbin,* normal

Fabric suggestion: 8″ × 12″ (20.3cm × 30.5cm) heavy white felt; white flannel for lining
Thread: white sewing thread; mauve, light green, and pale yellow rayon machine embroidery
Accessories: 2 tiny pearl buttons, vanishing marker, glue stick, dressmaker's pins
Stabilizer: fusible knit interfacing

First, press the fusible interfacing to the back of the felt. Then, with vanishing marker, transfer the pattern outlines in Fig. 11.18 to the heavy felt, but don't cut out the shoes yet.

With the open embroidery foot on and white sewing thread on top and in the bobbin, stitch around the shoe top and sole to stabilize all the edges. Change to white machine embroidery thread and stitch again around the sole, a presser foot's width from the first line of stitching, using stitch #17 or a straight stitch. Use the needle-down button, single pattern and the knee lifter when turning the fabric at heel and toe curves.

Next, using the same white machine-embroidery thread and the triple straight stitch (#10), stitch around the front instep

Fig. 11.18 Pattern for baby shoes. A. Remember to flip the top pattern piece for the right shoe. B. Sole of the shoe. Cut two and write in the date of birth on the other sole. C. Understrap for the top of the shoes. Cut two.

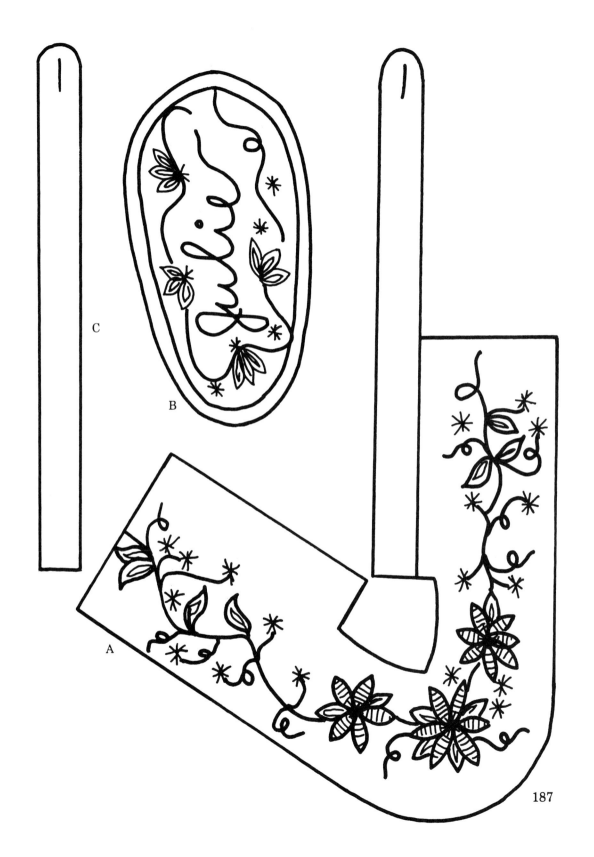

C

B

A

187

of each shoe on top of the line of straight stay-stitches.

Lower feed dogs, loosen top tension slightly, and with a darning or freehand embroidery foot, green thread on top and in the bobbin, freely stitch in the vines and leaves on the sides of both shoes as well as on the soles. Also stitch in the baby's name and date of birth if you wish.

Next, change to pale yellow thread and stitch in the flower petals (#21) and a scattering of daisies (#27) over the soles and shoe tops. Change to mauve thread and stitch in more daisies. Go back with green thread to add leaves and tendrils, and to connect some daisies with the vine.

Then cut out the shoes *outside* the white straight-stitching lines. Fold the shoe top in half the long way to find the center front. Mark it with a marker. Do the same with the sole, marking both front and back.

With right sides together, start from center front to baste the sole and shoe top together with ⅛″ (3.2mm) seam allowance, ending ½″ (12.7mm) from the center back. Go back to center front and baste around the other side, ending ½″ (12.7mm) from center back. Then lap the back edges (strap side will be on outside of the shoe) and adjust the top of the shoe to fit the sole. Pin overlapping sides together.

Then determine the center back of the shoe top, using the mark drawn on the sole as a guide. Measure ⅛″ (3.2mm) from each side of the center back and draw two lines down from top to bottom at these measurements. Then straight stitch or triple straight stitch (#10) down both lines from top edge of the shoe to the bottom. Trim back seam allowances to stitching lines on both inside and outside of the shoe (Fig. 11.19). First pin, then finish stitching the tops and soles of the shoes together. Turn shoes right-sides-out.

Place the top edge of the long strap piece along the top inside edge of the shoe and glue in place. Triple straight stitch (#10)

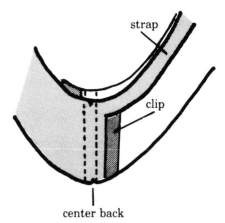

Fig. 11.19 *Pin top of the shoe to the sole, overlapping the shoe backs (strap on the outside), ending at center back. Stitch down both sides of center back, then clip at strap and cut off extra fabric back to stitching lines on the outside and inside of the shoe.*

or straight stitch, from the front around the strap to attach it. At the side of each shoe, opposite from the strap, sew a small pearl button. Change back to white sewing thread and the open embroidery foot (so you can see clearly), feed dogs up, tension normal. Stitch the buttonhole on the strap using the double needle limitation.

Construct the lining by first sewing the flannel pieces together as you did the shoe, eliminating the straps. Pin the flannel lining in the shoe, wrong sides together, while you custom fit the lining to the shoe. Fold under and pin the top of the lining at the bottom edge of the strap and around the front of the shoe. Use the vanishing marker to indicate the fold line. Take the lining out of the shoe and stay-stitch on the fold. Trim lining back to ⅛″ (3.2mm) from the stitching and clip curves. Then pin the lining into the shoe again and stitch in place by hand.

188

Project
Receiving Blanket

Another baby gift idea is this necessary, most welcome blanket (see color section). Instead of the skimpy receiving blankets we know and hate, this one is a generous size: warm, soft, and washable. It's a gift for both the new mother and new baby.

Stitch width: 0–widest
Stitch length: use machine setting
Needle position: center
Needle: #80/12
Feed dogs: up
Presser foot: walking foot, #560 (#1) multi-motion, #030 (#6) embroidery
Built-in stitch: #16, feather stitch; sewn-out zigzag; Fantasy Stitches; #9 or #16 on 830 model
Tension: *top,* normal; *bobbin,* normal
Fabric suggestion: two flannel squares, each 45″ (1.1m); one plain piece, one flowered
Thread: sewing or machine-embroidery thread to match fabric
Accessories: rotary cutter and mat, T-square, yardstick, vanishing marker, purchased satin blanket binding, quilter's pins, iron and ironing board

Flannel shrinks, so before you make this receiving blanket, wash both pieces of fabric and dry in the dryer. Next iron them, wrong sides together, starting at the top and pressing all the way to the bottom. This holds the fabrics together while you cut. Use a T-square, rotary cutter and mat to even up the top and bottom edges. Fold the square in half and press in a crease. Fold again and press, dividing the blanket into four parts. Open up the fabric. Turn it 90 degrees, fold in half, press, then fold in half and press again to divide the blanket into eight sections.

With a vanishing marker and yardstick, draw in lines at the folds. This is a small project, so I use only quilter's pins to hold it together while I stitch. If you have a walking foot, use it. If not, then use the #560 (#1) multi-motion foot or #030 (#6) embroidery foot. Choose a decorative stitch or Fantasy Stitch and sew the two pieces of fabric together, following the lines you've drawn in (Fig. 11.20) Remember that the lines will intersect and you may not want the jumble that can occur if the stitch is not chosen wisely. My favorite stitch to use is the feather stitch #16 or sewn-out zigzag. On my 830 I use #9 and #16, both symmetrical embroidery stitches.

When the embroidery is finished, double check to be sure the blanket is still even. If it isn't, take out the T-square, rotary cutter and mat again to trim any edges that need straightening. I'm not worried about whether the blanket is still an exact square. It won't even be 45″ (1.1m).

To hold the two flannel pieces together at the edges, straight stitch all around the outside, placing the outside edge of the presser foot at the edge of the blanket.

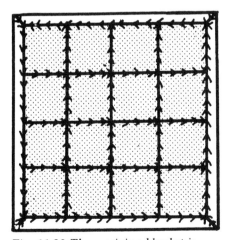

Fig. 11.20 The receiving blanket is divided in sections as shown, and bound with satin blanket binding using the same decorative stitch to hold the fabric together and attach the binding.

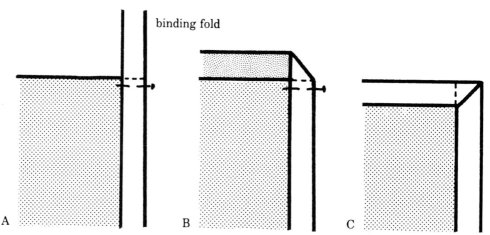

binding fold

Fig. 11.21 Miter the corners of the blanket binding. A. Slip blanket into binding and pin at the top corner. B. Fold a 45-degree angle from the corner to edge of binding on top of the blanket. Underneath, fold binding in as you make another 45-degree angle from corner to edge. C. Then fold binding down over the front edge of the blanket, creating the miter on the right side.

Start at one corner and slip the edge of the blanket down into the fold of purchased satin blanket binding and pin in place. Miter the corners as shown (Fig. 11.21). Baste, using the long stitch, or by hand, paying careful attention to the corners. Then stitch at the edge of the binding, using the same decorative stitch used to hold the blanket together (see Fig. 11.20). You may want to use ½ speed at this time. Remove the basting thread and press.

Project Badges and Awards

Sometimes I want to give a pat on the back or thanks to someone, so I stitch up an award for them (Fig. 11.22). Stitching on felt is the fastest, but I may also use woven fabric and finish them as I did the pendants (Chapter 2). After embroidering

my accolade, I cut another plain fabric piece for the back and stretch both fabrics over two circles of cardboard, with or without batting between the fabric and board. Using button forms the size of the pendants is also an idea, if you want a more conservative size. Jazz up the buttons with ribbons or fringe, slipping either between the two halves before you stitch them together.

Stitch width: 0–widest
Stitch length: varies
Needle position: center
Needle: #90/14
Feed dogs: up, lowered
Presser feet: #560 (#1) multi-motion, #030 (#6) embroidery, #528 (#12) bulky overlock (knitter's)
Built-in stitch: #26, #27, #13, satin stitch, Fantasy Stitches, embroidery stitches of choice
Tension: *top*, normal, slightly loosened; *bobbin*, normal
Fabric suggestion: medium to heavy-weight cotton, or felt

Fig. 11.22 Badges to thank, extoll, and commemorate.

Thread: rayon and metallic machine-embroidery; sewing thread
Accessories; circular embroidery device, heavy craft glue, mat board, ribbon, yarn, fringe, safety pins, hand-sewing needle, vanishing marker, fabric shears
Stabilizer: freezer paper

Before I began to stitch these three badges, I backed all the fabrics I chose with ironed-on freezer paper. Each of the circles, and circles within the circles, was stitched perfectly, using the circular embroidery device. It's not necessary to stitch only straight stitches or satin stitches when you use this accessory, and I experimented with several decorative built-in stitches. I didn't hesitate to stitch decorative stitches on top of satin stitches.

After I stitched circles on each badge, I took my fabric off the circular device and then removed the device from the machine. Using a vanishing marker, I drew in the placement for more decorative stitches and added names and greetings.

"Happy Birthday, Jenny" was decorated with daisies (#27, single pattern) and a few free machine-embroidered butterflies (Fig. 11.23). The greeting was done freely, too, with several passes of straight-stitch writing. Using a fringing fork, I made enough red fringe to encircle the edge. Instead of ribbons, I made Jenny two braids of red yarn and tied an orange ribbon at the end of each one. The last thing I added to the badge was a large safety pin. I stitched it by hand at the top back of the circle—the fringe will hide it. All three

Fig. 11.23 A birthday badge for Jenny.

Fig. 11.24 The recipient's name becomes part of the design when it's repeated around the circle.

badges were finished like this. Or add a loop of thread at the top of the circles so they can be hung on walls as decorations.

The next button was done in medium-weight cotton also, embroidered and finished like the first. The words "Thank You" are in the center of the badge, written freely in straight stitch (Fig. 11.24). Around the satin stitch circle I repeated the name of the young man I am thanking—in this case, Steve. The last flourish of the last letter "e" becomes the beginning of the first letter "S" and his name is a never-ending circle.

I often personalize gifts the same way. I used the name "Nancy," repeated in bold satin stitches, around the border of a quilt. A tote bag I made (Fig. 4.12) has a quilted lining that is folded inside at the top, and held in place by Pat Pasquini's name written freely in lower case letters for a border. Instead of a name, it looks like a design at the top of the inside edge. On Steve's badge, the name also looks like part of the overall design. It's not expected and I like that long-cut.

To decorate Steve's badge, I cut a strip of felt 2″ (5.1cm) wide and long enough to

Fig. 11.25 To tell a friend he's tops, give
him an award as a reminder.

stretch around the circle. It's clipped into
fringe and glued to the inside, between the
front and back of the circles. Grosgrain
ribbons of different colors, lengths and
widths were cut and slipped inside the two
halves before I stitched the circles together.

On the third badge (Fig. 11.25), I'm telling a friend he's "Tops," making his ini-
tials part of the design, even turning one
set backward to balance it. The upholstery
fringe I satin-stitched over sticks out in
spikes around the edge of the circle. To
stitch the fringe, I used a bulky overlock
foot, stitch width at the widest, and a satin
stitch length. I clumped together several of
the 3″ (7.6cm) long fringe cords and satin
stitched tightly up and back over them
with the same color thread as the cord. At
the ends I left a tuft of fringe. This strip
was slipped between the two cardboard
halves and glued in place like the other
fringes.

I hope I've achieved my goal in this chapter—to introduce you to the infinite possibilities of the Bernina so you will not only
use your machine more creatively, but
you'll enjoy using it more.

CHAPTER 12

Making the Tote Bag

The year I became program chairman for an embroiderer's guild, I began to assess previous programs: Why was one a success, another a failure? I remembered the many needlework workshops I had taken, the many projects I had started in those classes and never finished because they were too big or demanded too much of my time. And I knew I wan't the only one who felt this way, as other members also had boxes of half-finished needlework.

Fig. 12.1 The tote bag, with one of the squares in position on the pocket.

That's when I came up with the idea of the tote bag. I asked the teachers that year to gear their workshops toward making samples small enough to fit in a 6″ (15.2cm) square frame. The fabric squares could then fit into the frames made by the handles on a tote bag I designed. Each new square could easily slip in and out. Not only were the class projects small enough to complete easily, but they were useful and decorative as well.

I'm using the same tote bag for this book (Fig. 12.1; see front cover also). After you've made the tote bag, it can be used to show off the sample squares found in the lessons.

First, I'll explain how to finish the squares you made throughout the lessons in this book. Then I'll explain the tote bag.

Finishing the squares

Specific instructions for each square are included in the lessons. A brief recap: Start with a piece of fabric large enough to fit in a 7″ (17.8cm) hoop, if you will be working with one. I suggest starting with a 9″ (22.9cm) square, as it is better to have extra fabric than not enough. The finished square will be 6¾″ (17.1cm). The area that will show in the frame will be 6″ (15.2cm) square. Cut a piece of acetate or cardboard 6¾″ (17.1cm) square to use as a template.

After completing the embroidery, quilting, appliqué—whatever the lesson calls for—center the acetate pattern over the square. Draw a line at the edge of the acetate all the way around with a water-erasable marker or white chalk pencil.

Back the square with stiff fabric, fleece,

or iron-on interfacing if it is not stiff enough for the pocket. Stitch along the line you've drawn and cut off the extra fabric to that line.

Slip typing paper or heavy tear-away stabilizer under the square. Finish by satin stitching at a stitch width 3 or 4 setting around the edge. Dab the corners with Fray-Check to keep them from raveling.

Glue or stitch Velcro dots under the corner of each square to correspond to the ones in the pocket frame. (If the square is stiff enough, this will not be necessary.) An alternative to Velcro is an idea from Marilyn Tisol of Hinsdale, Illinois. She backs

each square she makes by first cutting a piece of plastic canvas the size of the square; then she attaches the fabric square to it by whipping the edges together. The plastic is rigid enough to keep the square in the frame.

Tote bag construction

My tote bag is made of canvas, but it can be made of any heavy-duty fabric. I used canvas because I wanted a bag that would stand by itself. If the fabric you've chosen is not heavy enough, press a layer of fusible webbing between two layers of material. Whatever you choose, pre-wash and press all fabrics before you cut.

Supplies:
1½ yards (1.4m) of 36" (0.9m) canvas (includes body of bag, handles, pockets, and bottom of bag)
3⅛ yards (2.9m) of 1" (2.5cm) wide fusible webbing
Teflon pressing sheet
Four Velcro dots
Sewing thread to match canvas, or monofilament
Rotary cutter and board are timesavers
24" × 6" (61 × 15.2cm) plastic ruler
Water-erasable pen, pencil or sliver of soap
#492 (#10) edge foot, #145 (#8) jeans foot
Jeans needle

My tote (see cover) is made up of many colors and looks as if Dr. Seuss invented it. It includes royal blue for the bottom, yellow pockets, green handles, and red for the body of the bag.

I chose those colors because the striped lining fabric included them all. I backed the lining with Pellon fleece and quilted down each stripe to give my bag even more body. I added pockets to the lining, too.

Lining is optional, but if you choose to include one, you will need another piece of fabric at least 34" × 20" (86.4cm × 50.8cm). Add 20" × 20" (50.8cm × 50.8cm) to this if you wish to make pockets for your lining.

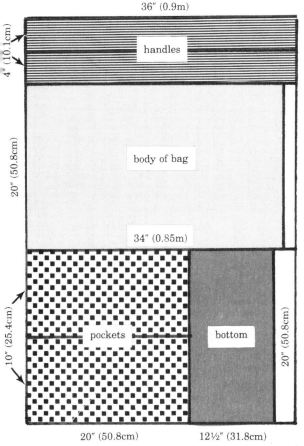

Fig. 12.2 Layout for the tote bag.

195

The layout of the bag is provided in Fig. 12.2; note that the layout is predicated on cutting all pieces from a single length of cloth, rather than several different colors.

Body of bag:
34″ × 20″ (86.4cm × 50.8cm)

1. Cut out fabric. Fold in half and notch bottom on both sides, 17″ (43.2cm) from top. Draw a line between the notches on the inside (Fig. 11.3).

2. Place a 1″ (2.5cm) strip of fusible webbing along both 20″ (50.8cm) edges on the right side of the bag and fuse in place using the Teflon pressing sheet. Fold at the top of the webbing to the backside. Press the fold, using the Teflon pressing sheet on top to protect your iron. Then fold over 1″ (2.5cm) again, using the pressing sheet *between* the fusible webbing and the body of the bag.

3. Mark a line down the length of this piece 6¼″ (15.8cm) from each side, as shown in Fig. 12.4 to use later as guidelines for construction of the bag.

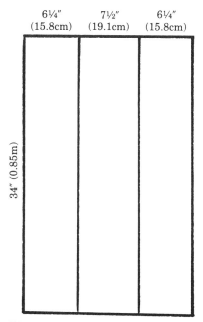

Fig. 12.4 Mark the outside of the bag.

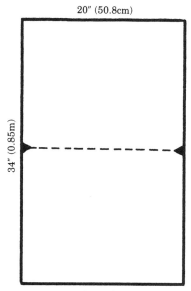

Fig. 12.3 Notch and mark the inside of the bag.

Pockets: 10″ × 20″
(25.4cm × 50.8cm); cut 2

1. Use the ruler and marking pen to indicate stitching lines from top to bottom–6¼″ (15.8cm) from each side. Center area will be 7½″ (19.1cm).

2. Cut slits 1½″ (3.8cm) down from the top on these lines. Make a mark ¾″ (19.0mm) from the top and another ¾″ (19.0mm) down from the first. Draw lines through those marks across the top of the pockets (Fig. 12.5A). It is easier if you mark the middle section on the *back* of the fabric, so you'll be able to see the lines as you fold. Fold on the lines as follows: Each side should be folded twice toward the inside of the bag. The middle 7½″ (19.1cm) should be folded twice toward the front of the fabric. This middle flap creates the top of the frame.

3. Stitch across the top of all three pockets ⅛″ (3.2mm) from the top edge. Do this on both pocket pieces.

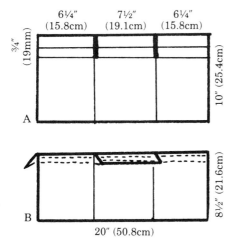

Fig. 12.5 Pocket construction. A. Mark lines to indicate the pockets. Then mark lines across the pockets, ¾" (19.0mm) and 1½" (3.8cm) from the top. Cut down 1½" (3.8cm) between the pockets. B. Fold the tops of the side pockets to the back, the top of the middle pocket to the front.

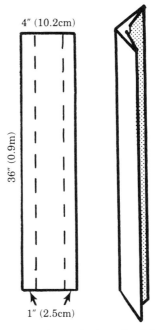

Fig. 12.6 Stitch down the length of the handles 1" (2.5cm) at each side. Fold down 1" (2.5cm) at each side, the length of the handle. Then fold the handle in half. Place strip of fusible webbing inside and press in place. Stitch the handles together.

4. Then stitch across side pocket sections through all three layers of fabric at ⅛" (3.2mm) from each bottom fold. Finish both side pockets on both pocket pieces this way (Fig. 12.5B).

5. Open out the top of the middle sections on both pocket pieces to enable you to stitch across the folds without stitching them to the pockets. Stitch across the 7½" (19.1cm) middle sections on both pocket pieces at ⅛" (3.2mm) from each bottom fold. This flap will create the top of the frames in which you'll slip the 6¾" (17.1mm) squares.

Handles: 4" × 36" (10.2cm × 0.9m); cut 2

1. Stitch down one long side 1" (2.5cm) from edge. Fold. Do the same with the other side. (This stitching is used as a guide to make folding the handles easier and more accurate.) Bring folded edges together and fold again, creating the 1" (2.5cm) wide handles. Place strips of 1" (2.5cm) fusible webbing inside the length of the handles and press to fuse. The handle is four layers (plus fusible webbing) thick (Fig. 12.6).

2. Topstitch both sides ⅛" (3.2mm) from edge. Use the #492 (#10) edge foot with needle position far left. Place the black bar at the edge of the handle and stitch. Then sew ¼" (6.3mm) in from those lines of stitches on both sides.

Bottom: 12½" × 20" (31.8cm × 50.8cm)

1. Fold over 1" (2.5cm) top and bottom along the 20" (50.8cm) edges and topstitch across ⅛" (3.2mm) from the fold. Draw a line ¾" (19.0mm) from each fold.

2. Fold the bottom in half the long way and notch on the fold on both sides, 6¼" (15.9cm) from top and bottom (Fig. 12.7).

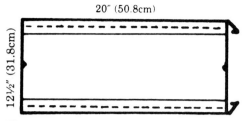

20″ (50.8cm)

12½″ (31.8cm)

Fig. 12.7 Follow this diagram to fold, mark and stitch the bottom piece of the bag.

Assembly

1. First sew pockets to the bag. The pockets will be 3″ (7.6cm) from the top. (Remember that the bag has been folded over 2″ (5.1cm) at the top. Measure from the top of the last fold. Line up the markings, 6¼″ (15.8cm) from each side on bag and pockets and pin in place. Stitch on the lines you've drawn to create pockets and, using a ¼″ (6.3mm) seam allowance, stitch down each side and across the bottoms of the pocket pieces.

2. Sew handles next. Find the center of the bag by folding it double the long way. Measure 3″ (7.6cm) from the center to each side of the bag and make a mark with the water-erasable pen; 6″ (15.2cm) will be open in center. Using the 24″ × 6″ (61cm × 15.2cm) ruler, draw guidelines through these marks the length of the bag. Pin handles in place outside those lines. Stitch across the bottom of the handles and up, ⅛″ (3.2mm) from the edge, on the existing outside stitching. Extend your stitching all the way to the top of the bag. Do this on the next outside lines as well (you will often stitch on top of other lines of stitching). The top edge of the bag will not be sewn down until later, but sew through the folds as you attach the handles.

3. To make the open frame, stitch only the top of the handles above the pockets on both sides. Leave ¾″ (19.0mm) around the frame to insert workshop squares (Fig. 12.8).

4. Attach bottom next. Match notches with those of the bag and pin the bottom in place. Stitch over the ⅛″ (3.2mm) stitching line to ¾″ (19.0mm) from each side of the center pocket (see Fig. 12.8). *Do not* stitch across the center pocket. Then stitch all across the bottom piece on the ¾″ (19.0mm) mark. This will create the bottom of the frame. Double check. Is the frame done correctly? Be sure you can slip a fabric square inside.

5. Finish the side edges of the bag with a zigzag stitch (Fig. 12.9). Then put it all together. Fold at center bottom notches with right sides together. Check to see that pockets and bottom meet at each side. Stitch in a ⅝″ (15.9mm) seam line from top to bottom. Now refold the top edge of the bag and press in place to fuse. Topstitch in place at the top edge and bottom fold.

6. Bag corners should be finished this way: On the inside, pinch the bottom by matching the side seam with the line drawn across the inside of the bottom of the bag (Fig. 12.10). Measure, on the seam line, 2″ (5.1cm) from the point. Draw a line across. Be sure it is exact on each side so stitching is perpendicular to the side seams. Stitch on drawn line for corners. This forms the bottom of the bag. If you wish to cut a piece of ⅛″ (3.2mm) Masonite or linoleum tile to fit the bottom, do so now before you line your bag.

7. Press one side of four adhesive-backed Velcro dots into the four corners of the frame.

Lining

If you line your bag, create the lining as if making another bag. Do not include bottom, pockets or handles. However, if you wish to add pockets to the lining, then cut out two pieces of 10″ × 20″ (25.4cm × 50.8cm) fabric, the same size as the bag pockets. At the top of each pocket piece, turn over 1″ (2.5cm) two times and sew down at the top and at the fold. Press up 1″ (2.5cm) at the bottom. Place the pocket

198

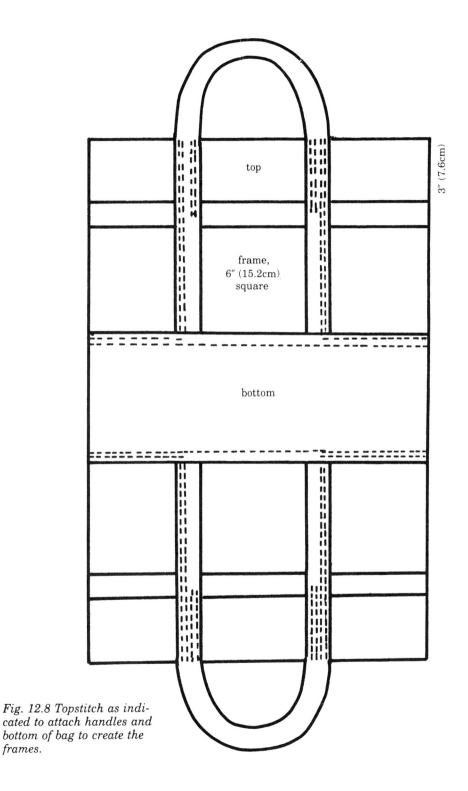

top

frame,
6″ (15.2cm)
square

3″ (7.6cm)

bottom

*Fig. 12.8 Topstitch as indi-
cated to attach handles and
bottom of bag to create the
frames.*

199

Fig. 12.9 Finish the edges with zigzag stitches. With right sides together, stitch each side of the tote bag.

Fig. 12.10 Make the tote bag corners by stitching lines perpendicular to the side seams, 2" (5.1cm) up from the points.

pieces 3" (7.6cm) from the top of the lining and pin in place. Sew across the bottom of the pocket at the fold and ¾" (19.0mm) from the first stitching line. (The double line of stitching will add strength to the pockets.) Then attach the pockets to the sides of the lining by stitching down on each side with a ¼" (6.3mm) seam allowance. With a ruler and water-erasable marker, draw lines down the pocket pieces to indicate where you will divide the fabric for pockets. Stitch those in place.

Sew up the sides of the lining, using a ⅝" (15.9mm) seam allowance, and create the bottom corner. Fold over the top as you did for the bag. I use the double fold for stability.

Whip stitch invisibly by hand around the top to keep the lining and bag together.

With heavy canvas, you may prefer to make the lining and then place wrong sides together (bag and lining) and machine stitch around the top.

AFTERWORD

Know Your Bernina could go on forever, as there is no way to include, in one book, everything that can be accomplished by this machine.

I hope you're as inspired as I am to experiment, to fill your notebook with samples, and to take those long-cuts, choosing decorative over mundane. If you aren't having fun, you aren't sewing on a Bernina.

The History of the Bernina Sewing Machine

MRS. ODETTE UELTSCHI-GEGAUF

Granddaughter, founder of Fritz Gegauf AG

In 1890, my grandfather, Friedrich Gegauf, settled in Steckborn on the Swiss side of the Lake of Constance. He started in his workshop by making attachments for sewing monograms and went on in 1893 to invent the first hemstitching machine. This was so quickly recognised and accepted by home sewers and experts alike that hemstitching or should I say "Gegauf's hemstitching" became a household word. This continued to such an extent that the name became a verb and one spoke of "gegaufing" instead of hemstitching. Gegaufing now meant a hem sewn by machine rather than one done by hand.

My father, Fritz Gegauf, took over the running of the factory in 1926 on the death of my grandfather. Towards the end of the twenties the demand for hemstitching machines began to decline as artificial silk was in vogue and this was not an ideal material to hem. It was high time for our firm to invent something new.

Every year 20,000 sewing machines were being imported into the country and most of them came from Germany. My father decided to compete in this market. The general idea was to bring out a first-class sewing machine for use by the housewife, that would be well constructed, strong and easy to handle. The first household sewing machines appeared on the market under the name of Bernina in 1932.

This was a tremendous success mostly because its technical capabilities were constantly being improved and it was of exceptionally good quality.

In 1938, Bernina produced the first Swiss zigzag sewing machine and in 1943 the first free-arm zigzag machine in the world. Each new model blazed its way straight on to the international market and the name of Bernina has since become a hallmark of top quality and precision.

In 1945, following the depression in the thirties and the second world war, the firm went into a frantic time of expansion. The factory, which in 1933 with sixty-five workers had produced 2,074 machines, now grew rapidly. By 1948 we put out 22,955 sewing machines with 515 workers and in 1981 with the help of 1,200 workers the firm was turning out over 150,000 Bernina machines per year.

Since it was founded in 1893, the firm of Fritz Gegauf AG has always been a family concern and will remain so in the future.

Nowadays, in Steckborn, we have centralised development, construction, production, marketing and sales. Bernina is officially represented in over a hundred countries and has eight subsidiary companies in the USA, Switzerland, Germany, France, Belgium, Sweden, Norway and Austria.

For me, as a woman, not only is the technical side important, both now and in the future, but also that represented by our slogan, "Bernina, a reputation for performance, reliability and good service". The technical side must meet the requirements of the market, but above all it must be what the average woman needs.

Reprinted by permission of Swiss/Bernina.

Chart of Presser Feet

Feet are in alphabetical order, reading down the columns.

187 short extension *177 long extension*

Adaptor shanks

189
Braiding foot

492
Edging foot

145
Jeans foot

181
Appliqué foot (clear)

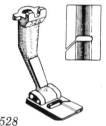

528
Bulky overlock foot

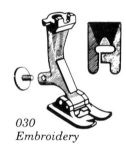

030
Embroidery

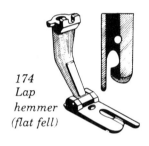

174
Lap hemmer
(flat fell)

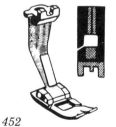

452
Automatic buttonhole

152
Button sew-on foot

508 (6mm)
179 (4mm)
Gathering foot

178
(8mm)
Lap hemmer
(industrial)

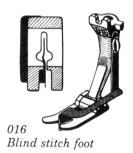

016
Blind stitch foot

285
Darning foot

003 (4mm)
Hemmer

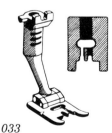

033
Non-auto buttonhole

147
Open embroidery

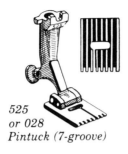

525
or 028
Pintuck (7-groove)

168
Roll and
shell hemmer

272
Wool darning

470
Overlock foot

164
or 589
Pintuck (9-groove)

038
Straight stitch

000
Zigzag

526
or 156
Pintuck (3-groove)

560
Red Dot foot (930)

419
Tailor tacking foot

007
Zipper foot

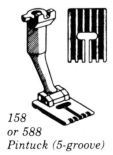

158
or 588
Pintuck (5-groove)

201
Roller foot

142
Teflon zigzag

Drawings reprinted
by permission from
Swiss/Bernina.
From parts manuals
for 840 and 930,
published by Fritz
Gegauf Ltd.,
Steckborn, Switzer-
land.

Bernina Feet in
1130 Number Sequence
Note: numbering for foot equivalents (if any)
on older machines appears in parentheses.

0	(000)	zigzag	32	(525)	pintuck, 7 groove
1	(560)	multi-motion	33	(569)	pintuck, 9 groove
2*	(470)	overlock	38	–	binding (cordless)
3*	(452)	buttonhole	51	(201)	roller foot
3a*	–	automatic buttonhole	52	(142)	Teflon zigzag
4*	(007)	zipper	53	(468)	Teflon straight stitch
5	(016)	blind stitch	54*	(547)	Teflon zipper
5	(030)	embroidery	55	(572)	leather roller foot
7	(419)	tailor tack	61	(166)	zigzag narrow hem, 2mm
8	(145)	jeans	62	(589)	straight stitch narrow hem, 2mm
9	(285)	darning			
10	(492)	edge	63	(252)	hemmer, 3mm
11	(499)	cordonette	64	(003)	wide hemmer, 4mm
12	(525)	bulky overlock (knitter's)	66	(415)	wide hemmer, 6mm
13	(038)	straight stitch	68	(168)	rolled hem, 2mm
16	(508)	gathering zigzag	70	(174)	lap hemmer (feller)
17	(179)	gathering zigzag	71	(178)	run and fell, 8mm
18	(152)	button sew-on	75	(177)	long extension (adaptor)
19	–	special button sew-on	77	(187)	short extension (adaptor)
20	(147)	open embroidery	83*	(018)	circular embroidery device
21	(189)	braiding	84	(121)	bias binder, 20–24mm
22*	–	couching	85	(077)	bias binder
23	(181)	appliqué	86	(165)	5 stitch ruffler
24	–	free-hand embroidery	90*	(578)	Cut'n'Sew
27	(033)	non-automatic buttonhole	91	(140)	zigzag for jersey
28	(272)	wool darning foot	92	(194)	English embroidery
29	–	special darning foot	94	(554)	binder
30	(526)	pintuck, 3 groove	99	–	zigzag with finger guard
31	(588)	pintuck, 5 groove	–	–	walking foot

*Not suitable for use on models older than 1130.

Sources of Supply

Bernina Information

Bernina of America
534 W. Chestnut
Hinsdale, IL 60521

(**Note**: The following listings were adapted with permission from *The Complete Book of Machine Embroidery* by Robbie and Tony Fanning [Chilton, 1986].)

Threads

Note: Ask your local retailer or send a pre-addressed stamped envelope to the companies below to find out where to buy their threads.

Extra-fine

Assorted threads
Robison-Anton Textile Co.
175 Bergen Blvd.
Fairview, NJ 07022

DMC 100% cotton, Sizes 30 and 50
The DMC Corporation
107 Trumbull Street
Elizabeth, NJ 07206

Dual-Duty Plus Extra-fine, cotton-wrapped polyester
J&PCoats/Coats & Clark
30 Patewood Dr., Ste. 351
Greenville, SC 29615

Iris 100% silk—*see* Zwicky

Madeira threads
Madeira Co.
56 Primrose Drive
O'Shea Industrial Park
Laconia, NH 03246

Mettler Metrosene Fine Machine Embroidery cotton, Size 60/2
Swiss-Metrosene, Inc.
7780 Quincy Street
Willowbrook, IL 60521

Mez Alcazar 100% Viscose rayon
Pfaff American Sales Corp.
610 Winters Ave.
Paramus, NJ 07653

Natesh 100% rayon, lightweight
Aardvark Adventures
PO Box 2449
Livermore, CA 94550

Paradise 100% rayon
D&E Distributing
199 N. El Camino Real #F-242
Encinitas, CA 92024

Sulky 100% rayon, Sizes 30 and 40
Speed Stitch, Inc.
PO Box 3472
Port Charlotte, FL 33949

Zwicky 100% cotton, Size 30/2
Viking White Sewing Machine Co.
11750 Berea Rd.
Cleveland, OH 44111

Ordinary

Dual Duty Plus, cotton-wrapped polyester—*see* Dual Duty Plus Extra-fine

Also Natesh heavyweight, Zwicky in cotton and polyester, Mettler Metrosene in 30/2, 40/3, 50/3, and 30/3, and Metrosene Plus

Metallic

YLI Corporation
45 West 300 North
Provo, UT 84601

Troy Thread & Textile Corp.
2300 W. Diversey Ave.
Chicago, IL 60647
Free catalog

Machine-Embroidery Supplies
(hoops, threads, patterns, books, etc.)

Aardvark Adventures
PO Box 2449
Livermore, CA 94550
Also publishes "Aardvark Territorial Enterprise"

Clotilde Inc.
1909 SW First Ave.
Ft. Lauderdale, FL 33315

Craft Gallery Ltd.
PO Box 8319
Salem, MA 01971

D&E Distributing
199 N. El Camino Real #F-242
Encinitas, CA 92024

Verna Holt's Machine Stitchery
PO Box 236
Hurricane, Utah 84734

Nancy's Notions
PO Box 683
Beaver Dam, WI 53916
    Free catalog

Patty Lou Creations
Rt 2, Box 90-A
Elgin, OR 97827

Sew-Art International
PO Box 550
Bountiful, UT 84010
    Catalog $2

Speed Stitch, Inc.
PO Box 3472
Port Charlotte, FL 33952
    Catalog $2

SewCraft
Box 1869
Warsaw, IN 46580
    Also publishes newsletter/catalog

Treadleart
25834 Narbonne Ave.
Lomita, CA 90717

Sewing Machine Supplies

The Button Shop
PO Box 1065
Oak Park, IL 60304
    Presser feet

Sewing Emporium
1087 Third Avenue
Chula Vista, CA 92010
    Presser feet, accessories

Miscellaneous

Applications
871 Fourth Ave.
Sacramento, CA 95818
    Release paper for appliqué

Berman Leathercraft
145 South St.
Boston, MA 02111
    Leather

Boycan's Craft and Art Supplies
PO Box 897
Sharon, PA 16146
    Plastic needlepoint canvas

Cabin Fever Calicoes
PO Box 550106
Atlanta, GA 30355

Ceci
PO Box 1602
Lemon Grove, CA 92045
    Thread holders, gadgets—$1 catalog

Clearbrook Woolen Shop
PO Box 8
Clearbrook, VA 22624
    Ultrasuede scraps

The Fabric Carr
170 State St.
Los Altos, CA 94022
    Sewing gadgets

The Green Pepper Inc.
941 Olive Street
Eugene, OR 97401
    Outdoor fabrics, patterns—$1 catalog

Home-Sew
Bethlehem, PA 18018
    Lace—$.25 catalog

Kwik-Sew
3000 Washington Ave. N
Minneapolis, MN 55411
    Knit and sweatshirt patterns

Libby's Creations
PO Box 16800 Ste. 180
Mesa, AZ 85202
    Horizontal spool holder

LJ Originals, Inc.
516 Sumac Pl.
DeSoto, TX 75115
    TransGraph

Lore Lingerie
3745 Overland Ave.
Los Angeles, CA 90034
    1 lb. of silk remnants, $9.45

Osage Country Quilt Factory
400 Walnut
Overbrook, KS 66524
    Washable fabric spray glue

The Pellon Company
119 West 40th St.
New York, NY 10018
    Machine appliqué supplies

The Perfect Notion
566 Hoyt St.
Darien, CT 06820
    Sewing supplies

Porcupine Pincushion
PO Box 1083
McMurray, PA 15317

Salem Industries, Inc.
PO Box 43027
Atlanta, GA 30336
    Olfa cutters, rulers

Sew Easy
2701 W. 1800 S
Logan, UT 84321
    Sweatshirt patterns

Solar-Kist Corp.
PO Box 273
LaGrange, IL 60525
    Teflon pressing sheet

Stacy Industries, Inc.
38 Passaic St.
Wood-Ridge, NJ 07075
    Teflon pressing sheet

Stretch & Sew
PO Box 185
Eugene, OR 97440
    Knit and sweatshirt patterns

Summa Design
Box 24404
Dayton, OH 45424
    Charted designs for knitting needle
    machine sewing

Susan of Newport
Box 3107
Newport Beach, CA 92663
    Ribbons and laces

Tandy Leather Co.
PO Box 791
Ft. Worth, TX 76101
    Leather

Taylor-Made Designs
PO Box 31024
Phoenix, AZ 85046
    Sweatshirt patterns

Theta's School of Sewing
2508 N.W. 39th Street
Oklahoma City, OK 73112
    Charted designs for knitting needle
    machine sewing, smocking directions
    and supplies for the machine

Magazines
(write for rates)

Aardvark Territorial Enterprise
PO Box 2449
Livermore, CA 94550
    Newspaper jammed with all kinds of
    information about all kinds of em-
    broidery, design, and things to order.
    I ordered the gold rings from them.

Creative Needle
1500 Jupiter Road
Lookout Mountain, GA 37350

disPatch
1042 E. Baseline
Tempe, AZ 85283
    Newspaper about quilting and ma-
    chine arts

Fiberarts
50 College St.
Asheville, NC 28801
    Gallery of the best fiber artists, in-
    cluding those who work in machine
    stitchery.

Needlecraft for Today
Ft. Worth, TX 76109
    Creative uses of the sewing machine

SewCraft
Box 1869
Warsaw, IN 46580
    Newspaper and catalog combination
    containing machine embroidery arti-
    cles, designs and supplies.

Sew News
PO Box 1790
Peoria, IL 61656
    Monthly tabloid, mostly about garment sewing

Threads
Box 355
Newton, CT 06470
    Magazine on all fiber crafts

Treadleart
25834 Narbonne Ave., Ste. 1
Lomita, CA 90717
    Bimonthly about machine embroidery

Books

Alexander, Eugenie, *Fabric Pictures*, Mills and Boon Ltd., London, 1967.

Bennet, dj, *Machine Embroidery with Style*, Madrona Publishers, 1980.

Brag, Rachel, *No-Sew Customized Sweatshirts* (Country Thread Designs, RR1, Box 27, Kindred, ND 58051), 1986.

Butler, Anne, *Machine Stitches*, BT Batsford, Ltd., 1976.

Clucas, Joy, *Your Machine for Embroidery*, G. Bell & Sons, 1975.

_____, *The New Machine Embroidery*, David & Charles Craft Book, 1987.

Coleman, Anne, *The Creative Sewing Machine*, BT Batsford, 1979.

Ericson, Lois, *Fabrics. . .Reconstructed* (Lois Ericson, Box 1680, Tahoe City, CA 95730), 1985.

_____, *Belts. . .Waisted Sculpture*, 1984.

Fanning, Robbie and Tony, *The Complete Book of Machine Quilting*, Chilton Book Co., 1980.

_____, *The Complete Book of Machine Embroidery*, Chilton Book Co., 1986.

Gray, Jennifer, *Machine Embroidery*, Van Nostrand Reinhold, 1973.

Hall, Carolyn, *The Sewing Machine Craft Book*, Van Nostrand Reinhold, 1980.

Harding, Valerie, *Textures in Embroidery*, Watson-Guptill, New York, 1977.

Hazen, Gale Grigg, *Sew Sane* (The Sewing Place, 100 W. Rincon Ave., Ste. 105, Campbell, CA 95008; $14.95 postpaid), 1985.

Hogue, Refa D., *Machine Edgings* (c/o *Treadleart*, 25834 Narbonne Avenue, Lomita, CA 90717).

Hoover, Doris and Nancy Welch, *Tassels* (out-of-print), 1978.

James, Irene, *Sewing Specialties*, I. M. James Enterprises, 1982.

Lawrence and Clotilde, *Sew Smart*, IBC Publishing Co., 1984.

_____, Supplement, IBC Publishing Co., 1984.

Macor, Alida, *And Sew On*, Alida Macor, 1985.

McNeill, Moyra, *Machine Embroidery—Lace and See-Through Techniques*, BT Batsford, 1985.

Mulari, Mary, *Designer Sweatshirts* (Box 87, Aurora, MN 55705), 1986.

Nall, Mary Lou, *Mary Lou's Sewing Tchniques* (c/o *Treadleart*, 25834 Narbonne Avenue, Lomita, CA 90717).

Nicholas, Annwen, *Embroidery in Fashion*, Watson-Guptill, 1975.

Ota, Kimi, *Sashiko Quilting* (Kimi Ota, 10300 61st Ave. So., Seattle, Washington 98178), 1981.

Pullen, Martha, *French Hand Sewing by Machine* (518 Madison St., Huntsville, AL 35801), 1985.

Sanders, Janice, *Speed Sewing Plus*, Speed Sewing Ltd., Centerline, Michigan, 1985.

Sewing Specialty Fabrics, Singer Sewing Reference Library, 1986.

Shaeffer, Claire B., *The Complete Book of Sewing Short Cuts*, Sterling Publishing Co., Inc., 1984.

Short, Eirian, *Quilting*, BT Batsford, London, 1983.

Skjerseth, Douglas Neil, *Stitchology*, Seth Publications (PO Box 1606, Novato, CA 94947), 1979.

Thompson, Sue, *Decorative Dressmaking*, Rodale Press, 1985.

Warren, Virena, *Landscape in Embroidery*, BT Batsford, 1986.

Wiechec, Philomena, *Celtic Quilt Designs*, Celtic Design Co., 1980.

Zieman, Nancy, *The Busy Woman's Sewing Book*, Open Chain Publishing, 1988.

Index